Moral Dilemmas

PRECEDENT STUDIES IN ETHICS AND THE MORAL SCIENCES

Moral Dilemmas

Philosophical and Psychological Issues
in the Development of Moral Reasoning

Edited by

Carol Gibb Harding

Precedent Studies in Ethics and the Moral Sciences
General Editor: Thomas E. Wren

Precedent Publishing, Inc.
Chicago, Illinois

Precedent Publishing, Inc.
737 North LaSalle Street
Chicago, Illinois 60610
Copyright © 1985 by Precedent Publishing, Inc.
Printed in the United States of America
All Rights Reserved
Distributed by Transaction Books, New Brunswick (USA) and
Oxford (UK)

Library of Congress Cataloging in Publication Data

Main entry under title:

Moral Dilemmas

Includes index
    1. Ethics – Addresses, essays, lectures. 2. Moral develop-
ment – Addresses, essays, lectures. I. Harding, Carol (Carol Gibb) II.
Wren, Thomas E.
BJ1012.M632 1985   170/:42   85-19286

ISBN 0-913750-35-2

This volume was supported in part by a grant from the Loyola-Mellon Fund
of Loyola University of Chicago.

Precedent Studies in Ethics and the Moral Sciences

The term "moral sciences," which is the rubric for the present series, originated with John Stuart Mill, who used it to cover what are now called the social and behavioral sciences. Accordingly, the Precedent Studies in Ethics and the Moral Sciences have as a general subject matter the rich and problematic interspace between philosophical ethics and such empirical but person- and society-oriented disciplines as developmental psychology, sociology, and anthropology, to cite a few of the more salient "moral sciences."

The essays in this volume each have their own philosophical orientations and background suppositions about the limits and procedures of psychological inquiry concerning morality. Nonetheless, they share a conception of human nature as inherently social, as well as a healthy respect for the problems or dilemmas which human sociality carries in its wake. Some of these problems are theoretical, such as those having to do with the ontogenesis of moral reasoning or the classic issues of values justification. Other problems are practical, such as those having to do with distributive justice or the methods of moral education. Only a few of these problems can be addressed in a single book, and the present volume is no exception. However, the importance of a discussion such as this one goes beyond its diverse examinations of specific theoretical and practical issues. Of course the discussions in these pages of such matters as the rational structures of moral discourse, the boundaries of the moral domain, the relationship of caring and justice, and so on, are extremely important in their own right. However, they also serve what might be considered a meta-theoretical function, since they demonstrate the reciprocity of two very difficult tasks: that of charting the flow of moral thought and that of making philosophical sense out of the undeniable psychological fact that we live in a world full of moral dilemmas.

Thomas E. Wren
General Editor

Contents

Contributors

Marvin W. Berkowitz
Department of Psychology; Marquette University; Milwaukee, Wisconsin

Marilyn Friedman
Department of Philosophy; Bowling Green State University; Bowling Green, Ohio

Carol Gibb Harding
Departments of Foundations of Education and Psychology; Loyola University; Chicago, Illinois

Lawrence Hinman
Department of Philosophy; University of San Diego; San Diego, California

Lawrence Kohlberg
Center for Moral Education; Harvard University; Cambridge, Massachusetts

Georg Lind
Department of Social Psychology; University of Konstanz; Konstanz, Germany

Larry May
Department of Philosophy; Purdue University; West Lafayette, Indiana

Larry P. Nucci
College of Education; University of Illinois at Chicago; Chicago, Illinois

Fritz Oser
Pedagogical Institute; University of Fribourg; Fribourg, Switzerland

Introduction

Carol Gibb Harding

The chapters in this volume are about moral dilemmas in two senses of that term. First of all, they deal with conflict situations, real and hypothetical, that require moral judgments. Several chapters focus explicitly on the well-known "Heinz dilemma" which is part of Lawrence Kohlberg's scoring system for levels of moral development. Problems related to the use of this particular dilemma as a scoring item are addressed, as are problems generated by similar dilemmas in real life. The kinds of decisions that such dilemmas engender, as well as the processes of reasoning that moral dilemmas require, have come to interest philosophers, psychologists, and educators.

There is a second sense in which these chapters are about moral dilemmas. At the present time, those who study moral reasoning and its development must struggle with their own dilemmas as they attempt to integrate information from the domains of philosophy and psychology, to investigate in varied cultural settings and across genders and age ranges what have been proposed as universals in moral judgment, and to formulate theories that reflect both empirical evidence and logical processes. The quandary in which moral philosophers and psychologists find themselves is certainly not eliminated by the essays in this volume, but may instead be intensified by the questions that are posed and the objections raised. Nevertheless, the process of scholarly discussion, dissent, and growth goes on.

This volume is an integration of philosophical and psychological approaches to moral reasoning. It grew out of an interdisciplinary colloquium series on moral development held at Loyola University of Chicago from 1983 to 1985, funded by a grant from the Loyola-Mellon Fund, whose support for the colloquia and this volume is here gratefully acknowledged. In the course of these discussions, a group of us, under the leadership of Thomas Wren who organized the series, found the process of "cross-pollination" across disciplines as well as across national frontiers to be an informative and exciting experience. With this book we hope to extend that process to the wider audience of researchers and educators for whom it is intended.

Marvin Berkowitz begins the volume by categorizing current theory and research concerning moral discussion according to four perspectives: Developmental, which describes the stages of development of moral argumentation competencies; Ethical, which describes and often justifies the ideal form of moral argumentation; Growth-Facilitative, which identifies the functions of moral argumentation, especially its capacity to promote moral development; and Instrumental, which focuses on practical functions of moral argumentation. Berkowitz offers a preliminary sketch of an integrative approach to moral argumentation which identifies the developmental path of moral argumentation as well as the ethical endpoint of such development. By calling for increased efforts in the consideration of an integrative understanding of moral discussion, Berkowitz's chapter provides a framework for the integrative approach of the volume.

In the second chapter Marilyn Friedman jumps into one of the philosophical dilemmas I mentioned above – that of apparent gender differences in moral reasoning – and emerges with an intriguing approach to the task of interpreting these differences. In fact, she manages to see beyond the gender differences and to recognize the importance of care and context (principles others have labeled as "female") in all moral reasoning. The significance of contextual detail is particularly emphasized, and Friedman points out some ways in which both Gilligan (1982) and Kohlberg (1983) seem to have been misled. According to Friedman, neither Kohlberg nor Gilligan seems to appreciate the difference it makes when moral dilemmas are specified in rich detail. This difference exists whether the reasoner shows a preference for care reasoning or for justice reasoning, and whether the dilemmas themselves invoke care considerations or justice considerations – or both. Creative variations on the Heinz dilemma are presented to illustrate Friedman's position.

In chapter 3, which is my own, I ask two questions: What are the characteristics of events that come to be interpreted as dilemmas; and (2) what is the process of human thinking that leads to that interpretation? The discussion of the first question is related to Friedman's concern with contextual detail, and describes characteristics of dilemmas, permitting an examination of the process of recognition. The second question is addressed from the developmental perspective, as called for by Berkowitz, and ends with a constructivist approach to the "invention" of dilemmas.

Lawrence Hinman's chapter 4 casts attention on the emotions and the role they play in the interpretation of dilemmas. Too often the emotions are considered unavailable for scientific examination, and this essay represents an attempt to provide a framework for future research. Hinman posits emotion as part of cognitive structure and proposes that "emotions are a way of structuring and understanding our world, a way of making sense of it." Given this cognitive framework, Hinman suggests an approach to educating the emotions so that those emotions which he labels "illuminating" – for example, compassion – can be cultivated in order to promote not only moral reasoning but also moral sensitivity.

Although most of the chapters in this book refer to and, in some cases, explicitly examine Lawrence Kohlberg's theory of moral development, Kohlberg's own chapter discusses a new approach to moral education – the just community approach. Kohlberg has always been concerned with the translation of theory into practice. However, his earlier efforts in moral education involved classroom discussions focused on hypothetical dilemmas, such as the Heinz dilemma. In this chapter, Kohlberg describes the just community which develops through the establishment of participatory democracy in the classroom or school. In the just community, there is an ongoing dialogue about the rights of the minority and the individual, and the rights of the community as manifested in majority vote. As Kohlberg describes it, the teacher in the just community advocates by presenting a rational point of view, instead of by dictating from a position of authority or power. Two instances of the application of the just community approach are reported. Descriptions are given of the process of resolving real-life conflicts within these school communities. Kohlberg concludes that the just community will lead not only to moral development but also to the development of active citizens for a democratic society.

In chapter 6 Georg Lind also addresses the issues of education and moral development. His empirical investigation was designed to test the question: Is cognitive growth in university students accompanied by moral regression? If regression does, in fact, occur, this finding would be problematic for Kohlberg's stage theory. The empirical research reported here focuses on 844 German university students who were followed longitudinally from their first to their fifth semesters. The assessment instrument used was Lind's *Moralisches Urteil Test*, a test based on Kohlberg's theory but employing a new methodology which Lind labels the "Experimental Questionnaire." This type of test allows for the subjective information derived from interviews, but also provides for objective quantitative analysis. Lind's findings corroborate Kohlberg's hypothesis of an invariant progression of moral judgment competency. Exceptions to this rule, according to Lind, may be traced to assessment methods of inadequate design. He concludes that a differentiated evaluation of students' moral judgment behavior shows that, when the personal significance of each stage of reasoning is neglected, highly competent individuals may be erroneously perceived as having regressed.

In the following chapter, Larry May examines the alleged moral superiority or adequacy of the higher stages of moral reasoning. After presenting several philosophical arguments which question the moral adequacy of Kohlberg's theory, May offers an alternate approach to moral development that may better describe the process of moral judgment than does Kohlberg's hierarchy. May argues that morality is based on a sense of the value of the self instead of on a concern for fairness to others, in which case moral development would be the result of a heightened sensitivity to self rather than the increased abstraction from self which Kohlberg and most developmental psychologists posit. Philosophical theories are presented to show that highly organized and functional moral systems do not necessarily have egalitarian justice as a base.

The last two chapters in this volume, by Larry Nucci and Fritz Oser respectively, extend the concept of moral reasoning by focusing on religious belief and the development of religious reasoning. Over the past decade, a body of research and theory has emerged which explicitly recognizes that people's conceptions of morality form a knowledge system distinct from their concepts of non-moral social issues. The focus of Nucci's chapter is on that account of social development, specifically, on the development of the concepts of morality and religious prescription. The research which he discusses asks two questions: (1) Does morality constitute a conceptual and developmental domain distinct from concepts of religious behavioral standards akin to societal conventions? and (2) Is one's identification of the moral ultimately independent of religious prescription? After presenting the results from several empirical studies, Nucci concludes that children's conceptions of morality are not reducible to their knowledge of religious rules or their adherence to them. Instead, his research indicates that children's moral, societal, and religious concepts articulate distinct facets of their notions of right and wrong. The findings of this research lend further support to the developmental hypothesis that children's conceptions of morality constitute a domain distinct from notions of societal convention and other non-moral behavioral norms.

In the final chapter of the volume, Oser discusses religious dilemmas and the reasoning process involved in attempting to resolve them. He proposes stages of religious development through which religious elements, such as the contrast between the "holy and profane," become integrated within conceptions of how human beings are related to "the ultimate." Oser approaches the topic of religious development with the assumption that "everybody has a religious judgment even if he or she does not know exactly what his or her ultimate is." He makes the case that although dilemmas can be resolved without reference to an ultimate, such unsolved problems as life and death issues trigger religious reasoning. Even in denying an ultimate, Oser concludes, we have used religious structures in order to come to what he labels "a cognitive religious equilibrium."

In the traditional sense, dilemmas are thought of as unresolvable situations, typically involving equally abhorrent alternatives. In life, one must at times face dilemmas and live through them by making choices. This volume is a study of dilemmas and the process of reasoning about them. If it serves to shed light on the process of resolving dilemmas – or inventing them – it will have served a useful purpose, both within the disciplines of philosophy and psychology and in our daily lives.

Four Perspectives on Moral Argumentation

Marvin W. Berkowitz

Over the past decade, moral argumentation has been examined from a range of diverse psychological perspectives. While these endeavors have remained largely isolated from one another, recent interest in the general phenomenon of moral argumentation has led to the beginning of cross-fertilization of these various perspectives. Little in the way of serious integration has been attempted, however. Therefore, I would like to examine the prevailing perspectives on such moral discourse, and, in so doing, to attempt to identify both the underlying communalities and the fundamental incompatabilities of these diverse viewpoints.

My interest is in the verbal interactions of individuals discussing issues of morality (Berkowitz, 1985; Berkowitz & Gibbs, 1983, in press). I refer to this as moral discussion, that is, the discussion of moral topics by two or more individuals. I have used the term moral discourse interchangeably with the term moral discussion and will continue to do so here. Moral argumentation I take to be moral discourse or discussion in which the discussants confront and attempt to resolve differences in their respective positions on the moral focus of the verbal interaction. It is certainly obvious that one may focus on a variety of aspects of this broadly defined phenomenon; indeed, that variability will be the primary concern of this paper. Unfortunately, this variability is also characteristic of the terminology commonly used in different disciplines. I will solve this problem simply by appealing to the reader's tolerance of my own idiosyncratic terminology.

It should be noted at this point that not all the perspectives to be expounded upon in this chapter are limited to *moral* argumentation. That is, some of the perspectives on moral argumentation can also apply to logical argumentation or to arguments concerning social conventions. However, in this chapter we shall consider only how these perspectives apply to the domain of morality.

The literature on moral argumentation can be categorized into three groups. This trichotomy is certainly not meant to be perfect in the sense of having clear and consistent definitional boundaries

between the categories. Nor is it exhaustive, since it does not
account for all possible, or even plausible, perspectives on the
phenomena in question. (Indeed, I shall shortly introduce a fourth
perspective that represents a somewhat different level of analysis.) I
do think, however, that it is a largely accurate and useful categorization of research and thinking about moral argumentation.
Furthermore, I would argue that it captures the most essential
features of the predominant perspectives on moral argumentation
currently influencing research, theory, and practice in moral developmental psychology and moral education today.

I have labeled these first three perspectives (1) *Instrumental*, (2)
Ethical, and (3) *Growth-Facilitative*. While all three are concerned with
discussions of morality, they have quite disparate orientations. Their
disparities include, but are not limited to, the fundamental questions
being investigated, the methods used in such investigations, the
disciplines primarily informing both the question-asking and the
method selection, and, consequently, the conclusions reached.
Because each of these forms of moral argumentation can be viewed
from both a simple descriptive standpoint and a more complex
developmental perspective, I shall also introduce a fourth,
Developmental perspective, which lies on a somewhat different plane
than do the other three, in that it can be applied to each of these
other perspectives. I will briefly define the four perspectives, after
which they will be treated more thoroughly and related to some of
the research now being done that exemplifies each perspective.

One difference between the Instrumental and Growth-Facilitative
perspectives taken in joint contrast to the Ethical perspective paral-
lels a classic contrast in ethical philosophy, especially as applied to
the question of human growth. This is the contrast between what
"is" and what "ought to be." Since the developmental significance of
this contrast has been discussed at length in Kohlberg's classic essay
"From 'Is' to 'Ought': How to Commit the Naturalistic Fallacy and
Get Away with It in the Study of Moral Development" (Kohlberg,
1981), I will say only that the Instrumental and Growth-Facilitative
perspectives are concerned with the "Is," the description of moral
argumentation, and the Ethical perspective focuses on the "Ought,"
the prescription of moral argumentation. The human growth question adds a new point of view to this contrast, a concern with the
issue of development toward a more adequate, or even ideal, end
state. The Developmental perspective represents this last point of
view.

More specifically, the Instrumental and Growth-Facilitative

perspectives refer to efforts to describe actual moral argumentation behavior forms. The former describes forms of moral argumentation whose goal is some instrumental or practical end, such as changing another's attitude or "winning" an argument. The latter has a quite different focus, i.e., to stimulate an individual to grow to a more mature level of moral understanding. That is, these two perspectives focus on the description of human moral argumentation and its function. The Developmental perspective expands that aim to include the developmental transformations through which the discussion of moral issues passes in the course of human growth. Typically, cross-sectional, but ideally also longitudinal (cf. Oser, 1984, p. 164), comparisons are made of moral discussion at different developmental stages.

In contrast, the Ethical perspective refers to the form that moral discussion ought to take. That is, the focus here is on the way individuals should discuss moral topics, as derived from ethical philosophy and social theory rather than from typical observed psychological patterns (although these patterns may be clearly implicated in the ethical justification). The Ethical perspective is oriented to an ideal end-state toward which human growth moves (although it may not reach it in all or even most individual cases). The Developmental perspective incorporates this theme of growth into the Ethical perspective.

The Instrumental, Ethical, and Growth-Facilitative perspectives are perhaps best differentiated by a functional analysis. The Instrumental perspective focuses on how moral argumentation can serve a desired goal, such as winning the argument. The function of Ethical argumentation is to take the rights of all discussants into account while searching for an ethical solution to the moral problem under discussion. Growth-Facilitative moral argumentation functions to produce individual development by means of the interaction. Correlatively, each of these first three perspectives can be construed as discourse competencies. We can talk about the competence to engage in ethically justified or in instrumentally effective forms of moral argumentation, and so on. By describing these aspects of moral argumentation as competencies, we invoke the fourth perspective, the Developmental perspective. If one can identify a form of competent moral argumentation from a particular perspective, it seems reasonable to ask whether there are varying degrees of such competence. Furthermore, one may question whether such variations in competency represent a developmental trend. However, the Developmental perspective cannot readily be classified functionally, as are the other three perspectives. Relative to these perspectives, it may best be viewed as a *meta*-perspective, since it describes the developmental path of moral argumentation. For instance, we can study how the ability to facilitate development itself develops, and can perhaps describe stages of the growth of such discourse behavior; or we may describe the development of the ability to win moral arguments, and so on. By now it should be at least minimally clear how these four perspectives are defined. The following sections will serve to elaborate these definitions and to concretize the perspectives via the examination of specific examples of each.

THE INSTRUMENTAL PERSPECTIVE

One way to describe the Instrumental perspective is in terms of conflict resolution. We have defined moral argumentation as discourse centered upon a moral disagreement. Similarly, Miller (1980) points out that "the constitutive task of an argumentation is to develop an argument which gives an answer to a disputed question" (p. 4). We may easily construe such a situation as a verbal moral conflict which the argumentation is intended to resolve. Psychologists have focused on two broad types of such conflict resolution: cooperative and competitive. The former refers to argumentations in which discussants share the same goal, and the latter to argumentations in which discussants have incompatible goals. This incompatibility need not be objectively real; it simply needs to be accepted as an orienting assumption by the discussants. In so-called "zero sum" situations, opponents are faced with objectively mutually exclusive goals, i.e., one's success implies the other's failure. However, most situations are not so clearly constrained. The theory of integrative bargaining (Pruitt & Lewis, 1977) is based largely upon the assumption that many apparently competitive situations can be reconstructed to allow for resolutions that fulfill the goals of each side of the conflict. Pruitt and Lewis suggest that a reorienting of the opponents may be all that is necessary to transform a competitive conflict into a cooperative enterprise. With this in mind, let us turn to the literature on Instrumental moral argumentation in order to identify the competitive and cooperative types.

An example of competitive moral argumentation is presented by Mall (1982), a rhetorician who has worked extensively on one side of the volatile social, political, and moral issue of abortion. He has helped bolster the anti-abortion perspective in this debate. In his book *In Good Conscience: Abortion and Moral Necessity*, he has undertaken the rather interesting task of demonstrating how Kohlberg's (1984a) theory of stages of moral development can be applied to an analysis of the moral adequacy of abortion argumentations. This may not seem an example of competitive moral conflict resolution, but the fact is that Mall does not fully divorce himself either from his personal position on the abortion issue nor from his training as a rhetorician who attempts to change other people's attitudes. Hence his book does indeed represent the competitive instrumental perspective, since it uses moral argumentation to help "win" the abortion debate.

Cooperative moral conflict resolution has also been represented in the moral argumentation literature. We will briefly introduce two examples here. First, there is the work of a group of philosophers and educators at Ohio State University who have applied the theoretical work of Bernard Rosen in normative ethics to classroom training in moral conflict resolution, a project entitled "Moral Negotiation as Moral Education: Rational Resolution of Moral Disagreements" (Reagan, 1984). Rosen's normative ethics model has been used in this project to produce means of argumentation that can be justified as leading to an ethically sound solution to moral disagreements. These forms of argumentation are taught in the classroom in order to increase the number of cooperative resolutions of moral conflicts. The goal, therefore, is to negotiate a shared solution to moral disagreements, and the orientation is cooperative because the means are based on normative ethics.

A different cooperative Instrumental analysis of moral discussion comes from organizational psychology. Argyris (Argyris & Schön, 1974) has analyzed the nature of organizational communication in an attempt to understand the failures and breakdowns that can be corrected through organizational intervention. Argyris and Schön (1974) have defined the goal of training for adequate moral argumentation in the title of their book *Theory in Practice: Increasing Professional Effectiveness.* Argyris has described two forms of organizational communication which can be considered success (Model II) and failure (Model I) cases. The success form includes three governing values and several behavioral strategies and norms. For Argyris,

the governing values or variables are valid information, free and informed choice, and internal commitment to the choices made. The behavioral strategies associated with Model II include advocacy coupled with inquiry, minimal (covert) face-saving actions, and the making of statements that are testable. The norms include trust, individuality, and openness *in such a way* that others can produce the same conditions. (Argyris & Argyris, 1978, p. 6)

Argyris claims that the more typical case (Model I) is one of failure to achieve these conditions and ultimately results in organizational breakdown, because in such "closed loop" interactions discussants cannot "step" out of the system and correct it. For example, a non-testable accusation will lead to a retaliation in kind, but cannot lead to a confirmable refutation or synthesis. Therefore, such a sequence cannot lead to a solution of a problem. In Miller's (1980) terminology, such moral argumentation cannot lead to a mutually acceptable end. Argyris argues that the success case (Model II) offers the potential for adequate moral argumentation. Furthermore, it should be clear that Model II argumentation is cooperative by the very nature of its values, strategies, and norms.

Two points need to be made concerning Argyris's model. First, Argyris is not centrally engaged in studying moral discourse. He is primarily concerned with organizational success. This leads him to the study of social interaction and to a prescription of the ethical bases of such communications, an extension which borders on the Ethical perspective of moral argumentation. His direct goal, however, is the adequate functioning of an organization, typically a large corporation, a goal similar to that of Habermas's (1979, 1984) perspective (which will be used to exemplify the Ethical perspective). Like Argyris, Habermas is more interested in the adequate functioning of a social organization than in moral argumentation per se, although in Habermas's case the organization in question is society as a whole and his orientation initially includes normative ethics along with critical social theory.

Secondly, Argyris has admitted (personal communication) that his theory is not sufficiently informed by a developmental perspective, even though his two models can be construed as representing a two-step developmental progression. Argyris seems to suggest that the only way to develop from the failure case to the success case is through intentional external intervention; the success case does not develop naturally. Here, then, we see a clear distinction between the Developmental perspective and the Instrumental perspective.

Instrumental perspective investigations of moral argumentation focus on how moral discussion can produce a specific desired outcome through the resolution of a moral conflict. The form of the moral argumentation may be either competitive or cooperative. We have presented only a few examples of this perspective here; however, the reader can probably imagine a variety of other examples that would serve equally well to illustrate this category. It should be noted that we have taken no position on the quality of the discussants' intentions, other than with reference to the competition-cooperation dimension. One could incorporate an ethical dimension into this motivation, differentiating, for example, a sociopathic con-artist's moral argumentation from a therapist's attempts to help a family find a fair and just alternative to its mutually destructive decision-making strategies. This kind of analysis, however, exceeds the intended scope of this chapter; we recommend to the reader Powers's (1982) study of family moral argumentation for an analysis of varying ego modes of orienting to such interactions.

THE ETHICAL PERSPECTIVE

In direct contrast to the Instrumental perspective on moral discussion, which tends to describe actual forms of moral argumentation, the Ethical perspective prescribes the ethically ideal form of moral argumentation. As noted earlier, these two perspectives have a potential relationship to each other in the same sense that Kohlberg's (1981) stages of moral development relate to the ethical justification of his highest stage, i.e., the relationship of "is" to "ought." I will briefly describe two endeavors that exemplify the Ethical perspective on moral discussion.

Perhaps the clearest and most highly developed position on the ideal form of moral discussion comes from the work of Jürgen Habermas (1979, 1984). From the perspective of a social theorist, Habermas has critiqued Marxist theory by pointing to the confusion between production and social interaction. The former, accentuated in Marxist theory, must be understood and evaluated according to standards of efficiency. Habermas argues that the latter, largely neglected in Marxist theory, should be understood and evaluated from the point of view of interactive competence. Habermas's reconstruction of critical theory is based largely upon this latter notion, which he terms "communicative competence."

Habermas delineates four essential components of ideal communicative competence (McCarthy, 1978). These four validity claims, which must be met for effective interactions to occur, are (1) comprehensibility, (2) truth, (3) truthfulness, and (4) appropriateness. Hence, Habermas has *prescribed* the form that communication ought ethically to take, whereas Argyris, Reagan, and Mall have *described* the forms that communication does instrumentally take. It should be pointed out, however, that Habermas has attempted also to tackle the Developmental question of the growth of ideal communicative competence. In so doing, he points to stages of moral and ego development, particularly to Kohlberg's stages of moral reasoning development (Habermas, 1979). He extracts from these models a three-step developmental sequence paralleling the Kohlbergian move from instrumental hedonist to conventional role adopter to postconventional role critic.

A second example of the Ethical perspective is the moral discussion component of Rawls's *Theory of Justice* (1971). Rawls has been regarded as offering the most comprehensive contemporary philosophical justification of justice as the preferred ethical basis for morality, a justification which has been used by Kohlberg as the philosophical ground of his arguments for the highest stage in his developmental scheme. In fact, Kohlberg's (1981) notion of moral argumentation as an element in his highest stage is firmly based upon Rawls's concept of ideal argumentation. Rawls uses the concept of the Original Position to describe the ideal state for generating just solutions to ethical problems. In this state, one adopts the "veil of ignorance" and proceeds to discuss the problem at hand as if one were blind to one's own identity (thus ensuring impartiality) while adhering in a rational fashion to principles of justice (roughly, liberty and equality).

Our interest, however, is in how Rawls conceptualizes moral argumentation. Indeed, his notion of the Original Position implies an ideal form of moral argumentation which is centrally rational and impartial. Kohlberg (1981) has termed it "ideal reversible role-taking" or, more colloquially, "moral musical chairs." According to Kohlberg's formulation, one must consider all positions (perspectives, protagonists) in a given moral dilemma and generate a fair (just) solution to the problem, as if the reasoner might be any one of those participants in the dilemma.

Here again we see a conception of an ideal form of moral argumentation. Exactly how one is to manage this highly sophisticated and complex task is never clearly laid out, either by Rawls or by Kohlberg, and the way it develops is apparently left to investigators of the development of social thinking skills, such as Selman (1980), Kohlberg (1981), or Piaget (1932/1965).

While Habermas and Rawls acknowledge the developmental nature of the phenomena whose endpoints they describe, they nonetheless are insufficiently focused on the developmental process (for obvious reasons of differing interests and purposes) to function as examples of the Developmental perspective. Where they do attempt to reconcile the development of moral discussion, they rely essentially on developmental psychology (e.g., Habermas's reference to Kohlberg's developmental scheme). This is altogether inadequate, because developmental psychologists have not as yet adequately charted the course of the development of moral discussion. Furthermore, while Habermas does acknowledge the existence of practical or pragmatic discourse, the two Ethical theorists are engaged in an endeavor that is quite separate from that of the Instrumentalists.

THE GROWTH-FACILITATIVE PERSPECTIVE

As noted earlier, the Instrumental, Ethical, and Growth-Facilitative perspectives can all be considered from a functional standpoint. We have also seen that at least the Ethical, and perhaps the Instrumental, positions on moral argumentation may incorporate the notion of individual development. However, only the Growth-Facilitative perspective integrates these diverse functional and developmental components.

The Growth-Facilitative perspective treats moral argumentation as a process or catalyst. In fact, it is understood to be a condition for the growth of moral maturity. This perspective stems from the large body of literature demonstrating the accelerating effects of participation in moral discussion in educational, rehabilitative, or family settings (see Berkowitz & Oser, 1985, and Mosher, 1980, for examples of such interventions). Once it was recognized that moral discussion could produce moral development, researchers began to investigate the phenomenon more closely. Early attempts looked principally at the contextual conditions of moral argumentation interventions, such as the developmental stages of the discussants (e.g., Colby et al., 1977) or the facilitators' instructions to the discussants (e.g., Maitland & Goldman, 1974). More recent investigations, however, have looked directly at the nature of the argumentation itself.

My own research (Berkowitz, 1985; Berkowitz & Gibbs, 1983, in press) has focused on the attempt to identify the growth-producing features of late adolescent moral dialogue. My colleagues and I have uncovered a form of moral argumentation that we have labeled "Transactive Discussion," and have demonstrated that it differentiates discussions that produce moral stage growth (according to Kohlberg's scheme) from discussions that do not. Such discussion behavior is defined as reasoning about the other's reasoning in the argumentation. It is assumed to produce cognitive disequilibrium and, consequently, to stimulate moral stage growth.

Damon and Killen (1982) have studied a parallel process in the justice discussions of young children. Similarly, they have demonstrated the relationship of moral discussion to subsequent moral stage development. Powers (1982) has also adapted the Transactive Discussion scheme and used it as part of a moral argumentation assessment in a study which was part of a larger project investigating the ego development of psychiatric and non-psychiatric adolescents and their parents. Powers has collected mother-father-child "trialogues" about Kohlberg's classic Heinz dilemma. Her analyses reveal that affectively supportive discussion behavior is related to higher moral stages and that cognitively inhibiting behaviors (such as rejection and distortion) are related to lower moral stage reasoning. There were some indications that transactive behaviors were also related to higher moral stages, although this pattern was not consistent.

Along the lines of the Powers study, there is a growing body of research that investigates the relationship of parenting behavior to child moral development. Typically, such behavior includes a strong moral argumentation component. One consistent finding is that democratic moral argumentation in the family is a strong correlate of the child's moral development (Hoffman & Saltzstein, 1967; Holstein, 1969; Parikh, 1980). Furthermore, Stanley (1980) has demonstrated that parents trained in such moral argumentation reduce their authoritarian decision-making in the family and that the children of these parents show gains in moral reasoning. This literature has been reviewed elsewhere, so I will not elaborate further (cf. Berkowitz, 1985; Higgins, 1980; Lickona, 1983; Powers, 1982; Speicher-Dubin, 1982).

Another sidelight on the issue of moral argumentation as a process of moral reasoning development comes from the work of Taranto (1984), who has reanalyzed the Berkowitz and Gibbs (1983) data for relationships between stages of specific utterances and mismatches between discussants' adjacent utterances. This microanalysis of the moral dialogues has revealed that less than a full stage mismatch is related to an equivalent degree of change in the same direction as the mismatch for the lower stage member of the dyad. Taranto directly relates this to the equilibration process that Berkowitz and Gibbs assume is produced by transactive discussion. This clearly raises the question of whether the structural microprocesses uncovered in Taranto's analysis are directly related to the discourse microprocesses described by Berkowitz and Gibbs. Such an analysis remains to be carried out.

The Growth-Facilitative studies present a consistent pattern, probably more so than do the sets of studies representing the first two perspectives. The Growth-Facilitative studies suggest that moral argumentation functions as a developmental catalyst for the growth of moral reasoning maturity. Three central elements in this process have thus far been described: logical discussion behavior, moral stage mismatch, and affective tone. While little of this research can claim to empirically demonstrate a causal relationship between the process variables and the structural outcomes, the overall pattern is certainly suggestive of such a conclusion.

THE DEVELOPMENTAL PERSPECTIVE

The developmental aspect of moral argumentation competence is probably the least developed of the four perspectives discussed in this paper. Nonetheless, significant efforts have been made in this direction, so I will be able to describe two completed investigations of this problem, as well as one proposed study. However, little systematic integration of such endeavors has been attempted so far, with the result that for the most part these stand as isolated studies of the development of moral argumentation competencies. Unfortunately, while such an integration is clearly needed, it is beyond the scope of this paper to provide.

In contrast to the Growth-Facilitative perspective, which focuses on how moral argumentation produces development of moral reasoning structures, the Developmental perspective focuses on the developmental path of forms of moral argumentation. This can apply to forms of Instrumental, Ethical, or Growth-Facilitative argumentation.

The first research concerning the development of moral argumentation appeared in the late 1970s with a paper by Miller and Klein (1979), followed shortly by a more thorough treatment by Miller (1980). Miller has been concerned with the development of moral argumentation in children and has focused upon the problem of moving toward a higher perspective in moral argumentation by confronting opposing perspectives. His research has attempted to identify the means by which children transcend differences in moral argumentation and move to dialectically more synthesizing positions. In investigating such discussion processes, Miller has studied young children (5-10 years of age) in discussion groups of four. Each discussion concerned Kohlberg's Heinz dilemma (see Colby et al., 1983, pp. 77-78).

The stages he has tentatively identified are defined by problems of argumentation ("coordination failures") that limit the adequacy of the moral discussion at each stage. These problems are, in increasing developmental order, problems of:

- Justification: the ability to provide an argument for one's position
- Coherence: the ability to agree on the relative weights or places of accepted propositions in the argument
- Circularity: the ability to differentiate between the criteria for relevance in a given problem and the criteria for validity of a proposition
- Language: the ability to apply ethical theory to explicate the meaning of terms central to solving a moral argumentation.

Even the 5-year-olds studied were able to solve the problem of justification. They were, however, unable to solve the problem of coherence. The 7- and 8-year-olds, while able to solve the problem of coherence, could not adequately solve the problem of circularity. Finally, the 10-year-olds were able to solve the problem of circularity, but were unable to solve the problem of language.

Miller is clearly engaging in a study of moral argumentation from the Developmental perspective. His goal is to describe the stages of the development of moral argumentation. He is concerned with how growth (of cognitive structures) leads to the specific form of moral argumentation, as opposed to how the form of moral argumentation leads to growth (of moral reasoning structures), as would be the case in investigations carried out from the Growth-Facilitative perspective. His method points to the Developmental perspective of his enterprise. He adopts a cross-sectional design to compare the moral discussions of children at different age groups. Then he classifies these discussions according to a stage development model. Two notable shortcomings of this study are: (1) the small sample size (only three groups of four children each), and (2) the limited range of ages (5-10 years; no children could solve the last problem, and all could solve the first one). Nonetheless, Miller's work is an important pioneering investigation of the development of moral argumentation.

Shortly after Miller first presented his case study, Oser published his large-scale investigation of the development of moral argumentation, *Moralisches Urteil in Gruppen* (1981). Given the complexity of the latter study, it is a bit difficult to categorize it according to the four perspectives we have identified here. Nevertheless, it does seem appropriate to describe it as most centrally concerned with the description of the development of moral argumentation. Oser (1984) explicitly acknowledged the Ethical or "philosophical" perspective, but criticized it for not being able to differentiate among different types of moral argumentation (p. 160). He further suggested that the traditional psychological perspectives on moral argumentation ignore the interactional processes that govern their form and outcome. His goal, therefore, is to identify the developing capacity to solve moral problems through discussion.

Oser studied the discussions of three moral problems by 120 groups of 15-year-old adolescents. These discussions were found to vary within two relevant dimensions, the first of which was termed "levels of interaction." These are summarized, in increasing developmental order, as follows:

– *Level 1: Functional perspective.* Solutions to the problem are proposed.
– *Level 2: Analytical perspective.* Proposed solutions are analyzed on the basis of relevant facts and conditions.
– *Level 3: Normative perspective.* Proposed solutions and their grounding facts and circumstances are evaluated on the basis of moral norms, rules, and principles.
– *Level 4: Philosophical perspective.* The moral evaluation of proposed solutions, facts, and norms is grounded in moral philosophy from a critical perspective.

Oser's second dimension is termed "communication compactness." The three levels, again in increasing developmental order, are:

– *Level 1:* Little or no coordination of perspectives
– *Level 2:* Intermittent coordination of perspectives
– *Level 3:* Units of communication are coordinated and clarified.

Oser's specific hypotheses concerned the differential impacts of three types of experimental-educational treatments on moral argumentations as assessed across the two dimensions. Supplying rules of justice to discussants increased their use of the normative perspective. Providing discussion strategy training affected communication compactness but not levels of interaction. There were also differences across the three dilemmas discussed.

Oser was thus able to describe the course of development, augmented by training, of moral argumentation. However, his design was tailored more for the identification of intervention effects than of developmental trends. For example, he studied only one age group. He therefore was not able to observe all of his hypothesized stages of discussion behavior. While Miller's design allowed the study of only a limited age range, he was at least able to demonstrate a cross-sectional age trend. In fact, Miller has collected data from a much larger age range, although he reports only the results of a limited part of that sample. Subsequent analyses may lead to a refinement of his developmental scheme.

In contrast to these two studies, the third Developmental study of moral argumentation to be described here is at this point only a proposal. Leadbeater (1984) has critically analyzed the research of Miller (1980), Habermas (1979), and Berkowitz and Gibbs (1983), concluding that none of these investigations captures the development of the truly intersubjective component of moral argumentation. Her conceptual analysis of this problem focuses both on psychological investigations of social understanding and on philosophical treatments of the concept of intersubjectivity. The planned empirical investigation should further illuminate our understanding of the development of moral argumentation.

These three investigations of the development of moral argumentation offer rich bases for follow-up research into that phenomenon. We still know very little about the course of development of moral argumentation. Later in this paper, some recent research will be presented that touches upon this issue while engaging aspects of one or more of the other perspectives. It is important to point out, however, that, as noted above, the Developmental perspective is different from the other three perspectives in that it is actually a *meta-perspective* on moral argumentation. To regard it as simply the development of moral argumentation is to ignore the important question of what type of moral argumentation is developing. We have already seen three other perspectives from which moral argumentation might be considered. For example, Miller is actually concerned with the study of Ethical moral argumentation from the Developmental perspective. Oser and Leadbeater, however, are more ambiguous about the type of moral argumentation whose developmental course they are attempting to chart. Later we will examine a study of the development of Growth-Facilitative moral argumentation.

THE FOUR PERSPECTIVES REVISITED

At this point the four perspectives on moral argumentation have been defined, and key examples of research and theory for each have been described. While some contrasts have been drawn between the perspectives, no systematic analysis of their interrelationships has been attempted. Consequently, I will now try to synthesize the preceding explanation by pointing to some central issues in the study of moral discussion evidenced in the category scheme which I have described.

It is important to recognize at the outset that we are not discussing four independent, alternative choices of perspectives. It is more fruitful (and certainly more appropriate to a constructivist approach to knowledge) to imagine these perspectives as alternative windows on the same phenomenon. In other words, I prefer to conceive of the four perspectives as representing four different vantage points from which the same phenomenon, i.e., moral argumentation, can be observed and understood. Epistemologically, I am assuming that moral argumentation exists and has a set of features which characterize its nature. Each of the four perspectives makes certain assumptions about the nature of moral discourse and employs certain methods of inquiry for its study. These choices determine the "window" through which moral argumentation is viewed. This is a rather lengthy way of claiming that we are not engaged in the task of determining which of these perspectives is "correct." Rather, we are concerned with how these four perspectives, taken together, may enhance our understanding of moral argumentation beyond what is revealed by their individual contributions.

Let me begin this section by raising two questions that these perspectives seem to address: (1) What are the forms of moral argumentation? and (2) What functions does moral argumentation play? It can easily be seen that the four perspectives relate differently to these two questions. The Developmental perspective predominantly addresses Question 1; that is, it describes the forms through which moral argumentation develops, but only minimally addresses the functions or roles of such discussion. For example, Miller (1980), who begins his investigation by raising the question of "how to contradict and still pursue a common end," focuses mainly on "the ontogenesis of moral argumentation." The Ethical perspective is also concerned primarily with Question 1, but includes some concern for the second question. While addressing Question 1 by focusing on the development of an ideal form of moral discussion, these investigators are typically interested in this issue because of the function of moral argumentation, as illustrated by the very title of Habermas's *Communication and the Evolution of Society* (1979). Finally, the Instrumental and Growth-Facilitative perspectives focus largely on the second question. The functions or effects of moral discussion are of greater interest here than is the origin of such skills. Berkowitz and Gibbs (1983) for example, while speculating about moral discussion as a developing skill, do not study this aspect but focus only on the effects of the argumentation process.

As noted above, this analysis is simplistic for three reasons. First, there is much intra-perspective variation among the different representatives of each perspective. While Miller (1980) is concerned with the function of moral argumentation, his fellow developmentalist Oser (1984) is largely unconcerned with this perspective. Secondly, even when different investigators agree on which of the questions is most important, they can differ widely as to the specifics of the question and the procedure for answering it. For example, while Habermas (1984) and Argyris and Schön (1974) agree that the function of ideal moral discussion is important, their concepts of such discourse, and of its functions, are quite different. (Nevertheless, given the different disciplines and orientations of these theorists, the similarity among their models of ideal moral discourse is most striking). Others have identified quite different functions of moral discussion. Finally, these two questions are logically interrelated. Indeed, both the nature of moral discussion and its roles develop. As Tamir (1979) has noted, "both the form and the function of the dialogue . . . become transformed as the individual advances through the stages of life" (p. xvii).

This leads us to acknowledge that moral argumentation is a multi-faceted phenomenon that warrants a variety of investigations. However, this acknowledgment still leaves us asking how best to conceptualize and study moral argumentation, a question which I will address in two ways. First, I will attempt to present an integrative model of moral argumentation, albeit a rather sketchy and tentative one. Second, I will present three examples of research that I feel offer some promise of moving the investigation of moral argumentation forward by approaching it simultaneously from at least two of the four perspectives introduced above.

A PRELIMINARY INTEGRATIVE MODEL OF MORAL ARGUMENTATION

As I have already pointed out, moral argumentation is best conceptualized as a multi-faceted phenomenon impinging on a broad range of aspects of human functioning. Hence, any simple model of moral argumentation would probably be incomplete and inadequate to the task of capturing the basis of moral argumentation. Returning to our four perspectives, we can begin by requiring that an adequate integrative model of moral argumentation successfully describe both (1) the development of such discourse toward an ideal (and explicitly delineated) endpoint, and (2) the various functions of moral argumentation, including how it produces development in moral reasoning. The work of Habermas (1979, 1984) is probably the best approximation of such an endeavor to date. However, Habermas's work only partially explicates the *development* of moral argumentation and its varied *functions*. Furthermore, the specific function defined by the Growth-Facilitative perspective, i.e., moral growth production, is totally absent from Habermas's work.

It is not enough merely to address each of these four perspectives in turn; a truly integrative study of moral argumentation must relate the four perspectives and their sub-components to one another in a theoretically systematic way. What, we must ask, is the logic of the developmental progression of moral argumentation competencies that leads necessarily to the ideal endpoint defined by the Ethical analysis? How do the specific forms of developing moral argumentation relate differentially to the functions uncovered by a Growth-Facilitative versus an Instrumental analysis? These are examples of the many integrative questions that must be raised about moral argumentation. We are not yet in a position to present a well-formulated theory of moral argumentation that encompasses all these issues. Nevertheless, it is useful to provide a sketch of such a model based upon what little we know at present. That sketch can be formulated as a set of six basic propositions, as follows.

1. Moral argumentation is a central component of human interactions. Because of the variability of human nature, it is inevitable that disagreements will arise in human intercourse. Even argumentation that is not explicitly focused on moral issues has a tacit moral component, constituted by the fact that human beings have certain intrinsic rights and derivative duties. Hence, one has certain ethical obligations when interacting with another person. *Moral* argumentation is, therefore, "doubly" moral because of (1) the implicit moral obligations in human intercourse and (2) the explicit moral focus of the topic of moral argumentation.

2. The ideal form of moral argumentation may be prescribed. If a normative argument can be presented for the intrinsically moral aspect of argumentation, then an ideal form of moral argumentation may be prescribed, as has been done by Habermas (1979, 1984), Rawls (1971), and Kohlberg (1981, 1984b).

3. Moral argumentation has a logical dimension. Moral argumentation is not simply a social skill. It is also a logical skill. The resolution of seemingly incompatible moral arguments can typically be realized through the use of logical modes of argumentation (cf. Keller & Reuss, 1985; Miller, 1980). Theoretically, all moral disagreements are logically resolvable. However, in reality human beings are not logic machines, and most disagreements are not solved, due to such obstacles as irrationality, defensiveness, immaturity, affect, and immoral or amoral motives.

4. *Less than ideal forms of moral argumentation must also be described.* Ideal argumentation must be understood as simply that – i.e., *ideal* and not *actual*. Because we are interested in analyzing actual human functioning, it is important to study less adequate approximations of the ideal. This can be done *functionally* by identifying how humans engage in moral argumentation, or *developmentally* by conceptualizing the approximations as less mature forms in a developmental sequence, with the ideal form as a teleological endpoint. While the ideal presupposes the actual, the reverse is not necessarily so. One can formulate a descriptive model of developmental stages without postulating an ethically ideal terminus. As noted previously, Kohlberg (1981) has extensively treated this "Is" to "Ought" problem. Hence, we must consider the functional and developmental analyses.

5. *Moral argumentation can serve a variety of functions.* It would be unduly narrow to define moral argumentation solely as the development toward an ethically justified form of human interaction. As Rest (1983) has pointed out, the same skills that constitute moral functioning can be used for a variety of alternative ends. Similarly, as we have argued here, moral argumentation can have a variety of functions. *Ideally,* moral argumentation can be described as having two central goals or functions: discovering the most just solution to the ethical problem under consideration, and doing so through means that adequately respect the intrinsic rights of the discussants and fulfill their derivative duties. However, one can entertain a variety of alternate, and even competing, goals. Moral argumentation may, in a compatible mode, function to stimulate individual moral reasoning; or, in an incompatible mode, it may function to circumvent or even subvert an individual's legitimate justice claims. Hence, as Rest has suggested in regard to moral decision-making, we must formulate a theory describing and explaining how an individual selects the functions toward which the moral argumentation will be directed, what those different functions may be, and how their developmental courses are or are not interrelated. Even when one is capable of a relatively mature approximation of the Ethical ideal of moral argumentation, questions

arise: How else might one use those skills? Which less mature levels of moral argumentation might the individual employ? How, and toward what purposes, would deviation from the Ethical track be justified? The answers to these questions are not yet available to us. Nonetheless, we can identify some of the functions of moral argumentation: conflict resolution, stimulating moral development, regulating human interaction, creating moral meaning, winning an argument, acquiring some instrumental goal, demonstrating another's "inferiority" or one's own "superiority," and so on. We can also assume that, as the form of moral argumentation develops, its functions will be transformed. For example, the relatively sophisticated logical modes of adolescent and adult moral argumentation may directly disequilibrate cognitive moral reasoning structures, as Piaget (1932/1965) suggested. Early childhood forms of moral argumentation, however, may better be explained by Vygotsky's (1962) notion of the zone of proximal development (cf. Forman & Kraker, in press; Rogoff & Wertsch, 1984). Vygotsky suggests that a child develops new skills in a social context before he or she can manifest the capacity alone. Thus, for young children, moral argumentation may function to provide a context for learning new skills through social interaction and collaborative problem-solving, rather than through direct cognitive disequilibration.

6. *Both the forms and the functions of moral argumentation follow a developmental path.* We have already suggested that acknowledgment of an ideal form of Ethical moral argumentation demands the charting of a set of less than perfect approximations of that ideal. The Developmental perspective expands this notion to suggest that the alternative forms themselves form a developmental sequence with increasingly more Ethical approximations of the ideal form. We can also attempt to chart the course of other aspects of moral argumentation described in our functional analyses. For example, we may wish to describe the development of Instrumental modes of moral argumentation, such as Argyris and Schön (1974) have done in their two-step model (although, as we have already noted, these authors do not consider their model as truly developmental). As we shall see shortly, researchers are currently attempting to chart the developmental path of Growth-Facilitative moral argumentation.

In summary, it should be clear that this is a preliminary attempt to present a model of moral argumentation. The goal of this chapter is to stimulate further consideration of this problem by presenting an initial organizing scheme and framework. The issues raised thus far are intended to suggest paths for future researchers to follow in their considerations of moral argumentation from whichever perspective(s) they adopt. In addition, this chapter attempts to high-light the need for more integrative considerations of moral argu-mentation. Toward this end, let us present some current research endeavors that are especially promising because of their integrative, multi-perspective orientations in the study of moral argumentation.

EXAMPLES OF INTEGRATIVE RESEARCH

I will present three examples of research that embodies the integra-tive approach to moral argumentation suggested above. It is impor-tant to point out that many of the examples already presented, e.g., Miller (1980) and Oser (1984), could have been included in more than one perspective. The three examples chosen for this section are, in addition, exemplary integrative approaches to the empirical study of moral argumentation.

Perhaps the most developed line of integrative moral argumenta-tion research is that presented by Keller and Reuss (1985). They are interested in the development of forms of moral discussion in chil-dren's responses to sociomoral dilemmas (Developmental perspec-tive). Relying upon the traditional methods of cognitive-structural psychology (especially the work of Kohlberg and Selman), they begin with the sociomoral interview which such theorists use for assessment purposes, and redefine it as a moral communication situation. Then, in charting the development of such communication, they turn to discourse ethics (most directly, to Habermas). They begin their anal-ysis by describing the philosophical components of ideal moral communication (Ethical perspective). Then they apply these princi-ples to the developmental analysis of moral argumentation. Finally, they apply such analyses to the problem of moral education, thereby capturing aspects of the Growth-Facilitative perspective. Hence, in one seemingly simple investigation these authors manage to employ at least three perspectives on moral argumentation.

A second example of integrative research concerning moral discussion comes from the program of research which I have been conducting concerning transactive moral discussion. In this case, the investigation came about somewhat inadvertently. Throughout our partnership, my colleague John Gibbs and I have disagreed as well as collaborated. While I have always focused, perhaps somewhat mono-maniacally, upon the Growth-Facilitative aspects of moral discussion, Gibbs has been more concerned with Developmental analysis. Recently we collaborated on a study (Gibbs, Schnell, Berkowitz, &

Goldstein, 1983) of the relationship which moral argumentation, specifically transactive discussion, has to cognitive development. We have discovered that, in general, transactive discussion requires a previous development of Piagetian formal logical thinking. In the very process of coming to this discovery, we were forced to integrate the Growth-Facilitative form of moral discussion, uncovered in our previous research, with a Developmental analysis of one stage of such discussion. This approach must to be expanded to identify the other developmental forms of the Growth-Facilitative aspects of moral discussion.

In a third and somewhat related study, Fritz Oser and I, along with our students, Wolfgang Althof, Marie-Madeleine Schildkneckt, and Joyce Caldwell, are attempting to describe the development of transactive discussion (Oser, Berkowitz, & Althof, 1985). Largely at Oser's urging, I have come to recognize the value of expanding the theory of transactive discussion to include a description of its development. We have collected matching sets of data in Switzerland and the United States by asking dyads at five age groups from 6 to 20 years of age to engage in moral and religious dilemma discussions. Thus far we have discovered a clear developmental increase in the usage of transactive discourse, with the greatest increase in early adolescence. We plan to analyze other aspects of these moral discussions by integrating findings on the development of transactive discussion, Oser's notions of what he calls "levels of interaction" and "communicative compactness," and Habermas's aspects of ideal communicative competence.

Future theory and research must address certain critical issues in moral argumentation. For example, theoretical efforts must focus on the integration of diverse perspectives on moral argumentation. Furthermore, empirical efforts must focus on tests of the causality of functional aspects of moral argumentation, as represented by the Instrumental and Growth-Facilitative perspectives. Also, longitudinal research about the developmental aspects of moral argumentation is sorely needed. Research in these and other areas offers the promise of a more integrative and accurate understanding of moral argumentation.

REFERENCES

Argyris, C., & Argyris, D. (1978). *Moral reasoning and moral action: Some preliminary questions.* Unpublished paper, Harvard University.

Argyris, C., & Schön, D. A. (1974). *Theory in practice: Increasing professional effectiveness.* San Francisco: Jossey-Bass.

Berkowitz, M. W. (1985). The role of discussion in moral education. In Berkowitz, M. W., & Oser, F. (Eds.), *Moral education: Theory and application.* Hillsdale, NJ: Lawrence Erlbaum Associates.

Berkowitz, M. W., & Gibbs, J. C. (1983). Measuring the developmental features of moral discussion. *Merrill-Palmer Quarterly, 29,* 399-410.

Berkowitz, M. W., & Gibbs, J. C. (In press). The process of moral conflict resolution and moral development. In M. W. Berkowitz (Ed.), *New directions for child development: Peer conflict and psychological growth.* San Francisco: Jossey-Bass.

Berkowitz, M. W., & Oser, F. (Eds.). (1985). *Moral education: Theory and application.* Hillsdale, NJ: Lawrence Erlbaum Associates.

Colby, A., Kohlberg, L., Fenton, E., Speicher-Dubin, B., & Lieberman, M. (1977). Secondary school moral discussion programmes led by social studies teachers. *Journal of Moral Education, 6,* 90-111.

Colby, A., Kohlberg, L., Gibbs, J. C., & Lieberman, M. (1983). A longitudinal study of moral development. *Monographs of the Society for Research in Child Development, 48*(1-2, Serial No. 200).

Damon, W., & Killen, M. (1982). Peer interaction and the process of change in children's moral reasoning. *Merrill-Palmer Quarterly, 28,* 347-367.

Forman, E. A., & Kraker, M. J. (In press). The social origins of logic: The contributions of Piaget and Vygotsky. In M. W. Berkowitz (Ed.), *New directions for child development: Peer conflict and psychological growth.* San Francisco: Jossey-Bass.

Gibbs, J. C., Schnell, S. V., Berkowitz, M. W., & Goldstein, D. S. (1983). *Relations between formal operations and logical conflict resolution.* Paper read at the meeting of the Society for Research in Child Development, Detroit.

Habermas, J. (1979). *Communication and the evolution of society* (T. McCarthy, Trans.). Boston: Beacon Press.

Habermas, J. (1984). *Theory of communicative action: Vol. 1. Reason and rationality in society* (T. McCarthy, Trans.). Boston: Beacon Press.

Higgins, A. (1980). Research and measurement issues in moral education interventions. In R. L. Mosher (Ed.), *Moral education: A first generation of research and development.* New York: Praeger Press.

Hoffman, M. L., & Saltzstein, H. D. (1967). Parent discipline and the child's moral development. *Journal of Personality and Social Psychology, 5,* 45-57.

Holstein, C. B. (1969). *Parental consensus and interaction in relation to the child's moral judgment.* Unpublished dissertation, University of California, Berkeley.

Keller, M., & Reuss, S. (1985). The process of moral decision-making: Normative and empirical conditions of participation in moral discourse. In M. W. Berkowitz & F. Oser (Eds.), *Moral education: Theory and application.* Hillsdale, NJ: Lawrence Erlbaum Associates.

Kohlberg, L. (1981). *Essays on moral development: Vol.1. The philosophy of moral development.* San Francisco: Harper & Row.

Kohlberg, L. (1984a). *Essays on moral development: Vol. 2. The psychology of moral development.* San Francisco: Harper & Row.

Kohlberg, L. (1984b). *The current status of Stage 6.* Paper presented at the Second Ringberg Conference on Moral Development, July, 1984, Ringberg, Bavaria, Germany.

Leadbeater, B. (1984). *The dynamics of intersubjectivity in adolescent and adult dialogues.* Unpublished dissertation proposal, Columbia University Teachers College.

Lickona, T. (1983). *Raising good children: Helping your child through the stages of moral development.* New York: Bantam Books.

Maitland, K. A., & Goldman, J. R. (1974). Moral judgment as a function of peer group interaction. *Journal of Personality and Social Psychology*, 30, 699-704.

Mall, D. (1982). *In good conscience: Abortion and moral necessity.* Libertyville, IL: Kairos Books.

McCarthy, T. (1978). *The critical theory of Jürgen Habermas.* Cambridge, MA: MIT Press.

Miller, M. (1980). *Learning how to contradict and still pursue a common end: The ontogenesis of moral argumentation.* Unpublished paper, Max Planck Institute, Starnberg, Germany.

Miller, M., & Klein, W. (1979). *Moral argumentations among children: A case study.* Paper presented at the Conference "Beyond Description in Child Language Research," Nijmegen, Netherlands.

Mosher, R. L. (Ed.) (1980). *Moral education: A first generation of research and development.* New York: Praeger Press.

Oser, F. (1981). *Moralisches Urteil in Gruppen.* Frankfurt: Suhrkamp.

Oser, F. (1984). Cognitive stages of interaction in moral discourse. In W. Kurtines & J. Gewirtz (Eds.), *Morality, moral behavior, and moral development.* New York: J. Wiley & Sons.

Oser, F., Berkowitz, M. W., & Althof, W. (1985). *The development of argumentative logic.* Paper presented at the meeting of the Society for Research in Child Development, Toronto.

Parikh, B. (1980). Development of moral judgment and its relation to family environmental factors in Indian and American families. *Child Development*, 51, 1030-1039.

Piaget, J. (1965). *The moral judgment of the child* (M. Gabain, Trans.). New York: Free Press. (Original work published in 1932)

Powers, S. I. (1982). *Family interaction and parental moral development as a context for adolescent moral development.* Unpublished doctoral dissertation, Harvard University.

Pruitt, D. G., & Lewis, S. A. (1977). The psychology of integrative bargaining. In D. Druckman (Ed.), *Negotiations: A social-psychological perspective.* New York: Halsted.

Rawls, J. (1971). *A theory of justice.* Cambridge, MA: Harvard University Press.

Reagan, G. M. (1984). *Resolution of moral disagreements in the classroom: The method of moral negotiation.* Paper presented at the National Conference of the Association for Moral Education, Columbus, Ohio.

Rest, J. R. (1983). Morality. In J. Flavell & E. Markman (Eds.), *Cognitive development*, in P. Mussen (General Editor), *Carmichael's Manual of Child Psychology* (4th Ed.). New York: John Wiley & Sons.

Rogoff, B., & Wertsch, J. V. (Eds.) (1984). *New directions for child development: Children's learning in the "Zone of Proximal Development."* San Francisco: Jossey-Bass.

Selman, R.L. (1980). *The growth of interpersonal understanding: Developmental and clinical analyses.* New York: Academic Press.

Speicher-Dubin, B. (1982). *Parent moral judgment, child moral judgment, and family interaction: A correlational study.* Unpublished doctoral dissertation, Harvard University.

Stanley, S. (1980). The family and moral education. In R. L. Mosher (Ed.), *Moral education: A first generation of research and development.* New York: Praeger.

Tamir, L. (1979). *Communication and the aging process: Interaction throughout the life cycle.* New York: Pergamon Press.

Taranto, M. A. (1984). *Microprocesses in moral conflict dialogues.* Paper presented at the Symposium of the Jean Piaget Society, Philadelphia.

Vygotsky, L. S. (1962). *Thought and language.* Cambridge, MA: MIT Press.

Abraham, Socrates, and Heinz: Where Are the Women? (Care and Context in Moral Reasoning)[1]

Marilyn Friedman

A number of researchers (cf. Holstein, 1976) have claimed that a moral "gender gap" is revealed by Lawrence Kohlberg's research into the stages of development in moral judgment: that women do not score as high as men on Kohlberg's scale of moral reasoning. If sound, such evidence would imply that women's moral judgment, on average, is deficient when compared to that of men. Carol Gilligan has become the best-known of Kohlberg's critics on this issue. The first chapter of her book, *In a Different Voice* (1982), compares the purported gender gap in Kohlberg's work to the work of a number of other theorists and researchers in psychology, for example Freud (1931) and Erikson (1950), whose conclusions all proclaimed the moral and psychological deficiency of women relative to men. Although highly controversial, Gilligan's research has nevertheless generated intense interest in a number of issues which are as important for moral philosophy as they are for moral psychology. Both of these fields are legitimate targets of Gilligan's accusation that there has been little serious study of what she regards as the distinctive moral reasoning of women – women's "different voice."

Gilligan argues that instead of regarding women's moral reasoning as an immature form of the development which men attain, we should recognize that women exhibit a *different* moral development altogether, one which she characterizes either as a "morality of care" or a "morality of responsibility." This alternative framework, this "different voice" for dealing with moral dilemmas, is contrasted with Kohlberg's stage sequence of moral reasoning which centers on the notions of justice and rights. Two of the major features which differentiate Gilligan's alternative, "female" moral framework are: first, that relationships predominate as the central moral consideration; and second, that moral reasoning is permeated by what Gilligan calls "contextual relativism."

As Gilligan explains, the importance of relationships, as women's central moral concern, makes care for and responsibility to persons, rather than rights and rules, the major categories of moral thinking for women. She identifies the concern not to hurt as a major theme of women's moral reasoning, thereby tacitly suggesting that she regards this concern as absent from Kohlberg's moral stages. Also, according to Gilligan, feelings of empathy and compassion abound for women, the expression of care is considered the fulfillment of moral responsibility, and principles of justice and rights are absent.

The "contextual relativism" which Gilligan attributes to women's moral judgment actually encompasses two distinct features: one, a great sensitivity to the details of situations; and two, a reluctance to make moral judgments. The feature which I shall emphasize is that of sensitivity to detail. Gilligan suggests that women more often than men will respond to stories such as the Heinz dilemma by changing it and by asking for more details before reaching a conclusion. Women are likely to seek the detail that makes the suffering clear and engages compassion and caring. In Gilligan's view, such responses have often been misunderstood by researchers on moral reasoning, who regarded them as showing a failure to comprehend the dilemmas or the problem to be solved. On the contrary, Gilligan says, these responses represent a *challenge* to the problem as it is posed: a rejection of its adequacy in allowing any real or meaningful choice.

In this paper, I will explore some philosophically important dimensions of the sort of reasoning to which Gilligan has drawn our attention. In the first part of the paper, I will attempt to show, through a sequence of hypothetical narratives, that considerations of care and relationships are more important in overall moral reasoning than Kohlberg, for one, has yet appreciated. The second, and final, part of the paper is a discussion of the role of contextual detail in moral reasoning. This, I believe, is the philosophically important core of the "contextual relativism" which has caught Gilligan's attention. After taking note of some research findings concerning the Gilligan-Kohlberg controversy over gender differences, I will attempt to move beyond that controversy and address the philosophical importance of the two features of moral reasoning which Gilligan's gender-based studies have highlighted: care and contextual detail.

CARE

Gilligan's claims about the differences between men's and women's moral judgments have become highly controversial. Most of the controversy has centered on two claims: one, that women tend to score lower than men when measured according to Kohlberg's moral reasoning framework; and two, that Kohlberg's framework is male-biased and fails to take into account the distinctly different moral orientation of women. Walker (1982) has recently surveyed all the empirical studies which were supposed to have revealed sex differences in scorings: his conclusion is that there is no significant difference. Some studies do show that adult males score higher on Kohlberg's scale than do adult females, but these differences appear to be explicable by differences in level of education and occupation rather than by differences in gender. In particular, it seems that housewives are the women who tend to score lower on Kohlberg's scale. In one of his most recent books, *Moral Stages: A Current Reformulation and Response to Critics* (Kohlberg et al., 1983; unless otherwise indicated, in the present essay page references to Kohlberg are to this work), Kohlberg has reminded us of his ongoing contention that the attainment of the higher stages of moral reasoning depends "upon a sense of participation, responsibility, and role-taking in the secondary institutions of society such as work and government" (p. 129), all of which, we are evidently supposed to believe, are unavailable to housewives.

If women do not score significantly differently from men on Kohlberg's scale when matched against men of similar educational and occupational background, then there would be considerably less evidence for a gender gap in moral reasoning. There would also be considerably less evidence for the second controversial claim, namely, that Kohlberg's framework is male-biased because it ignores the distinctly different moral orientation of women. However, and more important, even if there is no gender gap, a substantial bias in Kohlberg's framework seems to have been uncovered by Gilligan's work – not necessarily a bias toward male moral reasoning, but a bias toward certain particular moral considerations which constitute only a part of the whole range of our moral reasoning.

Kohlberg himself has acknowledged that Gilligan's research prompted him to take into account the importance to overall moral development of notions of care, relationships, and responsibility, and to consider how these moral concerns augment his own prior emphasis on reasoning having to do with justice and rights. He has suggested that his previous concern has been with "justice reasoning" only, and that it is unfortunate that it was simply called "moral reasoning," as if it represented the whole breadth and substance of the moral cognitive domain. Kohlberg has supported his contention that there is no gender gap in moral reasoning by arguing that both sexes use justice and care orientations, and that the type of orientation used depends on "the type of moral problem defined" and the environment in which the problem is located. Moral dilemmas located, for example, in a family context are more likely to invoke caring considerations from both sexes, whereas dilemmas located in a secondary institution of society, such as government, are more likely to invoke justice considerations from both sexes.

I leave to psychologists the task of assessing the empirical claim about differences in the moral reasoning of the two sexes. My interest is in the relationship between the two different moral perspectives which are now recognized by both Kohlberg and Gilligan. In *Moral Stages*, Kohlberg has argued that justice and caring are not "two different tracks of moral development which are either independent or in polar opposition to one another," that "many moral situations or dilemmas do not pose a choice between one or the other orientation, but rather call out a response which integrates both orientations," and that considerations of caring need not conflict with those of justice "but may be integrated into a response consistent with justice, especially at the postconventional level" (pp. 134, 139). Several decades ago, we learned that "separate" was inherently unequal; however, we cannot assume that "integrated" is inherently equal. In Kohlberg's most recent formulation, even though it is claimed that care can be integrated with justice, considerations of justice are still taken to be " . . . primary in defining the moral domain" (p. 91).

Kohlberg and his colleagues have portrayed a morality of care as pertaining to special relationships among particular persons, in contrast to the universalistic relationships handled by justice reasoning, suggesting that "central to the ethic of particularistic relationships are affectively-tinged ideas and attitudes of *caring, love, loyalty, and responsibility*" (pp. 20-21). In Kohlberg's estimation, special relationships should be regarded as supplementing and deepening the sense of generalized obligations of justice. For example, in the Heinz dilemma, Heinz's care for his wife would be regarded as supplementing the obligation which he has to respect her right to life. However, an ethic of care cannot, in Kohlberg's view, supplant a morality of justice, because an ethic of care is, in and of itself, not well adapted to resolve justice problems: problems which require principles to resolve conflicting claims among persons, all of whom in some sense should be cared about. (pp. 20-21)

Furthermore, "morally valid forms of caring and community presuppose prior conditions and judgments of justice" (p. 92).

Kohlberg has admitted that the primacy of justice has not been "proven" by his research, and that, instead, it has been a guiding assumption of the research, based on certain methodological and metaethical considerations (pp. 93-95). First, it is based on a "prescriptivist conception of moral judgment"; that is, moral judgment is treated not as expressing the interpretation of situational facts, but rather as the expression of universalizable "ought" claims. Second, it derives from a search for moral universality, for "minimal value conceptions on which all persons could agree." Third, the primacy of justice has stemmed from Kohlberg's cognitive, or rational, approach to morality. In Kohlberg's words,

justice asks for "objective" or rational reasons and justifications for choice rather than being satisfied with subjective, "decisionistic," personal commitments to aims and to other persons. (p. 93)

Finally, Kohlberg has claimed that the most important reason for the primacy of justice is that it is "the most structural feature of moral judgment." "With the moral domain defined in terms of justice," he has written, "we have been successful in . . . elaborating stages which are structural systems in the Piagetian tradition . . . " (p. 92). Kohlberg has suggested that care reasoning may not be capable of being represented in terms of the criteria which he takes to define Piagetian cognitive stages.

Kohlberg's grounds for according primacy to justice reasoning are unsatisfactory for several reasons. First, the methodological considerations to which he has appealed entitle us at best to infer that justice is primary in that domain of morality which *can* be represented in terms of Piagetian hard stages, but not that justice is primary to morality as such. Second, his appeal to certain *metaethical* considerations is controversial at best, question-begging at worst. Whether moral judgments express universalizable prescriptions rather than interpretations of situational facts, whether there are "minimal value conceptions on which all persons could agree," whether "personal commitments to aims and to other persons" are excluded as rational justifications of choice, as Kohlberg has seemed to suggest – all these are issues which cannot be resolved simply by *assuming* the primacy of a type of reasoning which has these features. Each of these issues is controversial and calls for considerably more reflection.

Kohlberg's primacy of justice in defining the moral domain is troubling for a third reason. I have noted Kohlberg's suggestion that higher scores on his scale of moral development are correlated with participation in the secondary institutions of society, such as government and the workplace outside the home. By contrast, care reasoning is supposed to be relevant only to special relationships among "family, friends, and group members" (Kohlberg et al., 1983, p. 131). It is tempting to characterize these two sorts of moral reasoning as pertaining, respectively, to the "public" or "political" realm and to the so-called "private" or "personal" realm. It seems that Kohlberg's primacy of justice reasoning coincides with a long-standing presumption of western thought that the world of personal relationships, of the family and of family ties and loyalties – the traditional world of women – is a world of lesser moral importance than the public world of government and of the marketplace – the male-dominated world outside the home.

Considerations of justice and rights have to do with abstract persons regarded as bound together by a social contract to act in ways that show mutual respect for rights which they possess equally. Considerations of justice do not require that persons know each other personally. Relatives, friends, or perfect strangers all deserve the same fair treatment and respect from one another. In Kohlberg's view, considerations of special relationships and of caring seem merely to enrich with compassion judgments which are based on *prior* considerations of justice. In no way would considerations of special relationship, for Kohlberg, override those of justice and rights. Unless caring and community presupposed prior judgments of justice, they would seem, in Kohlberg's terms, not to be "morally valid" (p. 92). In the discussion to follow, I shall begin to challenge Kohlberg's emphasis on the primacy of justice. I shall do so by telling some stories, the point of which is to suggest that sometimes considerations of justice and rights *are* legitimately overridden by considerations of special relationship. My stories will not, of course, show that special relationships *always* override considerations of justice; indeed, I do not believe that to be the case. But I hope to begin delineating in some detail just what the priorities and inter-connections are between these apparently diverse moral notions.

My first story is the biblical story of Abraham, asked by God to sacrifice Isaac, Abraham's only son. In this familiar tale, Abraham shows himself willing to carry out the command; only at the last moment does God intervene to provide a sacrificial ram and permission for Abraham to sacrifice it in place of Isaac. Abraham's faith in God has been tested and has proved unshakeable. Both Gilligan (p. 104) and Flanagan (1982) referred to this story in their discussion of the controversy about sex-differences in moral reasoning. They each used it as an illustration of what can go wrong with Kohlberg's highest, or principled, stage of moral reasoning, a stage, as Flanagan puts it, "where 'principle' always wins out in conflicts with even the strongest affiliative instincts and familial obligations" (p. 501). Kohlberg has disagreed with the Gilligan/Flanagan interpretation of the Abraham story as follows:

> By no stretch of the imagination could Abraham's willingness to sacrifice Isaac be interpreted by Gilligan or myself as an example or outcome of principled moral reasoning. It is, rather, an example of an action based on reasoning that the morally right is defined by authority (in this case God's authority) as opposed to universalizable moral principles. For both Gilligan and myself such judgment based on authority would represent conventional (Stage 4) moral judgment, not postconventional (principled) moral judgment. (p. 104)

However, there is at least one more way to interpret the Abraham story, and it is an interpretation which regards Abraham's choice to sacrifice Isaac as deriving from the considerations of a special relationship which is taken to override the duties derived from justice and rights. This third interpretation is suggested by Søren Kierkegaard in *Fear and Trembling* (Kierkegaard, 1941). Kierkegaard reminds us that Abraham's faith in and love for God were being tested by God's command that Abraham sacrifice his only son. In Kierkegaard's view, " . . . to the son the father has the highest and most sacred obligation" (p. 39). Thus Kohlberg is wrong, given this interpretation, to think that Abraham's act derives from the Stage 4 reasoning that whatever God says is right. There must be *some* sense in which what Abraham is asked to do remains morally *wrong*. The supreme test of the faith of a moral person is to ask that person to commit what he or she continues to regard as a grave moral wrong; only this sort of act would be the greatest sacrifice that such a person could be asked to make. If the command of God made the sacrifice of Isaac right in *all* senses, then it would be no sacrifice for a moral person such as Abraham to perform it, and hence, no test of his faith. Thus, one way of construing the story of Abraham, derived loosely from Kierkegaard's interpretation, is that it represents the moral dilemma of someone having to choose to uphold the right to life, thereby sacrificing relationship with a Supreme Being, or, rather to choose relationship with a Supreme Being, thereby sacrificing considerations of rights.

My second story is taken from Plato's dialogue, the *Euthyphro.* In this dialogue, Socrates encounters Euthyphro who has just arranged to prosecute his father for murder. The victim was a slave in Euthyphro's home who had killed another domestic servant in a drunken fit. Euthyphro's father tied up the slave who had done the killing, threw him into a ditch, and went to seek advice about what to do with him. Before the father could return, the slave died in the ditch from the cold, hunger, and chains. Socrates is astonished that Euthyphro would prosecute his own father for bringing about such a death. Socrates' reaction is complicated by certain troubling suggestions: an emphasis on the servant status of the man left to die by Euthyphro's father, and an emphasis on the father's status as "master," as if this role conferred privileges of life and death over servants. In this discussion, I will ignore these suggestions and focus only on Socrates' concern that a charge of murder is being brought against a father by his own son. Euthyphro tries to defend his action by appeal to universal rules, in particular, a rule of piety, which is something that both Socrates and Euthyphro accept as a part of justice. The rule, in Euthyphro's view, calls for "prosecuting anyone who is guilty of murder, sacrilege, or of any other similar crime – whether he be your father or mother, or some other person, that makes no difference . . . ." Against this universalizable, impartial injunction, Socrates continues to express strong reservations, as if the responsibilities deriving from family relationships outweigh even considerations of justice.

Socrates has been singled out by Kohlberg as one of the few human beings ever to have reached the highest stage of moral reasoning, now called the "hypothetical" sixth stage. It is, therefore, especially poignant to recall the story of the *Euthyphro,* in which it is the figure of Socrates who suggests that impartial and universalizable considerations of justice may be overridden by personal responsibilities arising out of familial relationships, relationships which are particular and non-universalizable.

It might be argued that the responsibilities deriving from particular relationships are universalizable. For example, if it is true that certain behavior is owed to someone simply because that person is my father, then such behavior is owed *by anyone* to whoever happens to be that person's father. Thus, more needs to be said in order to differentiate the responsibilities entailed by personal relationships from the duties which are based upon considerations of justice and rights. I have two suggestions to make about the differences between them. First, many of the personal relationships which matter to us do not originate in mutual consent, or with anything that can suitably be represented by the metaphor of a social contract – this is particularly true of most kinship ties. Yet, as one moves up Kohlberg's scale of moral reasoning, social contract becomes increasingly important as the justification of universalizability in moral reasoning. Therefore, the responsibilities arising out of personal relationships still cannot be derived from Kohlbergian justice principles. Second, justice does not seem to require as a duty the *special* treatment of one's kin. Certainly it does not require that one's kin be treated as exempt from the considerations of justice that *are* owed to all persons – the treatment suggested by Socrates in the *Euthyphro*.

Thus far my stories have all been about men. Yet Gilligan's work on *women's* moral development was the original stimulus for my investigation. My remaining stories will, therefore be about women. I shall take the liberty of performing a sex-change operation on the Heinz dilemma, the most famous of the dilemmas used by Kohlberg to measure the level of moral reasoning of interview subjects. The original dilemma is as follows:

> In Europe, a woman was near death from cancer. One drug might save her, a form of radium that a druggist in the same town had recently discovered. The druggist was charging $2000, ten times what the drug cost him to make. The sick woman's husband, Heinz, went to everyone he knew to borrow the money, but he could only get together about half of what it cost. He told the druggist that his wife was dying and asked him to sell it cheaper or let him pay later. But the druggist said, "No." The husband got desperate and broke into the man's store to steal the drug for his wife. Should the husband have done that? Why? (Kohlberg, 1969, p. 379)

Of course, there is already a woman in the Heinz dilemma, namely, Heinz's wife. She is easy to forget since, unlike Heinz, she has no name, and unlike both Heinz and the also unnamed druggist, she is the only person in the story who does not act. Instead she is simply the passive patient who is there to be saved, the one whose presence provides both Heinz and the druggist with their moral opportunities for heroism and villainy. Let us remove her from this oblivion. First, she needs a name: I will call her Heidi. Next, let us change her role from that of patient to that of agent. Finally, let us suppose that the druggist, another unnamed character in the original dilemma, is also a woman; I will call her Hilda. Now we are ready for our new story, the "Heidi dilemma":

> In Europe, a man was near death from cancer. One drug might save him, a form of radium that a druggist in the same town, a woman named Hilda, had recently discovered. The druggist was charging $2000, ten times what the drug cost her to make. The sick man's wife, Heidi, went to everyone she knew to borrow the money, but she could only get together about half of what it cost. She told Hilda, the druggist, that her husband was dying and asked Hilda to sell the drug cheaper or let her, Heidi, pay later. But Hilda said, "No." Heidi got desperate and broke into the woman's store to steal the drug for her husband. Should the wife have done that? Why?

It would be interesting to speculate whether any of our responses to the dilemma have changed as a result of the sex-change operation and the emergence of a woman as protagonist. However my real concern is with an even more modified version of the original dilemma. The first version involves only preliminary changes. Here is a second version of the Heidi dilemma:

> In Europe, a man was near death from cancer. One drug might save him, a form of radium that a druggist in the same town, a woman named Hilda, had recently discovered. The druggist was charging $2000, ten times what the drug cost her to make. A perfect stranger, a woman named Heidi, chanced to read about the sick man's plight in the local newspaper. She was moved to act. She went to everyone she knew to borrow the money for the drug, but she could only get together about half of what it cost. She asked the druggist to sell the drug more cheaply or to let her, Heidi, pay for it later. But Hilda, the druggist, said, "No." Heidi broke into the woman's store to steal the drug for a man she did not know. Should Heidi have done that? Why?

If Kohlberg's dilemma can indeed be resolved through impartial considerations of justice and rights, then the solution to the dilemma should not depend upon the existence of any special relationship between the person who is dying of cancer and the prospective thief of the drug. However, I suggest that the conviction which many of us have that Heinz should steal the drug for his nameless wife in the original dilemma, rests at least in part on our notion of responsibilities arising out of the special relationship called marriage, and that without this relationship, our conviction that theft ought to be committed might well – on grounds provided simply by the story – be much weaker than it is. If the patient and the prospective thief were absolute strangers, I suspect that we would be far less likely to say that a serious personal risk should be taken to steal the drug, break the law, and harm the druggist – even to save a life.

In *Moral Stages*, Kohlberg has already responded to the question of whether the solution to the original Heinz dilemma depends upon considerations of justice alone or upon considerations of special relationship as well. Kohlberg first explained why the issue is important, writing: "A universalizable judgment that appeals to norms implies a fair or impartial application of the norms" (p. 92). He then produced excerpts from an interview with an 11-year-old boy who was asked whether a "man" should steal a drug to save the life of a stranger "if there was no other way to save his life." The 11-year-old first responded that it does not seem that one should steal for someone whom one doesn't care about. But then the boy revised his judgment and said:

> But somehow it doesn't seem fair to say that. The stranger has his life and wants to live just as much as your wife; it isn't fair to say you should steal it for your wife but not for the stranger. (p. 92)

For Kohlberg, this example illustrates the way in which a concern for universalizing a moral judgment leads to a preference for justice reasoning rather than reasoning in terms of care and special relationship.

I shall conclude this section with several comments on Kohlberg's sample 11-year-old. First, the boy's reasoning is actually quite perceptive: it is *not* fair to steal the drug for one's spouse but not for a stranger. Considerations of *fairness* would not lead to this distinction among needy persons. If there is a distinction of this sort between what is owed to one's kin and what is owed to strangers, the distinction would likely derive from the special nature of the relationship to one's kin. If my duty to steal in order to save a life is owed to my kin in virtue of my kinship relationship to them, then the fact that it's *not fair* that I don't have this duty toward strangers does *not* entail that I therefore *have* the same duty toward strangers as I do toward my kin. The main point of my stories was to suggest that we cannot presuppose that considerations of justice have moral primacy, never to be outweighed by considerations of special relationship. Considerations of justice and rights do not necessarily lead to the conclusion that we owe to all persons the special treatment which is due to our family and friends. It may not be "fair" but, as I have been trying to suggest, fairness may not be our only moral concern.

Second, I suspect that the response of Kohlberg's 11-year-old is atypical and that few persons, even at the higher stage of justice reasoning, would sincerely judge that a person ought to steal, with all that this entails, to save the life of a stranger. If you are not persuaded that this is so, then I shall simply make one final modification to the Heinz dilemma. The result is the "You" dilemma:

> *You* are the perfect stranger who has just read in your morning paper of a man dying of cancer and of the only drug which can save him, yet which he cannot afford. *You* are the stranger who fails to convince the druggist to sell the drug more cheaply. Will *you* take the risk of stealing the drug to save the life of someone you don't know? What moral judgment will you make in *this* dilemma?

CONTEXT

The second point raised by Gilligan which I wish to explore is the importance to moral reasoning of a sensitivity to contextual detail. Gilligan suggests that women, more so than men, respond inadequately to such dilemmas as the Heinz dilemma because the dilemmas themselves are problematic. In Gilligan's view the problem is that they are hypothetical rather than real dilemmas; they are too abstract and, as she puts it, they separate "the moral problem from the social contingencies of its possible occurrence" (1982, p. 100). I shall try to strengthen Gilligan's insight by putting the point somewhat differently. What matters is not whether the dilemmas are real or hypothetical, but rather whether they are spelled out in great detail or simply described in a very abbreviated form. A substantial work of literature can portray a moral crisis with enough detail to make most of us feel that we know enough to judge what should be done by the protagonist. When Nora leaves her marriage home, her "Doll's House," many of us support her decision wholeheartedly; the hypothetical nature of her moral dilemma is simply unimportant.

Perhaps Gilligan has been distracted by the fact that when we learn of real moral dilemmas, we typically know the people and a good bit about their lives and their current situations. We rely upon our background information to help ourselves generate alternative possible solutions for those problems. Hypothetical dilemmas have no social or historical context outside their own specifications. Lacking any background information, we require longer stories in order to feel confident that we know most of the pertinent information that can be expected in cases of this sort. What matters is having enough detail for the story at hand – whether the story is of a real or a hypothetical moral dilemma.

Gilligan herself provides an example of how the hypothetical Heinz dilemma would be significantly altered were it to be enriched by some very plausible details. Commenting on the response to the Heinz dilemma given by one subject, Gilligan says:

> Heinz's decision to steal is considered not in terms of the logical priority of life over property, which justifies its rightness, but rather in terms of the actual consequences that stealing would have for a man of limited means and little social power.
>
> Considered in the light of its probable outcomes – his wife dead, or Heinz in jail, brutalized by the violence of that experience and his life compromised by a record of felony – the dilemma itself changes. Its resolution has less to do with the relative weights of life and property in an abstract moral conception than with the collision between two lives, formerly conjoined but now in opposition, where the continuation of one life can occur only at the expense of the other. (p. 101)

In order to make clear just how important contextual detail is, let us elaborate the Heinz/Heidi dilemma even further. The woman who dying of cancer is weary and depressed from the losing battle which she has been fighting with cancer for several years. It all began with cancer of the colon, and her doctors convinced her to resort to a colostomy. Now, several years later, it is clear that the malignancy was not stopped by this drastic measure. Disfigured in a manner which she has never been able to accept, weakened and in pain from the cancer which continues to poison her system, bedridden and dependent on others for her daily functioning, she has lost hope and grown despondent at a fate which, to her, is worse than death. How does this woman really measure the value of her own life?

And perhaps there is more to the druggist's story as well. Her husband deserted her and her three children years ago, and has paid not a penny of his court-ordered child support. So the druggist struggles mightily day after day to keep her family together and tend a small pharmacy which barely meets her material needs let alone those of her children. Moreover, she lives in a society which jealously guards the private ownership of its property. Were she and her children to fall into poverty, that society would throw her a few crumbs of welfare support, but only after she had exhausted all other resources, and at the cost of her dignity and the invasion of her privacy. In this society, the tiny share of goods on which she can labor and whose fruits she can sell are the slender means of livelihood for her and her family. The notion of property does not mean the same thing in regard to a single mother with dependent children who are living at the margin in a capitalist economy as it does in regard to the holdings of General Dynamics. The druggist, too, is a person of flesh and blood with a story of her own to tell.

There are other contingencies which could be explored. I have already referred to one of the interviews highlighted by Gilligan in which the subject ponders the risks and uncertainties of theft for a person who hasn't the skill or experience to bring the job off successfully – burglary is no mean accomplishment. Then there are the possible deleterious side-effects of drugs which are *proclaimed* as cancer cures in all the glittering hyperbole of the mass media before they have been adequately tested. And on and on. When the story is filled out in these ways, it is no longer possible to resolve the dilemma with a simple principle asserting the primacy of life over property. A restrictive economic context can turn property into a family's only means to life, and can force a competition of life *against* life in a desperate struggle which not all can win. Indeed, the most pervasive and universalizable problems of justice in the Heinz dilemma lie entirely outside the scope of its narrowly chosen details.

The significance of the *real* justice problem in the Heinz dilemma has apparently been missed or ignored by Kohlberg, whose construction of the dilemma as a problem in moral reasoning forces a choice between two alternatives which are, in fact, identical in at least one important respect: neither of them threatens the institutional status quo in which the situation occurs. The significance of this more fundamental justice problem has also not been commented on by Gilligan, even though she perceives the importance of grasping the situation in terms of rich contextual detail. Gilligan appears to think that contextual detail is a concern only of people whose moral reasoning centers on care and relationships. She does not appear to realize that in reasoning about justice and rights, it is equally inappropriate to draw conclusions from highly abbreviated descriptions of situations. Gilligan's position would be strengthened, I believe, by incorporating this insight.

In the Heinz situation, there are broad issues of social justice in the delivery of health care which are at stake. These issues cannot be resolved nor even properly understood from the scanty detail which is provided in any of Kohlberg's formulations of the so-called "dilemma." We must have background knowledge about the inadequacy of health care provided for people without financial resources, in a society which allows most health care resources to be privately owned, privately sold for profit in the marketplace, and privately withheld from people who cannot afford the market price. Before we can resolve the problem, we must know what the alternatives are, and must assess them for the degree to which they approximate an ideal of fair and just health care available to all, and the degree to which they achieve, or fall short of, other relevant moral ideals.

For example, should we allow health care resources to remain privately owned while we simply implement a Medicaid-like program of government transfer payments to subsidize the cost of health care to the needy? Or, should the government provide mandatory health insurance for everyone, with premiums taken from those who can pay, as a kind of health care tax, and premiums waived for those who cannot pay, as an in-kind welfare benefit? Or, should we instead abolish private ownership of health care resources altogether, and, if so, should our alternative be grassroots-organized health care cooperatives, or state-run socialized medicine? Selecting an answer to these questions and resolving the *real* justice dilemma which the Heidi/Heinz situation merely intimates requires an inordinate amount of detail as well as a complex theoretical perspective on matters of economics, politics, and social and domestic life. Thus, contextual detail is overwhelmingly important in matters of justice as well as in matters of care and relationships.

There is a second feature of Gilligan's emphasis on contextual detail in moral reasoning which I would change. Gilligan believes that a concern for contextual detail moves a moral reasoner away from principled moral reasoning in the direction of what she calls "contextual relativism." She suggests that persons who exemplify this form of moral reasoning have "difficulty at arriving at definitive answers to moral judgments" and show a "reluctance to judge" others (p. 101). Obviously, many people experience this reluctance at some time or other, and some people experience it all the time. But we misunderstand moral reasoning if we regard this as a necessary or inevitable outcome of becoming concerned with contextual detail.

At the same time, Kohlberg's response to Gilligan on this point is simplistic and unhelpful. In Kohlberg's view, the notion of a principle is the notion of that which guides moral judgment in a way which allows for exceptions. On this premise, a responsiveness to contextual details and a willingness to alter moral judgments depending upon the context does not imply an abandonment of moral principles or a genuine moral relativism (Kohlberg, 1983, pp. 145-148). For Kohlberg, an increasing awareness of context need only indicate an increasing awareness of the difficulties of applying one's principles to specific cases. There is something to this: sensitivity to contextual detail need not carry with it the relativistic view that there *are no* moral rights or wrongs, nor the slightly weaker view that *there is no way to decide* what is right or wrong. It need only be associated with uncertainties about which principles to apply to a particular case, or a concern that one does not yet *know* enough to apply one's principles, or a worry that one's principles are too *narrow* to deal with the novelties at hand.

However, this last alternative is quite significant. It is precisely the possibility of this narrowness of principle which Kohlberg seems not to appreciate. A rich sense of contextual detail awakens one to the limitations in moral thinking which arise from the *minimalist* moral principles with which we are familiar. A principle which asserts the primacy of life over property is obviously not wrong; in the abstract, few of us would be reluctant to make this judgment. But its relevance to a particular situation depends on countless details about the quality of *those particular* lives, the meaning of *that particular* property, the identity of those whose lives or property are at stake, the range of available options, the potential benefits and harms of each, the institutional setting which structures the situation and the lives of its participants – and the possibility of changing that institutional context. These details are ordinarily very complex; some sway us in one direction, some in another. In no time at all, we will need principles for the *ordering* of our principles. Kohlberg's suggestion that contextual detail helps one figure out which principle to apply simply does not get us very far in understanding how we finally decide what ought to be done in the complex, institutionally structured situations of our everyday lives. This is true whether the reasoning is about care and relationships or about matters of social justice.

Kohlberg has already acknowledged a variety of ways in which his scale of moral development does not measure the whole of moral reasoning; it is limited to what he calls structural stages in the development of reasoning about justice and rights. Drawing upon Gilligan's gender-based critique of Kohlberg, I have discussed two other limitations which I regard as highly significant: first, the absence of any real integration of moral considerations having to do with care and relationships; and second, the absence of an adequate account of how people reason about complex and richly specified situations in terms of moral rules and principles.

NOTE

1. Another version of this essay is to appear as a MOSAIC monograph
    under the title, *Care and Context in Moral Reasoning* (Bath, England:
    University of Bath Press).

REFERENCES

Erikson, E. (1950). *Childhood and society.* New York: W. W. Norton.
Flanagan, O. (1982). Virtue, sex and gender: Some philosophical reflections on the
    moral psychology debate. *Ethics,* 92, 501.
Freud, S. (1931). Female sexuality. In J. Strachey (Ed.), *The standard edition of the
    complete psychological works of Sigmund Freud* (Vol. 3). London: The Hogarth Press,
    1961.
Gilligan, C. (1982). *In a different voice.* Cambridge, MA: Harvard University Press.
Holstein, C. (1976). Development of moral judgment: A longitudinal study of males
    and females. *Child Development,* 47, 51-61.
Kierkegaard, S. (1941). *Fear and trembling* (W. Lowrie, Trans.). Princeton, NJ:
    Princeton University Press.
Kohlberg, L. (1969). Stage and sequence: The cognitive-developmental approach to
    socialization. In D. A. Goslin (Ed.), *Handbook of socialization theory and research.*
    Chicago: Rand McNally.
Kohlberg, L., Levine, C., & Hewer, A. (1983). *Moral stages: A current reformulation and
    response to critics.* Basel: S. Karger.
Walker, L. J. (1984). Sex differences in the development of moral reasoning: A crit-
    ical review. *Child Development,* 55, 677-691.

Intention, Contradiction, and the Recognition of Dilemmas

Carol Gibb Harding

When the moral development researcher confronts a child (or adult) with a hypothetical situation designed to present a dilemma (e.g., the Heinz dilemma), he or she typically asks questions to ascertain what the child thinks should be done in such a situation, and why. Some of the conclusions of this research concerning children's and adults' thinking about dilemmas are presented in this volume. For example: (1) decisions about dilemmas may be based on the principle of justice, or on care, or even on enlightened self-interest; (2) decisions, or at least their justifications, appear to change as children age, perhaps because of developing cognitive structures that allow for reversibility of thought, and perhaps also because of developing competence in employing emotions, particularly compassion, in the process of understanding; and (3) the decision-making process can be altered through education to become more effective in the resolution of dilemmas. Given this information, it seems that the process of reasoning about dilemmas has been well documented, if not entirely agreed upon. However, amid this plethora of inquiry, one aspect of the process has been neglected. I refer to the process of *recognizing* dilemmas. Although it is clear, given the general use of the concept, that most of us think we do recognize and can even agree on which events are dilemmas, it is not clear what it is about these events, or about our interpretation of them, that leads us to treat them as dilemmas.

My query concerning the recognition of dilemmas is twofold: (1) What are the characteristics of events that come to be interpreted as dilemmas? and (2) what is the process of human thinking that leads to that interpretation? The following discussion is organized around these two questions. The first part is a discussion of characteristics of dilemmas. These characteristics are presented as if they identify information intrinsic to certain events, although all such characteristics are presumed to be based on interpretations of the contexts in which events occur. It is also assumed that these characteristics have been generally agreed upon. It may be, in fact, that the process of recognizing dilemmas has not been neglected as a topic of study so much as it has been taken for granted. The assumption may be that all humans recognize all dilemmas in much the same way, and that it is only when they begin thinking about the resolution of dilemmas that the process becomes interesting. In any event, in this discussion the attempt is made to step back and consider what characteristics are used, and to develop both logically and psychologically a working definition of "dilemma."

This leads to the second part of the discussion: What is the process of thought through which individuals come to interpret events as dilemmas? This process must, of course, be related to characteristics of the events. However, this part of the discussion focuses on how the development of thought, through both cognitive construction and social interaction, leads to an interpretation of the meaning of, first, any event involving choices and, then, those events identified as dilemmas. A case is made that the development of the concept of "dilemma" requires the ability to act with intention and to interpret others' behavior as if it were intentional. A model for describing the development of intention is applied to the process of recognizing dilemmas.

A second aspect of development which relates to dilemma recognition is the interpretation of contradiction. It is proposed that through the cognitive achievement of reversibility, a person becomes able not only to recognize dilemmas in the traditional sense, but also to construct new dilemmas through the ability to invent negations for any event.

CHARACTERISTICS OF DILEMMAS

For the purposes of this discussion, I begin by assuming that there are characteristics common to all dilemmas and that those dilemmas labeled "moral" are a subset defined as dilemmas requiring moral reasoning for their resolution. I do not believe that events themselves are either moral or not moral, but rather that decisions about events may require reasoning about issues of morality. However, since I have limited my query to how dilemmas are recognized, I refer the reader to the other chapters in this volume for discussions of whether or not certain resolutions follow from moral reasoning.

In logic, any argument of the following form is defined as a dilemma:

Either p or q (but not both).

If p, then r.

If q, then s.

Therefore, either r or s.

Although we usually think of the two outcomes of a dilemma as being equally unpleasant, the logical requirement is only that they be equal, with no valid argument for choosing one over the other. This provides the first and most basic characteristic of a dilemma: *1. A dilemma is a valid argument which concludes with a choice between two equal alternatives.*

In theory the dilemma is unsolvable; in practice a resolution must be found. The first attempt at resolution may be avoidance of the dilemma. Avoidance, of course, is logically impossible if the premises are true. However, it is often difficult to know whether the premises are true. For example, the first premise, "Either p or q," appears straightforward until one begins to question its relevance to real life. Are there situations where there is no way of avoiding an either–or decision? Is there no way of including other options in the premise? Given the complexity of life, one hesitates to concede that there are situations in which options are truly limited to an either–or decision. For a simplistic example, consider a dilemma of the sort often presented in logic textbooks:

> Mr. Brown has been compelled to appear in court because he has been charged with a minor traffic violation of which he is innocent. The judge asks whether he pleads guilty or not guilty. This is Mr. Brown's dilemma:
>
> Either I plead quilty or I plead not guilty.
>
> If I plead guilty, then I must pay a fine of five dollars for an offense I did not commit.
>
> If I plead not guilty, then I must spend another whole day in court.
>
> Therefore, either I must pay a fine of five dollars for an offense I did not commit or I must spend another whole day in court.

The argument is a valid example of the form presented earlier. The problem is that one need not be in an either–or situation. There are other choices. Mr. Brown can plead guilty with extenuating circumstances and may not have to pay a fine; or he can petition to have someone else represent him in court so as not to spend another day there; or he can skip town and enter no plea at all. Any situation presented in the form given above is indeed a dilemma; one must, however, be certain that the premises are true. This insight is not profound. However, it appears to be critical when considering dilemmas, particularly those outside the logic textbooks. I offer this as the second characteristic of dilemmas, even though it appears redundant set beside the first characteristic: *2. A dilemma assumes that there is no way to avoid choosing one of the alternatives.*

With this characteristic I have moved from a discussion of the form of the state of affairs called a dilemma to an interpretation of the truth or meaningfulness of that state of affairs. Although it may be that true dilemmas do not exist in real life, it is certainly evident and observable that humans act as if dilemmas do exist. In his book *After Virtue,* MacIntyre (1981) gives three examples of contemporary moral dilemmas: (1) just war vs. peace; (2) the unborn's right to life vs. the pregnant woman's right to free choice; and (3) the provision of public services as a means for equalizing opportunity vs. the provision for the free enterprise of physicians, teachers, and other service providers. Within each of these debates is what MacIntyre labels an interminable argument. Having described the characteristic rival moral arguments, he concludes:

> Every one of the arguments is logically valid or can be easily expanded so as to be made so; the conclusions do indeed follow from the premises. But the rival premises are such that we possess no rational way of weighing the claims of one as against another. For each premise employs some quite different normative or evaluative concept from the others, so that the claims made upon us are of quite different kinds. In the first argument, for example, premises which invoke justice and innocence are at odds with premises which invoke success and survival; in the second, premises which invoke rights are at odds with those which invoke universalisability; in the third it is the claim of equality that is matched against that of liberty. It is precisely because there is in our society no established way of deciding between these claims that moral argument appears to be necessarily interminable. From our rival conclusions we can argue back to our rival premises; but when we do arrive at our premises argument ceases and the invocation of one premise against another becomes a matter of pure assertion and counter-assertion. Hence perhaps the slightly shrill tone of so much moral debate. (p. 8)

Although MacIntyre presents his interpretation of the philosophical stance best suited to serve society in addressing these arguments, it is the recognition of such dilemmas, not their resolution, that is pertinent here. The interminable arguments that MacIntyre so aptly describes lead to the third characteristic of dilemmas: *3. There is no way, given the present knowledge base, to know the truth of the premises a priori.*

Our acceptance of one set of premises over another becomes what Reese and Overton (1970) described in their classic article, "Models and Theories of Development" – that is, a product of the assumptions of our personal "world view." The arguments are interminable because the premises are unprovable.

The fourth and last characteristic follows from the third. Although in MacIntyre's discussion of these contemporary examples one can easily recognize the situations as current dilemmas for society, at a personal level they become dilemmas only when the decision becomes necessary in one's life. Cocktail party conversation is made up of interminable arguments; dilemmas exist when the argument must be terminated and a decision made – for example, when the fetus whose life is at stake is within your own body; when the war to be avoided or espoused is one into which you have been conscripted; when the health services discussed are ones that are vital to your life. The fourth characteristic may be an arbitrary one, but it becomes essential when we consider the psychological impact of dilemmas: *4. To be a dilemma, an argument must demand resolution in the course of daily life.*

The implicit value judgment is that all the "interminable arguments" can exist only because those of us who argue these issues do not have to resolve them to get on with our lives. It is only when individuals are able to concern themselves with dilemmas that overwhelm others (e.g., Third World starvation; the Cambodian holocaust) to such an extent that those dilemmas require resolution in their own lives that this problem develops beyond egocentric problem-solving.

THE INTERPRETATION OF EVENTS AS DILEMMAS

Given the array of potential behaviors, all actions in life require choices. How is it, then, that some of these choices take on special meaning, posing a dilemma, while others do not? I have attempted to outline characteristics of dilemmas. However, the question remains of how humans come to think about events as dilemmas. Developmentally, there appear to be two processes which play a major role in the recognition of dilemmas. These are (1) the development of intention and (2) the interpretation of contradiction.

The development of intention

All actions require a selection from among the available potential behaviors. This selection process has led, throughout history, to attempts to understand the role of intention in making selections and to grasp what Cazden (1977) discussed as "the *why* of human behavior" (see Harding, 1981). Although any one of us can discuss intentions as explanations of our own behavior and as sources for our interpretation of others' behavior, these introspections have not led to a consensus in the inference of intention as a basis of behavior. Anscombe (1957) attempts to demonstrate that some behavior occurs because of preconceived goals or intentions. She concludes that as long as "the question 'Why?' exists, with answers that give reasons for acting," the concept of intention must also exist (p. 34). The answers need not be verbal (see her discussion of animals and infants behaving with apparent intention, p. 5) and may not accurately explain the behavior, since these answers are, in Anscombe's terms, only the expression of intention. However, the fact that for the actor there can be an answer affirms that the behavior was based on intention.

In addition to the compelling psychological reality of the actor's own intentions, Anscombe presents, as evidence of the existence of intention, interpretations of behaviors which require the inference of intention. One such interpretation is implicit in the act of signaling. In order to interpret one's own behavior or another's as a signal, one must assume that one organism can attempt intentionally to affect another. Not all signals are intentional, but in order to possess a concept of signaling, one concedes the possibility that such behaviors can be intentional. Although Anscombe does not discuss it, the interpretation of dilemmas is another act which implies the assumption of intention. Conflicting choices and outcomes have no meaning unless intentional choice is assumed. Given the assumption of intention, it is interesting to examine when and how individuals recognize the possibility – and responsibility – of intentional choice.

Elsewhere I have proposed a model for describing the developmental process of intention (Harding, 1982). This model is based on various components or facets of the concept "intention" (cf. Anscombe, 1957; Ryan, 1970) which may have distinct developmental courses dependent on the cognitive abilities necessary for their occurrence. The development of the components may follow a sequence similar to that described for intentional behavior by Ryan (1970; cf. Miller et al., 1960). This description included four basic components of intention: (1) an initial arousal or tension when the individual perceives a situation and becomes aware of a goal; (2) the formation of a plan for achieving the goal; (3) an attitude of necessity leading to the formation of alternate plans, if necessary; and (4) persistent behavior in striving for the goal.

The model based on these components has been used to examine the developmental process of the ontogenetic emergence of intentional behaviors and their prerequisite cognitive abilities, and to examine the development of communication as a goal (Harding, 1984). This model may also be useful in examining the development of the recognition of dilemmas. Although the question remains whether we can find empirical verification for the developmental sequence described below, the model can provide a framework for understanding what is required in the recognition of dilemmas.

According to the model, the first component in the gradual development of intention involves awareness of a goal, in this case the awareness that there is a situation demanding a choice between conflicting outcomes. It is interesting to consider what developmental skills are involved in this awareness.

Piaget's extensive investigations of sensorimotor development (1952) and moral judgment (1965) serve as a starting point. In addition to the sensorimotor accomplishments involving the concepts of object permanence, time, space, and causality, which are required for any intentional act, Piaget (1965) discussed abilities, developing out of both the social and nonsocial environments, which are necessary for the development of what I interpret as social decision-making – the "rules of the game." The basic condition necessary for the awareness of situations involving choices appears to be a concept of regularity, including both consistent "physical events such as alternation of day and night, sameness of scenery during walks, etc." (Piaget, p. 51) and ritualized social activities, games such as peek-a-boo (cf. Bruner, 1974), which become "rites defined by their regularity" (Piaget, p. 52). This notion of regularity is the basis for understanding events; only when children begin to see disruptions and contradictions against a background of previously perceived regularities does the need for choices become apparent. (The concept of contradiction is discussed more thoroughly below.)

Component 2 of the model focuses on the development of a plan for achieving a goal. Since the goal in this case is to recognize that an event poses a dilemma, the plan for achieving that goal must represent a means for moving from the initial tension engendered by an event to the recognition of the conflict or discrepancy in the event. Developmentally, this "plan" is accomplished through (1) expectations of outcomes based on perceptions of regularities derived from experience in both the physical and social environments, and (2) recognition of the possibility of multiple outcomes, one of which may be more acceptable than the others. Often the physical and social environments collaborate in the development of these expectations. Piaget (1965) gave an example of the impact of regularities and, in addition, called attention to a developmental issue: separating necessary physical outcomes from necessary and arbitrary social outcomes. Piaget wrote:

> Heat burns (physical law), it is forbidden to touch the fire (moral law) and the child playing about in the kitchen will amuse himself by touching every piece of furniture except the stove (individual ritual). How can the subject's mind distinguish at first between these three types of regularity? (p. 52)

Recent research (e.g., Trevarthen & Hubley, 1978; Kaye, 1982; Stern et al., 1984) indicates that caregivers begin this process by establishing with the child a context of shared meanings and intentions, which allow not only for the perception of regularities but also for the shared interpretation of possible outcomes. Kaye (1982) has provided the following examples of situations in which parents "frame" for the child a plan for choosing between actions. Both examples indicate how parents demonstrate for their children that there are choices to be made in the course of their behavior and that these choices have various meanings and consequences.

> *Example 1:* More is involved than the parent merely making the physical consequences of certain actions salient to the infant. The most important thing is that social consequences are introduced even into nonsocial actions. "Good girl!" someone shouts, and a simple product of maturation and solitary practice is marked as a social occasion. Similarly, parents' "No!" or "Hot!" when the child approaches too near the fire (which must occur a hundred times for every one time a child actually gets burned) does more to build the edifice of approving and disapproving caretakers, and to lay the foundation for perception of self, than it teaches about physical safety.

> *Example 2:* I am holding a 3-month-old in my lap. She stares at the toy about 6 inches in front of her on the table. Her fingers scrabble on the table surface, then she extends her arm toward the toy but, with her fist closed, knocks it a few inches away. I reach for it and move it back to where it was. I have no lesson plan, in fact I act without really thinking. I

don't care much whether the baby succeeds. I enjoy watching her clumsy failures, but I cannot do that when the toy is out of her reach. So I move it back. Yet in doing so, I have demonstrated the correct way to reach and grasp the rattle. Adults perform dozens of demonstrations like that for infants every day without realizing it. (Kaye, 1982, pp. 80-81)

Component 3 of the model refers to the development of "an attitude of necessity leading to the formation of alternate plans." To some extent, at least when recognition of a dilemma is the goal, this component represents the development of a meta-cognitive ability. The child must not only be able to recognize the tension engendered by an event requiring resolution and have a concept of making correct and incorrect choices; she must also be able to think about her own thinking about the event, compare it to her thinking about other such events and their resolution, and conclude that a particular kind of decision is required this time. It may be that at this point the child knows (albeit implicitly) the form of the dilemma, can recognize that a choice is called for, and can begin to evaluate the truth of the premises as an alternative to making the initially perceived choice. Other choices may then become necessary, but developmentally it is probably at this level that the child is able to break from traditional, learned solutions and construct alternatives to both the choices and their outcomes.

Component 4, persistence, is one which exists at all levels of development but in different degrees. If we intend to achieve a goal, we typically persist until we do. However, if it is the case that the ability to recognize a dilemma develops through a gradual process (perhaps the one described above), then at certain developmental points persistence can be observed only within the context of the component(s) of intention thus far achieved. For example, when the child's developmental repertoire includes only the awareness (component 1) of variation from expected regularities, persistence is probably evidenced through confused activity, frustration, and perhaps withdrawal. When the child has the ability to recognize the available choices (component 2), then a known choice is probably attempted over and over again. It may be that at this point the concept of obligation as described by Piaget (1965) begins to reveal itself developmentally. According to Piaget, obligation develops out of the

pleasure of regularity . . . and intervenes [in behavior choice] as soon as there is a society, i.e., a relation between two individuals. As soon as a ritual is imposed upon a child by adults or seniors for whom he has respect, or as soon as a ritual comes into being as a result of the collaboration of two children, it acquires in the subject's mind a new character which is precisely that of a rule. (p. 33)

It may be this rule, this obligation, that establishes the first routine (or plan) for recognizing that a choice must be made. At this developmental level, persistence would involve the rigid use of this rule.

Developmentally, the expected ultimate achievement for the goal of recognizing dilemmas (component 3) is persistence in the evaluation of *all* events as potential dilemmas and in the examination of the truthfulness of premises and the alterability of outcomes. Alternate interpretations of the situation, as well as alternate solutions, would be constructed and considered in the course of recognizing dilemmas.

This model of the development of intention has been used to examine the developmental process of recognizing dilemmas. Age periods for the development of certain components have not been estimated, and further theoretical justification and empirical verification of this model are necessary if it is to be used for any other purpose than as a framework for discussion.

Interpretation of Contradiction

This framework describes how the developing ability to act with intention relates to the recognition of events involving choices. However, one dimension of this process – the interpretation of contradiction – requires further discussion, since it is the ability to interpret contradiction that allows one to discriminate dilemmas from other events requiring choices. The choices inherent in a dilemma are not just two different options; they are incompatible alternatives requiring a recognition of the contradictory nature of their outcomes.

Developmentally there are two aspects of interpreting contradiction that are of interest: (1) the ability to compare objects or events and to recognize that they are incompatible, and (2) the ability to invent or construct an opposite or a negation of an event where none has previously existed (cf. Piaget, 1980; Murray, 1983). The developmental process of the first ability is one which has been well documented (e.g., Inhelder & Piaget, 1964; Langer, 1980; Sugarman, 1984). The literature on the development of the concept of conservation is particularly useful in describing the process through which children come to interpret and act on incompatible information, and I refer the reader to the work of Murray (1981) and Pinard (1981) for further study of this topic. It is the second aspect – the invention of negations – on which I wish to focus here.

In *Experiments in Contradiction* (1980), Piaget described how children changed in their ability to experience contradiction cognitively. At one level, potentially conflictual events are seen not as inconsistent but rather as independent. It is only through the cognitive construction of a link between the two events, in this case a link based on the negation of one event by the other, that they become contradictory and, in fact, indissociable from each other in their contradiction. It is this inability to dissociate an action and its negation that allows for the recognition of dilemmas. For example, recognition of the dilemma posed by abortion does not require only the recognition that the fetus's right to life conflicts with the pregnant woman's right to free choice; it also requires the interpretation that, in each instance, an action in support of one human right negates the other – and that the negation of any human right poses a contradiction for the principled thinker. The dilemma does not exist, however, for those who either (1) do not consider the removal of a fetus from the uterus a violation of its rights; or (2) the denial of choice to a woman a violation of her rights. The decision to abort or not to abort becomes, in those cases, either right or wrong.

Individuals – and societies – develop in their ability to invent negations for actions and, in the process, to invent dilemmas. An example of an action which has come to pose a dilemma for most societies is the oppression of sub-culture groups. Recognition of the dilemma posed by any oppression requires the ability to imagine its negation – freedom – for the group involved. When it is taken for granted that certain groups are born to be oppressed, freedom for that group is not considered and there is no dilemma. In an example of how otherwise moral people could justify the violation of the rights of a sub-culture group, in this case the American Indian, Jovanovich (1971) writes:

> As Cotton Mather reminded his faithful, the Red Man was a creature of the Devil himself; therefore, in exploiting the Indian, the Puritans could be confident that they were fulfilling their obligations not only to themselves but also to God." (p. viii)

A dilemma is constructed only when it appears possible that the oppressed group could – and perhaps should – be free. The possibility of freedom becomes indissociable from the action of oppression, setting up a contradiction for an individual or a society that espouses freedom and yet practices oppression. Whether or not such contradictions are constructed probably depends not only on the developmental status of the human mind but also on the social and emotional context within which the event is perceived.

Dilemmas, it is proposed, exist only in a context in which people are cognitively, socially, and emotionally able to see the possible negations of what then become alterable events. Given this conclusion, dilemmas are interesting not only in their resolution but also in their invention. It may be, in fact, the recognition – and invention – of dilemmas that suggests the significant developmental and cultural questions.

REFERENCES

Anscombe, G. E. M. (1957). *Intention.* Oxford: Basil Blackwell.

Bruner, J. S. (1974). Organization of early skilled action. In M. Richards (Ed.), *The integration of a child into a social world.* London: Cambridge University Press.

Cazden, C. B. (1977). The question of intent. In M. Lewis & L. A. Rosenblum (Eds.), *Interaction, conversation, and the development of language.* New York: John Wiley & Sons.

Harding, C. G. (1981). A longitudinal study of the development of the intention to communicate. Unpublished dissertation, University of Delaware.

Harding, C. G. (1982). The development of the intention to communicate. *Human Development, 25,* 140-151.

Harding, C. G. (1984). Acting with intention: A framework for examining the development of the intention to communicate. In L. Feagans, C. Garvey, & R. Golinkoff (Eds.), *The origins and growth of communication.* New York: Ablex.

Inhelder, B., & Piaget, J. (1964). *The early growth of logic in the child.* London: Routledge and Kegan Paul.

Jovanovich, S. (1971). Introduction. In A. F. Bandelier, *The Delight Makers.* New York: Harcourt Brace Jovanovich.

Kaye, K. (1982). *The mental and social life of babies: How parents create persons.* Chicago: University of Chicago Press.

Langer, J. (1980). *The origins of logic: Six to twelve months.* New York: Academic Press.

MacIntyre, A. (1981). *After virtue: A study in moral theory.* Notre Dame, IN: University of Notre Dame Press.

Miller, G., Galanter, E., & Pribram, K. (1960). *Plans and the structure of behavior.* New York: Holt, Rinehart and Winston.

Murray, F. B. (1981). The conservation paradigm: The conservation of conservation research. In I. Sigel, D. Brodzinsky, & R. Golinkoff (Eds.), *New directions in Piagetian theory and practice.* Hillsdale, NJ: Erlbaum.

Murray, F. B. (1983). Equilibration as cognitive conflict. *Developmental Review, 3,* 151-160.

Piaget, J. (1952). *The origins of intelligence in children.* New York: International University Press.

Piaget, J. (1965). *The moral judgment of the child.* New York: The Free Press.

Piaget, J. (1980). *Experiments in contradiction.* Chicago: University of Chicago Press.

Pinard, A. (1981). *The conservation of conservation: The child's acquisition of a fundamental concept.* Chicago: University of Chicago Press.

Reese, H., & Overton, W. (1970). Models and theories of development. In L. Goulet & P. Baltes (Eds.), *Life-span developmental psychology.* New York: Academic Press.

Ryan, T. A. (1970). *Intentional behavior: An approach to human motivation.* New York: Ronald Press.

Stern, D. N., Hofer, L., Haft, W., & Dore, J. (1984). Affect attunement: A description of the intermodal communication of affective states between mothers and infants. In T. Field & N. Fox (Eds.), *Social perception in infants.* Norwood, NJ: Ablex.

Sugarman, S. (1983). *Children's early thought: Developments in classification.* Cambridge: Cambridge University Press.

Trevarthen, C., & Hubley, P. (1978). Secondary intersubjectivity: Confidence, confiding, and acts of meaning in the first year. In A. Lock (Ed.), *Action, gesture, and symbol: The emergence of language.* New York: Academic Press.

Emotion, Morality, and Understanding

Lawrence Hinman

We all approach questions with certain presuppositions, with a certain web of beliefs and interests which influences what we see and the way we see it. This paper is no exception to this general rule, and a word of preface about my own initial presuppositions and interests may be useful in setting the stage for the remarks which follow.

Although this is a paper about the place of emotions in moral education, it arises originally out of an interest in, and work on, the emotions, especially the cognitive dimension of the emotions (see Hinman, 1983a; 1984a; 1985). This work led me to at least one important conclusion which underlies the following discussion: our emotions are a way of structuring and understanding our world, a way of making sense of it, and they are thus cognitive, given a broad understanding of the term "cognitive." My work on the cognitive dimension of the emotions led to a reconsideration of the role of emotions in morality – if the emotions are more cognitive than is usually acknowledged, then perhaps they should be accorded a more positive role in the moral life than is customary. I found myself particularly dissatisfied with the place which Kantian morality accorded to the emotions, since it seemed that Kant excluded the emotions from his concept of the moral agent and that, consequently, he left open the possibility of a conflict between the requirements of morality and the demands of personal integrity (see Hinman, 1983b). This led to a fundamental conviction which lies at the heart of the critique of Kohlbergian moral education offered toward the end of this paper: we must develop a conception of the moral agent which is sufficiently broad to encompass and integrate the agent's emotions as well as his or her thoughts and choices. Education of the moral agent includes education of the emotions as well as of the understanding.

The first step in this process of developing a fuller understanding of the nature of the moral agent is to re-examine our understanding of the emotions. Once that task has been accomplished, we can turn to sketching a more positive account of the role which the emotions play in the moral life, especially in moral education. Obviously, this can hardly be done in a single paper. What we can do here, however, is take four steps – important ones, I hope – toward that goal. The first step involves attacking some false beliefs about the emotions, which have gotten in the way of our understanding of the role that they play in morality. The second step involves outlining a more positive account of the emotions, which recognizes their cognitive structure. Step three consists of applying the concept developed in the preceding step to the area of morality. The fourth and final step involves drawing the consequences of this view for our understanding of moral education. In the following remarks, I shall take the first three steps rather quickly, realizing that they cover a lot of ground, in order to take the final step more slowly and deliberately.

SOME MISCONCEPTIONS ABOUT THE EMOTIONS

There are three important misconceptions about the emotions which, taken together, have resulted in the exclusion of emotions from our understanding of the moral self and have thus profoundly affected our understanding of the role of emotions in morality. These are the beliefs that emotions are: (1) non-cognitive; (2) causally determined; and (3) passive. If the emotions possess these characteristics, and if the essential moral self is a being capable of knowing and acting freely, then it follows that the emotions are not part of the essential self. Let me deal with the cognitive dimension of the emotions first, and then treat the questions of determinism and passivity together.

Emotions and Knowledge

The story of how the emotions came to be excluded from the cognitive domain is a long and complex one that cannot be told in detail here, but we can summarize the contents of some of the main chapters of that tale. The story begins with the subject seen as essentially an isolated self over and against a world comprised of external objects. The problem then becomes one of trying to provide a plausible account of how this isolated subject gains access to this external world: the central problem of classical modern philosophy since Descartes. If we presume that this access is gained through some kind of picturing activity – the mind as the mirror of nature, a powerful metaphor in modern philosophy, as Richard Rorty (1979) has pointed out (see also Hinman, 1984b) – then it is easy to understand why the emotions were excluded from cognition. They are not the kinds of things which can depict or picture anything, whether internal or external. It is this ocular metaphor for describing knowledge which, perhaps more than any other single factor, has excluded emotions from the cognitive domain. Yet this metaphor, useful though it is in certain contexts such as the natural sciences, is hardly sufficient to cover all cases of knowing.

Once the emotions are seen as non-cognitive, they are easily excluded from the moral domain insofar as that domain is seen as a rational one. If morality is a matter of reason, and if emotions are non-rational because they are not cognitive, then emotions simply have no positive place in the moral realm. If emotions are admitted to a legitimate place in the moral life, it can be only at a very high price, one which emotivists seemed initially too ready to pay: morality ceases to be a matter of reason. Yet there is another option here, namely, to challenge the premise that the emotions are non-cognitive.

If one wants to challenge that premise and maintain that the emotions are in fact cognitive, two alternatives present themselves. First, one can accept the ocular metaphor and claim that the emotions have a component which is a candidate for knowledge within this model. This, I take it, is essentially the move made by many of those who defend a "component" approach to the analysis of emotions. They claim that many emotions have particular kinds of belief components which are subject to epistemic assessment in the standard fashion (see Thalberg, 1977). Emotions can then be factored into their belief and affective components, and the former can be scrutinized in the same way that other beliefs are examined. Yet at least two objections can be raised against pursuing this path. First, it is far from obvious that this presents a phenomenologically accurate description of our actual experience. It seems far more likely that we are dealing with a single, unitary act which is not adequately captured in the language of the component approach. Second, as Stephen Ross (1984) has recently argued so effectively, the actual way in which we evaluate the emotions bears little resemblance to the way the component approach suggests. If the component approach were correct, it would be very difficult to explain the variance of feelings about a single object among otherwise rational beings.

The second alternative is more radical, for it involves rejecting the unrestricted validity of this visual metaphor for knowing, and exploring alternative metaphors which more directly accord the emotions a cognitive role, rather than restricting that cognitive dimension solely to a belief component. If we take love, for example, as an emotion, this approach would maintain that there are not two separate components, my set of beliefs about the beloved and my loving feelings toward that person, but rather that the emotion of love is a unitary phenomenon in which feeling and knowing are present in a single act. In loving the other person, I come to know the other through the very act of loving, and I may well come to know myself better at the same time. Infatuation, to take a contrasting emotion, presents the same kind of unitary structure, but in this instance I deceive myself about the other person and, quite often, about myself as well. Infatuation and love are both cognitive, related to one another as are error and knowledge.

It is this latter approach to the cognitive dimension of the emotions which seems to me the more promising one, but it is important to note that it involves a radical restructuring of the basic metaphors in terms of which we understand our relationship to the world. While it may well be that the best metaphors for under-standing natural scientific knowing are visual, other metaphors may be more helpful in understanding the type of knowing which occurs in the emotions.

Determinism and Passivity

The second and third major stumbling blocks to according the emotions a more positive role in morality stem from our tendency to view emotions within a deterministic framework, and thus to see ourselves as fundamentally passive in relation to them. Since the ground here is familiar, I shall try to move over it quickly.

If freedom is a necessary condition of the possibility of moral action and responsibility, and if our emotions are not things that are freely chosen but rather things that simply happen to us, then we can see the way in which the emotions are necessarily excluded from the moral domain, insofar as that domain is a realm of freedom. Thus we are, for example, responsible for our actions because they are freely chosen, but we cannot be responsible for our emotions, because they are things that just happen to us, things about which we have no choice. We are passive, rather than active, vis-à-vis our emotions. Moreover, emotions do not provide an acceptable basis, at least within Kantian morality, for moral action, since they cannot be freely adopted in the same way that reasons can. We give the moral law to ourselves freely, in Kant's eyes, but our emotions simply happen to us.

Once again, there are two ways to attack this claim. We can either accept the premise that the emotions are causally determined and passive, but deny that this means that they should be excluded from the moral domain, or we can challenge the truth of this key premise. It is this latter course which is, I think, the more fruitful one. Part of that attack involves a criticism of purely causal accounts of the emotions (see A. Rorty, 1980; Nussbaum, forthcoming). Such accounts are unable to handle key characteristics of emotions, such as their intentional structures, in an adequate manner. Moreover, insofar as such accounts are part of a larger commitment to determinism in general, they are open to the objection that they are self-defeating. Yet such a critique, valuable though it may be in itself, will carry little weight if it is not complemented by an alternate, non-deterministic account of the emotions which brings out their cognitive and active dimensions. Let us now turn to developing precisely such an account.

EMOTIONS AS WAYS OF UNDERSTANDING OUR WORLD

Instead of looking at emotions as non-cognitive, causally-determined, passive responses to our environment, I suggest that we think of them as active ways of structuring our experience, as ways of making sense out of ourselves and our world. Let me illustrate this by taking a pair of emotions, compassion and pity, which are particularly interesting in regard to morality. Both, I shall argue, are possible means through which we can structure our experience of another person, means by which we come to know – or fail to know – the other person in a way that cannot be reduced simply to a set of categorical beliefs to which is added a particular type of feeling.

Consider, to begin with, some of the differences between typical cases of compassion and pity. When we feel pity, we implicitly make some judgment through which we look down on the other person; it is difficult to imagine feeling pity for someone whom I at the same time admire. Compassion, on the other hand, seems to involve an identification with the suffering of the other, an identification that presupposes a fundamental equality. If I pity another individual, I am usually assuming that on some level he is responsible for or deserves his suffering. Yet if I feel compassion for another individual, I usually make no such assumption about her being in any sense to blame for her suffering. In pity, I may or may not be moved to action to relieve the pitiful condition, but it would in any case be highly unlikely that I would be moved to share the pain that the other is experiencing. Compassion, if not always oriented toward action, does seem to be oriented toward reaching out to the other person, to touching him, to share her suffering. Pity seems to view its object as the intersection of a set of circumstances: whoever is found in those circumstances is an object of pity. Compassion, on the other hand, usually appears to be directed toward the specific individual as an individual. We feel compassion for this particular individual, not for whoever might be in those circumstances.

Consider the differences in how we feel when we are the objects of pity or compassion. If someone feels pity toward me, I may well feel that he is devaluing me in some way, that he is failing to make contact with me. Yet if I think the other person is showing compassion, my feeling would more likely be one of a shared bond with the other person, of a contact made in which we encounter each other as equals. If I am an object of pity, I may well feel that the other person does not understand me. Indeed, I may be angry at being perceived in that fashion. Yet if I am the object of compassion, I am more likely to feel that the other person knows me, in and through the act of compassion, in a quite important way. Similarly, if I am the object of pity, I may well question whether the other person is genuinely interested in *me;* but if a person feels compassion toward me, I can hardly doubt the genuineness of his interest in me at that moment.

Both compassion and pity are, I believe, ways of coming to understand the other person, ways of structuring our experience. Both exhibit conceptually complex structures, and an adequate understanding of them cannot ignore these differing conceptual structures. (This is but one of the reasons a purely causal account of such emotions falls short of the mark.) Both are ways of understanding another person, if we apply two qualifications to the meaning of the word "understanding." First, "understanding" is not used here as a success verb; rather, it covers both succeeding and failing to understand another person. Second, "understanding" is not a purely cognitive activity in the narrow sense of "cognitive"; rather, it involves a unitary act of grasping an object in such a way that it has, for the purposes of analysis, both cognitive and affective dimensions. When I feel compassion toward another person, it is not as though I have a set of pre-existent beliefs to which I then add a feeling of, say, concern. Rather, to feel compassion toward another individual is precisely to grasp that individual compassionately in a single act which is both knowing and feeling.

Our language makes it very difficult to state this point at once clearly and simply. The split between the cognitive and the emotive runs so deep in our language that any simple locutions are almost invariably dichotomous, turning this unitary act into either emotion or cognition. (This is not to maintain that this thesis about a unitary act is in any way mysterious or unclear or ineffable. It simply means that the thesis cannot be stated clearly and *simply*. Clear statements of it will of necessity be more complex than one would wish.) We could resort to adverbial formulations, but these, too, are often dichotomous. We could say, for example, that I know the other person compassionately, or that I knowingly feel compassion for the other person. Each of these formulations, however, forces us to put primacy on either the cognition or the feeling. What I am suggesting, in contrast to these formulations, is that we have here a single, unitary act, of which understanding and feeling are aspects that can be separated for the purposes of analysis, but that the act itself is a unitary one in which understanding and feeling are one.

TWO MODELS OF MORALITY

So far we have taken two important steps in the development of our argument. First, we have criticized certain mistaken but still pervasive presuppositions about the emotions, namely, that they are non-cognitive, causally determined, and passive. Second, we have sketched an alternate account of the emotions which suggests that emotions are active ways of structuring our world, ways which contain aspects of understanding and feeling in a single, unitary act. This opens the door to a much more positive account of the role of the emotions in morality, but such an account cannot be realized if we simply retain the dominant utilitarian or Kantian models of morality. Such models have little room for the emotions, even when we have developed a more sophisticated understanding of the emotions.

Let me suggest a contrast here between two views of what morality is about, a contrast which opens up the possibility of an account of morality in which the emotions can play a much more positive role. On the one hand, we have those models of morality – for the sake of discussion, this will be called the standard view – which view morality as a matter of the articulation and justification of fundamental moral principles and the impartial application of those principles through choices in particular contexts. Certainly Kant and Mill differ on what our fundamental moral principles should be and on how they are to be justified, but they are at one in the basic conviction of the standard view that the main concern of ethics is the justification of such principles and that the primary focus of the moral life is the application of those principles to specific problems in as impartial a manner as possible. On the other hand, we have a view of morality, going back to Aristotle (see A. Rorty, 1980; Nussbaum, forthcoming), but also represented today by the work of Murdoch (1956; 1970), Williams (1973; 1981; 1985), Blum (1980), and others (see Kekes, 1984; Diamond, 1983), which proposes that morality is a matter of cultivation of virtue, the formation of character, the education of our emotions, and the development of moral sensitivity and vision. This alternative view, which in this discussion we will call virtue ethics, is concerned with understanding virtues instead of justifying principles, with looking at the particularities of specific situations in which actual individuals find themselves instead of with concentrating on the impartial application of principles, with the cultivation of moral sensitivity rather than with the development of a foolproof decision procedure for dealing with moral problems, and with the quality of an individual's entire life rather than with the assessment of isolated choices.

I certainly do not want to argue that the standard view of morality is completely wrong. Clearly, it captures something important about the moral life, namely, that it is in part constituted by rules, impartiality, and specific choices. Yet at the same time, it is equally clear that it leaves out an important aspect of the moral life, namely, the development of character, moral sensitivity, and vision. Iris Murdoch (1970) suggests the following case, one intended to illustrate precisely what is omitted by the standard view of morality. She sets the stage for the example in the following way.

A mother, whom I shall call M, feels hostility to her daughter-in-law, whom I shall call D. M finds D quite a good-hearted girl, but while not exactly common yet certainly unpolished and lacking in dignity and refinement. D is inclined to be pert and familiar, insufficiently ceremonious, brusque, sometimes positively rude, always tiresomely juvenile. M does not like D's accent or the way D dresses. M feels her son has married beneath him. Let us assume for the purposes of the example that the mother, who is a very "correct" person, behaves beautifully to the girl throughout, not allowing her real opinion to appear in any way. We might underline this aspect of the example by supposing that the young couple have emigrated or that D is now dead: the point being to ensure that whatever is in question as *happening* happens entirely in M's mind. (p. 17)

Having sketched the situation, Murdoch then asks us to imagine the following change taking place in M's attitude toward D.

> Time passes, and it could be that M settles down with a hardened sense of grievance and a fixed picture of D, imprisoned (if I may use a question-begging word) by the cliché: my poor son has married a silly vulgar girl. However, the M of the example is an intelligent and well-intentioned person, capable of self-criticism, capable of giving careful and just *attention* to an object which confronts her. M tells herself: "I am old-fashioned and conventional. I may be prejudiced and narrow-minded. I may be snobbish. I am certainly jealous. Let me look again." Here I assume that M observes D or at least reflects deliberately about D, until gradually her vision of D alters. If we take D to be now absent or dead this can make it clear that the change is not in D's behavior but in M's mind. D is discovered to be not vulgar but refreshingly simple, not undignified but spontaneous, not noisy but gay, not tiresomely juvenile but delightfully youthful, and so on. And as I say, *ex hypothesi*, M's outward behaviour, beautiful from the start, in no way alters. (pp. 17–18)

In advancing this example, Murdoch is focusing attention on the fact that an important change – indeed, a morally important change – takes place in M, but that there is virtually no room within the standard view to account for this change. It does not issue in any outward *behavior*, any publicly observable *choice*, so it cannot be picked up and recognized by the standard view. Insofar as morality is seen primarily as a matter of the impartial application of moral principles to choice situations, this change in perception will have virtually no moral significance. Yet Murdoch's claim here is that the real business, as it were, of the moral life is precisely the development of our moral vision, the sharpening of our moral perceptions. Morality, she is arguing, is primarily a matter of the inner life, not of the external choice, primarily a matter of the way in which we see things, not of what we actually do.

None of this is meant to deny that morality involves actions, not just vision. Yet what it suggests is that the actions we take, and the moral significance which they should be accorded, will depend upon our moral vision. The example of M and D is intended to eliminate action from the picture in order to focus attention on M's inner life. However, Murdoch's point holds equally well in situations in which overt choices are made. The morally significant process may not be in the actual choice, but rather in the development of the moral awareness which leads to the choice. Thus we might well have had an example in which M's behavior toward D actually changed, yet the significant thing might still be the change in M's perception of D. Indeed, if Murdoch is right, by the time we get to the point of an overt choice, most of the story is already over, for the choice is but the final result of the change in perception. Morality becomes, then, primarily a matter of the development of our vision, of our moral perception.

It would be difficult to present a conclusive argument here to show that Murdoch and others are correct in claiming that what morality is really about is the development of moral vision and sensitivity. Yet it is possible to show that this view of morality allows us to deal with a central problem which has plagued the standard view of morality, whether in its Kantian or its utilitarian variants (see Williams, 1981). Roughly, the problem is this. Neither Kantian nor utilitarian accounts of morality have a notion of moral agency sufficient to prevent a conflict developing between the demands of morality and the demands of personal integrity. In Kantian morality, the reason for this is clear: one is obligated to act in the way in which any rational being would act. However, to act in that way is precisely to set aside one's own individual history, personal loyalties, fundamental projects, and basic desires. All of these things are excluded from Kant's notion of the moral agent as purely rational. Consequently, the door is opened for a conflict between the purely rational moral agent and the full person who I am. In utilitarian morality, there is an analogous problem. My own emotions, projects, etc. are taken into account in the utilitarian calculus, but the utilitarian framework fails to provide any way of recognizing that these bear a special relationship to my own actions. For a utilitarian, it is only the consequences of an action which are important. It is irrelevant whether the action is *mine* or not. Thus an action may be necessary, and it may happen to be the case that I am the one who is obliged to perform it, even though it may entail a violation of my most fundamental commitments, a negation of my own character. In both Kantian and utilitarian morality, there is thus the possibility of a conflict between character and the demands of morality, and in both cases this possibility is grounded in an inadequate notion of moral agency.

One of the primary advantages of the view of morality espoused in this section is that it seems to diminish, and perhaps even eliminate, the possibility of such a conflict between morality and character. It does so precisely by enlarging our understanding of the moral agent. The moral agent is not just a Kantian rational self or a utilitarian calculator, but rather a whole person, a person who not only thinks and acts, but also feels and perceives. Morality then becomes not the impartial application of principles, but the moral cultivation of the entire self: the development of moral perceptions and emotions as well as the sharpening of our moral reasoning skills. It is precisely with this view of morality that the account of the emotions offered in the second part of this paper is most compatible.

THE ROLE OF EMOTIONS IN MORAL EDUCATION

At this juncture, my criticism of the Kohlbergian program of moral education should be evident. Precisely because of the stress which it places on the impartial application of moral principles and on the importance of choices made largely in isolation from questions of individual character, Kohlberg's approach puts far too little emphasis on the cultivation of the moral emotions, the sharpening of moral perceptions, and the development of moral sensitivity. This is evident not only in the cognitive structure of the stage theory of moral development that Kohlberg defends, but also in his extensive use of moral dilemmas. Let us examine each of these issues in turn.

First, the thrust of Kohlberg's theory of the stages of moral development is clearly one which places its highest value on universality and impartiality in moral judgments, and in this respect Kohlberg's stage theory typifies the standard view of morality criticized above. Emotions come to be seen as characteristic of an earlier stage, as something to be put aside as one moves to the higher stages of moral development. Acting on principle involves acting in the manner that any rational agent, whatever he or she may feel, would act. Emotions can only cloud the picture or weaken the resolve of the will to impose the moral law on itself.

This, of course, is not a problem inherent in any stage theory of moral development, but is an issue because the highest stages are defined in terms of impartial actions based purely on principle. A stage theory which made the cultivation of certain emotions characteristic of the higher stages could retain a developmental approach and yet accord the emotions a much more prominent and positive role than the Kohlbergian schema has been able to do.

The second way in which Kohlberg's approach places too little emphasis on the role of the emotions in the moral life emerges in his use of moral dilemmas. There are at least two important ways in which this occurs. First, the use of dilemmas places a heavy emphasis on overt behavior and choice rather than on perception and moral vision, and it is precisely this which Murdoch and others have quite rightly criticized as ignoring the importance of the inner life in morality. Second, the use of dilemmas demands that individuals prescind from their individual history, that they assume another role (e.g., that of Heinz) which is itself almost completely lacking in individual history. This effectively suggests that the agent's own personal history is largely irrelevant to moral deliberation. Yet insofar as the development of character is a matter of one's personal history, considerations about character fall by the wayside when dilemmas ignore individual history.

If the viewpoint outlined in the second and third parts of this paper is sound, it opens the way for a much more important role for the emotions in moral education than Kohlberg has recognized. Indeed, one of the primary concerns of moral education then becomes the education of the emotions, which includes the cultivation of what I have been calling moral sensitivity (see Kekes, 1984). There are several points to be made here about this process of educating the emotions within a moral context.

First, we must recognize that we are beginning with emotions which have been significantly deformed in our own society. Here the influence of advertising is of the utmost importance, for it has had a deep and pervasive influence on our emotions. Joy, one of the most important of human emotions, has become associated with a dishwashing liquid. Happiness is the feeling you get when successfully preventing a waxy build-up on your floors. Feelings of friendship come from buying Löwenbräu beer. The feeling one gets on the first real day of spring is now tied up with a menthol cigarette. The feeling of freedom is now the feeling of drinking a Pepsi without caffeine. Important moral emotions are connected, time after time, with inappropriate objects or actions. This cannot help but create a very basic confusion for many of us at the level of our feelings, a confusion which leads us to buy beer when we want friendship, Pepsi when we want freedom, and cigarettes when we want a new season. Part of the task of educating the moral emotions involves freeing them from the distortions to which they have been subjected in contemporary advertising.

Second, educating the emotions involves doing more than just ensuring that our emotions are based on well-founded beliefs. Consider what it takes to develop a feeling of compassion. We can certainly have the beliefs upon which compassion is based without feeling that emotion at all. Indeed, imagine a person who wants to see other people suffer. He may be just as perceptive about the suffering other individuals endure, but his feeling may be the opposite of compassion. We need to learn when and how to feel compassion, when compassion needs to be balanced by other feelings, such as a feeling of responsibility. Indeed, one of the most difficult tasks in educating the emotions is teaching persons how to balance conflicting emotions and when not to be overwhelmed by one particular emotion.

Third, educating the emotions involves more than ensuring that they are not irrational. Steven Ross (1984) has pointed out that, while we may criticize a person's feelings by saying that they are irrational, we are hardly inclined to praise them by saying that they are rational. Irrationality provides a negative criterion for judging the emotions, but we are still in need of a set of positive criteria to indicate the ideals toward which education of the emotions should strive.

Fourth, we must realize that the education of the emotions involves the cultivation of an entire view of the world, not just of a single feeling taken in isolation from all else. I cannot learn to appreciate a Mozart piano concerto without learning how to appreciate at least some other piano concerti and, presumably, some other musical forms. In a similar way, I cannot learn the proper weight of one emotion without having some grasp of the weight to be accorded to many of the others. Loyalty, for example, may be an important if somewhat neglected moral feeling, but we would hardly want to acquire it in isolation from other moral emotions such as compassion and a sense of fairness. Part of the process of a moral education of the emotions involves the development of the full range of the moral emotions.

Finally, the moral education of the emotions involves in particular the cultivation of the illuminating dimension of the emotions, in contrast to the concealing and distorting dimensions of emotions. Some emotions are particularly associated with blindness or distortion – hatred, envy, jealousy, and greed are standard examples – but this is not limited to those emotions alone. Love can be as blind as hatred, and an excess of trust can be as distortive as jealousy. The task of educating the emotions involves fostering the development of the illuminating dimension of all the emotions and revealing the ways in which every emotion has a potential for falsifying our view of a situation. What is to be stressed here, however, is that falsifying emotions are not to be dealt with by eliminating emotions, but by cultivating illuminating emotions.

REFERENCES

Blum, L. A. (1980). *Friendship, altruism and morality.* London: Routledge & Kegan Paul.

Diamond, C. (1983). Having a rough story about what moral philosophy is. *New Literary History,* 15, 155-169.

Hinman, L. (1983a). Heidegger, emotions and truth. Paper presented at the annual meeting of the American Philosophical Association, Eastern Division.

Hinman, L. (1983b). On the purity of our moral motives: A critique of Kant's account of the emotions and acting for the sake of duty. *The Monist,* 66, 251-267.

Hinman, L. (1984a). Metaphors of truth. Paper presented at the annual meeting of the American Philosophical Association, Eastern Division.

Hinman, L. (1984b). Transcendental feelings. Paper presented at the annual meeting of the American Philosophical Association, Western Division.

Hinman, L. (1985). False feelings. Paper presented at the annual meeting of the American Philosophical Association, Pacific Division.

Kekes, J. (1984). Moral sensitivity. *Philosophy,* 59, 3-20.

Murdoch, I. (1956). Vision and choice in morality. *Proceedings of the Aristotelian Society.*

Murdoch, I. (1970). *The sovereignty of good.* London: Routledge & Kegan Paul.

Nussbaum, M. (Forthcoming). *The fragility of goodness.*

Rorty, A. O. (Ed.). (1980a). *Essays on Aristotle's Ethics.* Berkeley: University of California Press.

Rorty, A. O. (Ed.). (1980b). *Explaining emotions.* Berkeley: University of California Press.

Rorty, R. (1979). *Philosophy and the mirror of nature.* Princeton, NJ: Princeton University Press.

Ross, S. L. (1984). Evaluating the emotions. *The Journal of Philosophy,* 76, 309-326.

Solomon, R. (1983). *The passions.* Notre Dame: University of Notre Dame Press.

Thalberg, I. (1977). *Perception, emotion, and action.* New Haven: Yale University Press.

Williams, B. (1973). *Problems of the self.* Cambridge: Cambridge University Press.

Williams, B. (1981). *Moral luck.* Cambridge: Cambridge University Press.

Williams, B. (1985). *Ethics and the Limits of Philosophy.* Cambridge, MA: Harvard University Press.

Resolving Moral Conflicts within the Just Community[1]

Lawrence Kohlberg

MORAL EDUCATION THROUGH DISCUSSIONS OF DILEMMAS

The just community approach assumes a much different relationship between theory and practice than did our first efforts in moral education, which took the form of classroom discussion of hypothetical dilemmas. Moral education in terms of moral stages was launched in 1968, when Moshe Blatt conducted research (published in Blatt & Kohlberg, 1975) in which children discussed hypothetical moral dilemmas, demonstrating that through Socratic discussion children developed according to our stage model (what I have henceforth called "the Blatt effect"). The Blatt effect has now been replicated in over one hundred different classrooms. Some of these interventions are reported in Mosher (1980); others are summarized by Lockwood (1978). The Blatt approach followed the traditional method of applying research to practice: it simply imported to the classroom classical Piagetian developmental psychology theory and the results of experimental training studies that used cognitive conflict and exposure to the next higher stage. The Blatt approach had a pure research basis, which included the studies of Rest (1973) on comprehension, preference, and assimilation, and the experimental studies of Turiel (1966) and his colleagues. In these studies, children were exposed to advice at different stages, given pro and con arguments on an issue, and then post-tested for change, which proved to be mainly to the next higher stage. Blatt took this research-based approach to the classroom and found, somewhat to my surprise, that even a limited amount of Socratic moral discussion would move children up a third of a stage. After several replications we were finally convinced that the stages were influenced by this kind of Socratic moral discussion.

The philosophic rationale for the practice of Socratic dilemma discussion also seemed theoretically sound (Kohlberg, 1981). It

TABLE 1
The Six Moral Stages

Level and Stage	Content of Stage		Social Perspective of Stage
	What Is Right	Reasons for Doing Right	
Level I: Preconventional Stage 1—Heteronomous Morality	To avoid breaking rules backed by punishment, obedience for its own sake, and avoiding physical damage to persons and property.	Avoidance of punishment, and the superior power of authorities.	Egocentric point of view. Doesn't consider the interests of others or recognize that they differ from the actor's; doesn't relate two points of view. Actions are considered physically rather than in terms of psychological interests of others. Confusion of authority's perspective with one's own.
Stage 2—Individualism, Instrumental Purpose, and Exchange	Following rules only when it is to someone's immediate interest; acting to meet one's own interests and needs and letting others do the same. Right is also what's fair, what's an equal exchange, a deal, an agreement.	To serve one's own needs or interests in a world where you have to recognize that other people have their interests, too.	Concrete individualistic perspective. Aware that everybody has his own interest to pursue and these conflict, so that right is relative (in the concrete individualistic sense).
Level II: Conventional Stage 3—Mutual Interpersonal Expectations, Relationships, and Interpersonal Conformity	Living up to what is expected by people close to you or what people generally expect of people in your role as son, brother, friend, etc. "Being good" is important and means having good motives, showing concern about others. It also means keeping mutual relationships, such as trust, loyalty, respect, and gratitude.	The need to be a good person in your own eyes and those of others. Your caring for others. Belief in the Golden Rule. Desire to maintain rules and authority which support stereotypical good behavior.	Perspective of the individual in relationships with other individuals. Aware of shared feelings, agreements, and expectations which take primacy over individual interests. Relates points of view through the concrete Golden Rule, putting yourself in the other person's shoes. Does not yet consider generalized system perspective.

Content of Stage

Level and Stage	What Is Right	Reasons for Doing Right	Social Perspective of Stage
Stage 4—Social System and Conscience	Fulfilling the actual duties to which you have agreed. Laws are to be upheld except in extreme cases where they conflict with other fixed social duties. Right is also contributing to society, the group, or institution.	To keep the institution going as a whole, to avoid the breakdown in the system "if everyone did it," or the imperative of conscience to meet one's defined obligations. (Easily confused with Stage 3 belief in rules and authority; see text.)	*Differentiates societal point of view from interpersonal agreement or motives.* Takes the point of view of the system that defines roles and rules. Considers individual relations in terms of place in the system.
Level III: Postconventional, or Principled Stage 5—Social Contract or Utility and Individual Rights	Being aware that people hold a variety of values and opinions, that most values and rules are relative to your group. These relative rules should usually be upheld, however, in the interest of impartiality and because they are the social contract. Some nonrelative values and rights like *life* and *liberty*, however, must be upheld in any society and regardless of majority opinion.	A sense of obligation to law because of one's social contract to make and abide by laws for the welfare of all and for the protection of all people's rights. A feeling of contractual commitment, freely entered upon, to family, friendship, trust, and work obligations. Concern that laws and duties be based on rational calculation of overall utility, "the greatest good for the greatest number."	*Prior-to-society perspective.* Perspective of a rational individual aware of values and rights prior to social attachments and contracts. Integrates perspectives by formal mechanisms of agreement, contract, objective impartiality, and due process. Considers moral and legal points of view; recognizes that they sometimes conflict and finds it difficult to integrate them.

Table 1 (Continued)

	Content of Stage		
Level and Stage	What Is Right	Reasons for Doing Right	Social Perspective of Stage
Stage 6—Universal Ethical Principles	Following self-chosen ethical principles. Particular laws or social agreements are usually valid because they rest on such principles. When laws violate these principles, one acts in accordance with the principle. Principles are universal principles of justice: the equality of human rights and repect for the dignity of human beings as individual persons.	The belief as a rational person in the validity of universal moral principles, and a sense of personal commitment to them.	*Perspective of a moral point of view* from which social arrangements derive. Perspective is that of any rational individual recognizing the nature of morality or the fact that persons are ends in themselves and must be treated as such.

Table 2

Examples of Responses at Each Stage

In Europe, a woman was near death from a very bad disease, a special kind of cancer. There was one drug that the doctors thought might save her. It was a form of radium that a druggist in the same town had recently discovered. The drug was expensive to make, but the druggist was charging ten times what the drug cost him to make. He paid $200 for the radium and charged $2,000 for a small dose of the drug. The sick woman's husband, Heinz, went to everyone he knew to borrow the money, but he could get together only about $1,000 which was half of what it cost. He told the druggist that his wife was dying, and asked him to sell it cheaper or let him pay later. But the druggist said, "No, I discovered the drug and I'm going to make money from it." Heinz got desperate and broke into the man's store to steal the drug for his wife.

STAGE 1. (Tommy at age 10):

"Heinz shouldn't steal; he should buy the drug. If he steals the drug, he might get put in jail and have to put the drug back anyway."

"But maybe Heinz should steal the drug because his wife might be an important lady, like Betsy Ross, she made the flag."

STAGE 2. (Tommy at age 13):

"Heinz should steal the drug to save his wife's life. He might get sent to jail, but he'd still have his wife."

Tommy, you said he should steal the drug for his wife. Should he steal it if it were a friend who was dying?
"That's going too far. He could be in jail while his friend is alive and free. I don't think a friend would do that for him."

STAGE 3. (Tommy at age 16):

"If I was Heinz, I would have stolen the drug for my wife. You can't put a price on love, no amount of gifts make love. You can't put a price on life either."

STAGE 4. (Tommy at age 21):

"When you get married, you take a vow to love and cherish your wife. Marriage is not only love, it's an obligation. Like a legal contract."

STAGE 5. (Kenny at age 25):

"I think he was justified in breaking in because there was a human life at stake. I think that transcends any right that the druggist had to the drug."

Table 2 (Continued)

Did the druggist have the right to charge that much when there was no law setting the limit?
"He has a legal right, but I don't think he had a moral right to do it. The profit was excessive, it was 10 times what he bought it for."

Is it the husband's duty or obligation to steal the drug for his wife if he can get it no other way?
"Again, I think the fact that her life was in danger transcends any other standards you might use to judge his actions."
Why? "Well, supposedly man is the supreme being and we are the most valuable resource on the planet. It is important to preserve a human life."
Suppose it was someone dying who wasn't even close. But there was no one else to help him. Would it be right to steal drug for such a stranger?
"It's something he should do. In order to be consistent, yes, I would have to say...something he should do, again from a moral standpoint."

What is this moral standpoint?
"Well, I think every individual has a right to live and if there is a way of saving an individual, I think an individual should be saved if he wants to be."

What does the word morality mean to you?
"I think it is acting so as to...I have to get my thinking straight on that. Nobody in the world knows the answer. I think it is presuming or recognizing the right of the individual to do...well, basically it is recognizing the rights of other individuals, not interfering with those rights, act as fairly–it is going to sound corny–but as you would have them treat you, as you would expect them to treat you, fairly and honestly. I think it is basically to preserve the human being's right to existence. I think that is the most important. Secondly, the human being's rights to do as he pleases, again without interfering with somebody else's rights."

STAGE 6. (Joan at age 32):

Now the first question is, what do you see as the problem in this situation?
"The problem for Heinz seems to be that his wife is dying and that he's caught in between obeying a societal law of not stealing and committing a crime that would result in saving his wife's life. I would like to think that there's a conflict for the druggist as well. Anytime there are conflicts in a situation... As soon as more than one person knows about a situation, O.K., that there's shared conflicts and the conflicts of each person sort of play off one another. And I think that the conflicts can be resolved to some extent by kind of pooling–so that as soon as more than one person becomes aware of the conflict that there are automatically problems to be resolved by each, things to be considered by each; and each person then has the power to affect what happens in the conflict. If I were Heinz I, you know, would keep trying to talk with the druggist...I have a hard time thinking of any

Table 2 (Continued)

decision as being static and it seems to me that dialogue is very important and a continuing dialogue in this kind of situation. But if it comes to a point where nothing else could be done, I think that on consultation with his wife, if he and his wife decided that that would be an acceptable alternative for Heinz, then yes he should. Because I think that ultimately it comes down to a conflict of duties. On the other hand, Heinz, I think as, just by virtue of being a member of the human race, has an obligation, a duty to protect other people. I guess that's a way to put it. And when it gets down to a conflict between those two, I think that the protection of human life is more important."

Is it important for people to do everything they can to save another's life?"
"No. I have this natural responsibility I'm talking about–to preserve your dignity, integrity, as an autonomous human being. And now when I think 'Do I have a responsibility to save your life?' I think that depends a lot. If I'm walking down the street, yes. I would do anything I could to save somebody else's life. I mean if I saw somebody walking in front of a car, I would jerk that person out of the way of the car. That would be the way I would react automatically. But, in other situations it depends. If you are terminally ill and you have decided that you would prefer rational suicide, or would prefer to not go through any more chemotherapy, any number of those things, I don't feel that I have the right to intrude on that position of yours, to say that you must take this chemotherapy, it's going to extend your life for a week longer, or a month longer or something. I don't see myself doing that, no."

Let me ask you this question: in looking at the original situation of Heinz and the drug and deciding whether to steal or not, is there any one consideration that stands out in your mind above all others, in making a decision of this sort?"
"I would say that there are two things. The first thing is that no person has the right to make a decision that affects the dignity and integrity of another person without there being cooperative discussion among the people involved. Number one. The second thing is that, you know, in this very strange situation where it would come down to being, you know, the single person's decision, and I have trouble conceiving that as every happening, then it comes down to preserving the dignity and integrity...and for the reason of life usually is involved in that, of another person. So I guess I'm saying that, well...I'm not saying that preserving life is *the* essential or ultimate thing. I think that preserving a person's dignity and integrity are the important things."

If Heinz doesn't love his wife, should he steal the drug for her?"
"I don't think that he should steal it out of a sense of love. I think that Heinz should steal the drug, if it comes down to that far-reaching point, out of a sense of responsibility to preserve life, not out of love. I think responsibility, as I'm using it here, means a recognition of dignity, on the part of every living being, but I could narrow it down, if you like, to

Table 2 (Continued)

persons. And responsibility is really something that's entailed in that recognition. If I respect you as a creature with dignity and your own unique, special being, in recognizing that I won't intrude on you, I won't purposefully harm you–there's this whole series of negatives that go along with being responsible and there's also some positives. And that's to recognize you as being unique, important and integral, in some sense, and to do what I can to preserve all that."

Suppose the person dying is not his wife but a stranger. Should Heinz steal the drug for a stranger?"
"Yes."

Is it a duty or obligation for Heinz?"
"When I think of my being obliged to do something, I think of another person as having a special claim, a claim that goes beyond the sort of minimal claims we all have on one another. To me that's obligation. And resensibility is what I naturally feel for every person. It's not imposed on me from the outside, it's part of my nature as a human being."

rested on two arguments about moral development as the aim of moral education. The first argument, which is reminiscent of Dewey, considers that development defines the process of education. It claims that the developmental approach is a third alternative to relativistic individualism on the one side and indoctrination on the other. Relativistic individualism is well illustrated by the values clarification, or values realization, approach of Rath and Simon. Like Protagoras the Sophist in the days of Socrates, the values clarifiers helped the individual student express and organize his values while being relativistic about recognizing that other students had other values. Given its premises and procedures, the values clarification approach offered no grounds for objection if the student's values included genocide at the extreme, or cheating on exams at the more likely, level.

At the other extreme was the alternative of indoctrination, often called character education, usually rationalized as what I have somewhat irreverently termed the "bag of virtues" approach. In the American studies of Hartshorne and May (1928-1930), the three cardinal virtues were honesty, service, and self-control. Their studies suggested that preaching and reward had no effect in increasing behavioral measures of these three virtues. Today in the People's

Republic of China, the cardinal virtues include courtesy, cleanliness with regard to the environment, loyalty, and cleanliness of thought. The character education approach is arbitrary in its content and doctrinaire in its method. In contrast, the developmental approach appeals to rational autonomy in both its intent, or theory, and in its use of the Socratic method.

The second, more debatable argument, is that a higher stage is a better stage, culminating in stages of principled moral reasoning. These are (1) a Stage 5 which is based on universal human rights and democratic agreement or contract -- i.e., a liberal philosophy basic to any constitutional democracy – and (2) a Stage 6 which, in Jürgen Habermas's version, represents discursive will-formation in a paradigm of universal dialogue, and in my version represents ideal role-taking or "moral musical chairs." In Kohlberg (1981) I called this endpoint "Justice as Reversibility" and likened the sociomoral operations of justice, such as reciprocity and equality, to the reversibility which Piaget found in operational logico-mathematical thought. Higher stages are not only formally more adequate, but lead empirically in some situations and under some conditions to a universal consensus on choice, a consensus which is the aim of reasoning and argumentation about justice. This lends support to the Socratic belief in the universality of rational justice.

What I have actually described is a straight movement from developmental psychology and philosophy to practice, a movement whose representation is what I call the one-way street model. A psychologist takes a theory that has been developed and tested by pure research, then makes prescriptions from the theory and applies it to classroom practice, and finally evaluates the effect by summative rather than formative research. I have never felt that this was a viable way of relating research to practice in moral education. Rather I believe that theorists had to be in reciprocal collaboration with teachers. The theorist, as consultant and researcher, should search for concepts and methods which aid the teacher in making the decisions he or she faces instead of making prescriptions to teachers based on deductions from developmental psychology and research. The one-way street model of relating theory to practice rests on what I have called the "psychologist's fallacy," i.e., the belief that what is important for developmental psychology research is what is important for practitioners in the classroom. I think Skinnerian behavior modification was, at least until recently, a good example of the psychologist's fallacy of developing prescriptions for educational practice from preformed theory based on pure research findings. I came to a practical realization of the lack of utility of the one-way street approach from a Stone Foundation study (Colby, Kohlberg, Fenton, Speiker-Dubin, & Lieberman, 1977), in which Fenton, a curriculum expert, and I trained a number of social studies teachers to facilitate hypothetical moral discussion, using Fenton's textbooks. We found a Blatt effect in about half the classrooms. The classrooms in which we found that effect were ones in which two things had occurred: first, a Socratic approach by a teacher who asked probing questions to elicit reasons, and second, a stage mixture in the classes. To achieve developmental change, children had to be reasoning at more than one stage, or a class had to have a sizeable number of members who reasoned on at least two stages. Our research results indicated that the teacher-training operation was a success in that at least half of the ordinary classroom teachers reproduced the Blatt effect even though they were not elaborately trained and motivated psychology graduate students. However, while the intervention operation was a success, the patient died. When we went back a year later, we found that not a single teacher had continued to engage in moral discussion after the commitment to the research had ended. Our intervention apparently did not speak sufficiently to the teachers' and students' own needs and expectations, even though it did lead to a one-third stage change.

One response to this problem was to integrate moral discussion with teachers' curriculum goals in English and social studies. Some teachers were quite innovative about curriculum, and would include moral discussion, not with the purpose of increasing the level of moral reasoning (as in the Stone study), but in order to relate moral discussion to the way in which children experienced and thought about literature and history. Such integration of moral discussion with curriculum was carried out in the 1970s and is summarized in Ralph Mosher's (1980) book on moral education. It became clear that one way of getting moral development theory into education and into practice is by having teachers relate it to already accepted curricular goals, such as sensitivity to literature.

INDOCTRINATION OR ADVOCACY

Besides integration with the curriculum, there were more fundamental limits to the dilemma discussion approach which needed to be surmounted before we would really have a viable kind of intervention. In the first place, there was the question of the relationship of judgment to action, or what might be called the relationship of reasoning in hypothetical dilemmas to reasoning in real-life dilemmas. Empirical studies showed certain relationships between judgment and action (Kohlberg, 1984). However, it is not clear from those studies whether changes in moral judgment that were produced in educational programs would actually lead to changes in moral action. Therefore, the first issue was the concern for action, a concern shared by the teachers and ourselves. The second related issue was the concern for content and structure. The teachers I consulted, including the philosopher of education Richard Peters, said that moral education has to deal with content as well as with structure, and that the traditional "teaching of virtues" approach is, in a sense, justified.

For me the philosophic problem involved in education for content as well as for structure is the issue of indoctrination. Common sense would say that teachers should help children see that stealing is a violation of certain fundamental rights of others and is therefore wrong. In all likelihood, some would be willing to accept an indoctrinative approach to this content. Although we are unwilling to accept indoctrination, we have come to accept what we now call an advocacy approach to the teaching of moral content. I have accepted the idea that the teacher is and should be an advocate for certain moral content. But what are the limits of advocacy? The teacher in real life has to go beyond being a Socratic questioner or a Carl Rogers type of reflector and supporter of development. This stance of teacher as process facilitator is quite workable for hypothetical moral dilemmas, but if there is, for example, an actual episode of stealing, the teacher is going to become an advocate for what we hope is the right answer.

Following Downey and Kelley's (1978) review of the indoctrination issue in moral education, we may consider indoctrination in terms of (1) the content of what is taught, (2) the method of teaching, and (3) the intent of the teacher. Within broad limits I believe that principles of justice represent *content* on which it is possible to reach some rational consensus, as expressed in the Declaration of Independence, which enumerates equal rights to life, liberty, and opportunity in the pursuit of happiness. In terms of manner or *method*, moral advocacy of justice can be carried out through the appeal to reasons which the teacher himself or herself accepts, rather than through the use of the teacher's authority. In terms of *intention*, advocacy of justice by the teacher can and should be based on an attitude of respect for the student as an autonomous moral agent. Advocacy should be just in its method and intent, not only in its content. For me the thing that prevents teachers' advocacy from being indoctrination is the establishment of participatory democracy in the classroom or in the school. The teacher should advocate as an individual, the first among equals, speaking from a rational point of view and not from one that relies on authority and power. In short, the teacher should be one member of a democratic political community in which each person has one vote. Effective teacher advocacy in what we have called a just community school rests on the use of appeals to reasons of fairness or community, usually at a relatively advanced stage, in a context of controversy about the rightness of a particular rule or policy. Later in this essay, I shall illustrate cases in which teachers have strong moral opinions about use of drugs, school attendance, or cheating, which in a just community school cannot be imposed directly on students through authority but must instead become influential insofar as they are couched in terms of consideration of justice or community. In addition, I shall illustrate that there is an ever-ongoing dialogue about the rights of the minority or the individual and the rights of the community manifested in majority vote. In these schools, this dialogue includes discussion of what some students in one just community which we studied, Scarsdale Alternative School, call teacher intimidation, i.e., the fact that when a teacher advocates, he or she is also perceived by students as having power through academic authority in grading, college recommendations, etc.

JUSTICE AND COMMUNITY

The linkage of democracy to the justice side of the just community approach, and to that aspect of justice we call non-indoctrination, is quite clear; it is the linkage of justice to a small political community based on equal political rights. It is also clear why school democracy might succeed in developing just action as well as just judgment where hypothetical dilemma discussions seem to have failed. First, in a democratic school students would make decisions about real-life dilemmas and actions, ones they had to make for the school's survival as a community. They would have to take responsibility for rules and a discipline process, all of which they would come to through discussion, reasoning, and argumentation about fairness. Second, they would be confronted by teachers and peers about discrepancies between their public judgments or reasoning and their actual action. If they agreed to adopt a rule, violating it could be counted by teachers and peers as a gap in the violator's self-consistency, as "hypocrisy" rather than as ignoring an authority-made rule. While non-indoctrinative, our approach might be called "socialization" because, unlike hypothetical moral dilemma discussion, it does involve the use of group criticism, reward, and discipline.

We have so far discussed the philosophy and psychology of the "right," the conception which guides our thinking about the just community. We now turn to the philosophy and psychology of "the good," the conception which guides our efforts, a philosophy of community. Going beyond respect for rights, "the good" includes the ideals of altruism, or responsibility of persons to and for one another, and of participation in the affairs of the community, a point recognized during the French Revolution by those who, inspired by Rousseau, added the watchword "Fraternity" to those of "Liberty" and "Equality." Community as a central moral ideal has been defined in various ways by more "organic" moral philosophers from Plato to Rousseau and Hegel, and in our century, Durkheim (1973), Royce (1982), Dewey (1966), Macmurray (1961), and Habermas (1979).

There is a powerful reason for concern about the lack of motivation and ability of youth to participate actively in the larger democratic community. In 1978, Lasch described this phenomenon as "The Culture of Narcissism," more popularly known as the "Me Generation." Not necessarily unjust or immoral, the youthful student and citizen is often privatistic or apathetic about the civic community and the public good, centering instead on his or her own personal concerns and ideals of happiness.

John Dewey spoke forcefully of the need for school democracy to educate toward a sense of responsibility for participating in the civic community for the public good. In Dewey's developmental or progressive view, democracy in the school is a bridge between the family and outside society, which is necessary for providing experiences of democratic participation and community, leading to the development of social responsibility:

> The term community has both a normative or eulogistic sense and a descriptive sense. In social philosophy society is conceived as one by its very nature. The qualities which accompany this praiseworthy community of purpose and welfare and loyalty to public ends are eulogized. On a more descriptive level, community is (1) the number and variety of commonly shared interests in a group and (2) a certain amount of inter-action and cooperative intercourse with other groups. These two elements both point to democracy. The first signifies not only more numerous and varied points of common interest, but greater reliance upon the recognition of mutual interests as a factor in social function. A democracy is

more than a form of government, it is a mode of living such that the persons who participate in an interest have to refer their own action to that of others. (Dewey, 1966, pp. 82-83)

Elsewhere I have relied on Dewey in articulating a general view of "development as the aim of education" (Kohlberg, 1981, ch. 3). Similarly, as the present essay shows, I have relied on Dewey's idea of democratic community as the means of moral education. However, I have also been much influenced by another concept of community, one which is even more vivid than Dewey's, though not so democratic. This is the concept of community once proposed by Durkheim (1973), whose central ideas are that (1) the group, society, or community is a whole or collectivity greater than the sum of its individual parts, and (2) the experience of membership in the collective whole induces in the individual moral sentiments capable of generating moral actions. On the one side these moral sentiments are sentiments of respect for group norms and rules, the "spirit of discipline," a respect which is derived in turn from respect for the group which makes them. On the other side, they are "the spirit of altruism," the willingness freely to give up the ego's interests, privileges, and possessions to the group or its other members because of a sense of solidarity in and with the group. We have found Durkheim's theory very useful in both practice and theory, in spite of what I consider some philosophic mistakes. It explains why a classroom or small school community is often able to promote in adolescents a sense of altruism and responsibility not generated by friends and family. Similarly, norms experienced as collective may inspire feelings of obligation which the individual adolescent's own judgment or that of other individuals may not produce of themselves. Following Durkheim, then, we have stressed that "the good" as altruism is cultivated by a "sense of community," by a feeling of group cohesion or solidarity, by a shared valuing or attachment to the school community and each of its members.

Recently Gilligan (1982) has criticized my moral theory as ignoring altruism, care, or "response." Like Durkheim's, and unlike Gilligan's, our theory of the just community does not make a typological dichotomy between justice and care, or assume that both are not present in each sex. For Durkheim, the collectivity was both the authority behind "the right" of rules and obligations and the object of altruistic aspiration toward "the good." Durkheim's double-aspect theory of morality is even clearer in our just community theory. Through participatory justice and democracy, a sense of the group as valuable and united, the source of altruism and solidarity, is enhanced. Through collective acts of care and responsibility for the welfare of the group and each of its members, the sense of justice is enhanced. Both are advocated by teachers in a community designed to include both teachers and peers, who in most American schools constitute two morally different groups. Moral development occurs in the just community not so much by advocacy on the part of teachers and students of the ideals of justice and community as by the discovery of a small world which is in fact fair and communitarian. Following Durkheim, the teacher's role is largely to help students "discover" the existence of this "moral reality," thereby helping to create a good moral atmosphere. However, I should add here that although our concept of the just community has been inspired by Durkheim's theory of moral education, the non-democratic and indoctrinative aspects of his theory are not part of our concept. Unlike Durkheim, we do not regard the teacher as the supreme authority in the classroom, the dispenser of punishment and reward, and the representative or priest of the national society which is the major collective source and object of morality.

MORAL EDUCATION IN THE JUST COMMUNITY: TWO CASES

Our first effort at using "Dewey-Piaget" democracy and Durkheimian collective moral education focused heavily on remedial moral education for preconventional adolescents. Founded in 1974 the Cambridge Cluster Alternative School focused heavily on disadvantaged or street youth, 50% black, who were at risk in terms of success in school or in conventional society. On entrance, most were Stage 2 or 2/3. The school succeeded by means of certain criteria. All the students moved to the conventional stages and by graduation were, on the average, at Stage 3/4. Furthermore, more than three-fourths of them went on to college, a striking result given their slim prospects for higher education at the time they entered the school.

One episode from the just community process implemented at the Cambridge Cluster School illustrates the intervention theory and the method of research on moral atmosphere tied to that theory. In accordance with my interpretation of Durkheim, my role in community meetings, and the role which I strove to teach the staff to adopt, was to speak not for myself but rather as a representative of the spirit, traditions, and future of the community. In this role my task was a double one: (1) to advocate the making of a rule or the developing of a collective norm important to the school, and (2) to attempt to tie this norm to the group's welfare and spirit of community.

In the first year at Cluster School, there were repeated episodes of theft. The issue was raised in a community meeting by the staff. Students agreed it should be made a disciplinary offense, although they voiced the Stage 2 opinion that "if someone was stupid enough to leave something around it was his or her fault if it was ripped off." Not willing to leave the matter there, I said, "Maybe somebody can explain why the stealing is going on? Don't people think it's wrong and a violation of the community?" The students were non-responsive to this appeal. One said: "I don't think you should worry about that. The fact is that it happened. To worry about why it happened isn't worth it." Yet I persisted: "I think ripping off is not an individual business; it is a community business. It is not a discipline issue so much as a feeling in the community that people must have some level of trust, which is inconsistent with anybody ripping off from anybody else in the community." Only one student saw my point. The others believed that making a rule against stealing was the best that could be done. They voted for the rule and with that the meeting ended, but the problem of stealing persisted. Discussions about the necessity for building trust and mutual care continued throughout the first year.

Cluster members began the second year optimistically. However, in October there was another stealing incident. Nine dollars was taken from a student's purse during a class, and no one would say who took it. At a community meeting convened to discuss the theft, one group of students proposed that each member of the school chip in fifteen cents, to add up to the nine dollars stolen from the girl's purse. Phyllis, a girl from this group, offered an elaborate rationale for reimbursing the stolen money: "It's everyone's fault that she don't have no money. It was stolen because people just don't care about the community." They think "they are all individuals and don't have to be included in the community. Everybody should care that she got her money stolen," and therefore, "We decided to give her money back to her."

Not everyone agreed with this proposal. Bob was worried that if they adopted the proposal, "Then anyone can say 'I lost ten dollars,'" adding "If a bank is ripped off, we don't pay." Jill asked, "How do you know whether to believe someone who says her money has been stolen?" Bob and Jill both thought the fault lay not with the community but with the girl, for having left her purse unattended. "She gives you a chance to steal it; if you had it in your arms, wouldn't you be thinking about stealing it?" In response, Phyllis reiterated her point. She began with the assumption that Cluster School ought to be a community and its members ought to trust one another. If people could not be trusted, it was the group's failure, and they would have to pay for the fault. Both staff members and students pointed out that the community should put pressure on the guilty party to return the money. Thus they adopted a compromise: "If the money is not returned anonymously by a certain date, everyone will be assessed fifteen cents." The combined proposal was voted in and, in fact, proved effective. The person who stole the money eventually admitted it. There were no thefts in the school in the three years after the meeting.

In comparing these two meetings, it does not appear that the change in stealing behavior can be accounted for solely in terms of development in individual moral judgment between the first and second years. A review of the transcripts shows some individual reasoning at Stage 2 and Stage 3 in each meeting. What changed dramatically was the social or collective norms within whose context the judgments were being made. In its second year, Cluster School began the process of becoming a just community. Phyllis's statements marked the change. They revealed a Stage 3 structure not only of Phyllis's individual moral judgment but of the moral atmosphere of the Cluster community. Phyllis did not simply speak for herself as an individual with personal opinions; she spoke for the whole school, exhorting the other members to live up to the normative values of caring and trust. In her view students were obligated as members of the community to live up to these expectations. Thus caring and trust were no longer perceived simply as the staff's bag of virtues, but were seen as values that the community as a whole was beginning to share. These shared values can be referred to as "collective normative values," to distinguish them from values expressed in individual moral judgments.

What gave force to these normative values was that they were perceived as necessary for creating a community in the school. During the first year, some of the staff and I had suggested that the issue of stealing be viewed as "a violation of the community," but only one student responded. By the second year, students were concerned with whether the Cluster School was "really a community," a concern which presupposed their recognition that "this school is supposed to be a community." We believe this recognition was crucial for the resolution of the stealing problem. In the

Table 3

Phases of the Collective Norm

Phase 0: No collective norm exists or is proposed.

COLLECTIVE NORM PROPOSAL
Phase 1: Individuals propose collective norms for group acceptance.

COLLECTIVE NORM ACCEPTANCE
Phase 2: Collective norm is accepted as a group ideal but not agreed to. It is not an expectation for behavior.
   (a) Some group members accept ideal
   (b) Most group members accept ideal

Phase 3: Collective norm is accepted and agreed to but it is not (yet) an expectation for behavior.
   (a) Some group members agree to collective norm
   (b) Most group members agree to collective norm

COLLECTIVE NORM EXPECTATION
Phase 4: Collective norm is accepted and expected. (Naive expectation)
   (a) Some group members expect the collective norm to be followed
   (b) Most group members expect the collective norm to be followed

Phase 5: Collective norm is expected but not followed. (Disappointed expectation)
   (a) Some group members are disappointed
   (b) Most group members are disappointed

COLLECTIVE NORM ENFORCEMENT
Phase 6: Collective norm is expected and upheld through expected persuading of deviant to follow norm.
   (a) Some group members persuade
   (b) Most group members persuade

Phase 7: Collective norm is expected and upheld through expected reporting of defiant to the group.
   (a) Some group members report
   (b) Most group members report

Table 4

Stages of Collective Normative Values and the Sense of Community Valuing

COLLECTIVE NORMATIVE VALUES	SENSE OF COMMUNITY VALUING

STAGE 2

There is not yet an explicit awareness of collective normative values. However, there are *generalized expectations* that individuals should recognize concrete individual rights and resolve conflicts through exchange.	There is no clear sense of community apart from exchanges among group members. Community denotes a collection of individuals who do favors for each other and rely on each other for protection. Community is value insofar as it meets the concrete needs of its members.
EXAMPLES:	*EXAMPLES:*
1. Do not "rat" on another group member. Ratting or reporting another group member to authorities is disapproved of because it exposes the rule breaker to likely punishment.	1. The community is like a "bank." Members meet to exchange favors, but you cannot take more than you give.
2. Do not bother others. Live and let live.	
3. Help others out when you want to.	

STAGE 3

Collective normative values refer to relationships among group members. Membership in a group implies living up to *shared expectations.* Conflicts should be resolved by appeal to mutual collective normative values.	The sense of community refers to a set of relationships and sharings among group members. The group is valued for the friendliness of its members. The value of the group is equated with the value of its collective normative expectations.
EXAMPLES:	*EXAMPLES:*
1. Members of a group should be able to trust each other with their possessions.	1. The community is a family in which members care for each other.
2. Members of a group should care about other members of the group.	2. The community is honorable because it helps others.

students' past experience, stealing had been a common occurrence. Given their stages of development, they could not be expected to take responsibility for the property of others unless they valued the school as a social context different from the city streets or from the larger school which housed the Cluster School. Participating in a community which drew them into close association with one another allowed them to realize that their actions had consequences for a group solidarity that they really cared about.

The issue of stealing led to the creation of a collective norm which was able to prevent stealing behavior because it was linked to communitarian norms – the norm of trust and the norm of collective responsibility – and hence was linked to the value of community itself. This did not happen spontaneously, but was a response to advocacy by me and other members of the staff. Our advocacy was ineffective in the first year of the school but meaningful in the second year. Our research report (Power, 1979) documents in detail the longitudinal formation of the collective norms of property, trust, and collective responsibility at Cluster for four years. The growth of these collective norms is documented both in stages (from Stage 2/3 to Stage 3/4) and in phases or degrees of institutionalization. At a high phase of institutionalization, not only is a norm expected for the self and others, but so is active enforcement of the norm through persuasion or through taking a stand when others are deviating. Analyses of both community meeting statements and longitudinal interviews of individuals showed similar patterns of development. Our research also defined the stages of collective norms, although the fact that one norm would develop in stage and phase was no guarantee that another norm would. For instance, the Cluster School never developed a norm against smoking marijuana or coming high to class, but was satisfied with the more modest norm or maxim, "Be cool, be discreet" in drug use.

The second case of the just community approach which I would like to discuss is the Scarsdale Alternative School, to which students come from homes with higher socioeconomic status and where family and community socialization and lack of economic need ensure that there are no major issues of stealing. Since 1978, when the just community approach was inaugurated at Scarsdale, the only episode of "stealing" involved the disappearance of a few students' lunch sandwiches from the communal refrigerator. However, while stealing was not an issue at Scarsdale, another form of injustice was: cheating.

In the case of cheating at schools like Scarsdale High School, most students and teachers are aware of a "hidden" or unspoken curriculum about cheating which presents a double message. On the one hand, teachers, parents, and even peers have high academic expectation and positively evaluate competitive achievement for grades, a pressure which influences students to use illicit means (i.e., cheating) to achieve. Peers, in particular, not only condone the use of illicit means to get good grades but may actually expect each other's help and cooperation in cheating. Thus there is a peer "counter-norm" to help and ignore cheating, conflicting with official or teacher-based norms against cheating. A student in the regular Scarsdale High School described it in an anonymous letter to the local newspaper, which said in part:

> Scarsdale's biggest problem is that nobody is happy. Priding itself on being a great prep school, they have created a hellish atmosphere . . . The past year three to five students tried to kill themselves and at least four students were institutionalized for mental problems . . . Most of these problems were due to the unbearable pressure. This pressure is evident in many facets of the school. What people do for good grades is unbelieveable. Obviously, there is much cheating in Scarsdale. As an aware student, I approximate that 95 percent of the students will cheat without guilt whenever they need something. This habit is something that is taught to them by the school, not dissuaded at all . . .

It should be noted that developing a peer-supported norm against cheating is more difficult than developing one against stealing. Peer group norms against stealing from one another develop readily because peers are clear victims of unfairness in stealing. In the case of cheating, those most obviously concerned or victimized are the teachers, so that peer group norms in favor of cheating can develop in an atmosphere in which students are a "we-group" distinct from a "they group" of teachers. Strong collective norms against cheating can usually develop only if the peer group and the teacher group are seen as members of a common community making community norms fair to teachers as well as to students. This is, in fact, what happened at Scarsdale.

In 1982 Judy Codding, the director, held a core or advisory group meeting in which students talked about the cheating that took place when they had been in the regular Scarsdale High School and about the moral atmosphere that made it acceptable there. In answer to her question: "Is cheating widespread at the school?" Sam answered, "It's very common at the high school, there's the opportunity to cheat and get away with it. Teachers can't really keep their eyes on every student. There's a feeling that your friend is going to help you if you don't know the answer."

The norms of friendship and affiliation, especially strong at Stage 3, create a peer counter-norm to honesty. In the cheating situation, not only peer norms but parental expectations act as "quasi-obligations" which actually prevent students from making judgments of responsibility to do "the right thing." In the core group just mentioned, Richy experienced the Stage 3 "quasi-obligation" of fulfilling parental expectations and "making them feel happy." He said, "I got a lot of pressures from my parents and in the ninth grade I was saying, 'OK, it's your first year of high school, you have to do well,' and I was just cheating because I wanted to do well and make my parents happy." Going on to describe how other students acted, he said, "I just know there has to be in other people's minds that parental pressure of 'I have to do good on this test or my Dad is going to kill me.' That's how it was for me, so I cheated."

The net combination of these factors was to create in the regular high school a moral atmosphere which suggested that no one had a responsibility to refrain from cheating. A female student said," I'd think the atmosphere at the high school was that everyone around you is cheating. It pressures you into it because they're going to get a ninety and you're going to get an eighty. It's a lot of pressure to be like them and to get a good grade, too."

In the Scarsdale Alternative School, a community meeting was held about making and enforcing a rule against cheating. One student said, "I disagree that under pressure people have to cheat. I was under a lot of pressure and I was hysterical I was going to fail this test. It was just memorization and I had these crib sheets and this teacher said, 'No cheating goes' and I couldn't cheat, so I got a 67. What I'm saying is that cheating isn't necessary. The reason for cheating is that people are lazy and don't want to study so they make up crib sheets. It's not responsible."

Other students spoke against cheating not in terms of fairness or justice but in terms of community values. A male student said, "It goes with being in a community. Ending cheating is a good direction for our community; it's for the benefit of our community." Speaking for "we, the community," this student proposed a collective norm against cheating. Judy, the director, advocated a shared norm against cheating by invoking the value of such a norm for the mutual trust and solidarity of a community, including teachers and peers. She said:

Cheating is an issue that can really divide our community, students against teachers in terms of cheating. There are students who join teachers' ranks, but it sounds like on this issue that it's me and you, because obviously teachers don't participate in cheating. Peter, you were asking for reasons in this school. It's because it's fundamental to our school that there's trust within the community. You know my attitude when I give a test. It's based on trust. I would hate to mistrust people in the community. When people say it's not so bad cheating on a little test, because you won't ever take it again and it's not relevant to your later life, it ignores a decision about trust which can divide the community.

Just as at Cambridge Cluster School when a collective norm against stealing arose through advocacy of the norm as necessary for community trust and solidarity, at Scarsdale Judy advocated a norm against cheating. Another teacher advocated a norm against cheating less in terms of community and more in terms of the injustice of cheating. He said, "You have to see that cheating is hurting other people as a way to get ahead. I can't imagine you can think that's a principle you can live by, despite all the temptation we talked about." While making a rule against cheating was soon agreed upon, the question of how to enforce this rule was extremely controversial. The teachers proposed that both the faculty and the students had the responsibility to enforce the rule by confronting a student they saw cheating. From the start the faculty was concerned that the students share responsibility for enforcement of agreed upon norms. In our theoretical language, they were determined that the norm should reach Phase 6 or 7, persuasion to desist from rule violation or to confront someone who had violated the rule. The rationale for the faculty's expectation that students confront one another over cheating was that teachers and students belonged to a common community and that it was not fair to the faculty to leave it to them to be the police officers or enforcers of a rule arrived at democratically. As stated by one of the teachers:

> Is it fair in a democratic school to make these rules and then shuffle down to the teacher's corner for their enforcement? There are certain rules that we make and the problem of who finds out about violation of them and who enforces them doesn't arise. But for others that are hard to enforce, like this one, I would say if we can't enforce it together we can't make it together. We don't own it. It's all our responsibility to deal with the cheating problem. If John sees someone cheating, why is it any different from my seeing someone cheating?

Using this logic the faculty made the following proposals:
- If students know that another student has cheated, it is their responsibility to confront the cheater.
- The student who cheated should discuss the situation with the teacher of the class.
- If the student who cheated refuses to discuss the matter with the teacher, the students who did the confronting have the responsibility to discuss the issue with the teacher.
- The teacher has the responsibility to fail the student for the assignment.
- The teacher has the responsibility to bring the student before the Fairness Committee.

This stance proved controversial not only for the students but also for me as an outside observer and consultant. The effort of the staff to make students responsible for enforcing the cheating rule and being loyal to the school as a whole contradicts powerful norms of loyalty and trust among friends. While it is possible to conceptualize these norms of loyalty to friends as being at a third stage of caring for individual mutual relations and loyalty to the community as fourth stage, norms of interpersonal loyalty and trust are also basic to fourth and even fifth stage concerns about friendship, as well as to concerns about solidarity in the school community.

A less controversial episode of conflict resolution among community rules and personal caring occurred during a 1983 community meeting. The issue at hand was whether or not to expel Lisa, a first year tenth grade student; this meant that she would return to the regular high school, where she had been very unhappy and done quite poorly. The staff, in a staff meeting, had unanimously decided that such a return would be best for the school community, and possibly for Lisa herself. Until the threat of expulsion became imminent, she had regularly cut classes in spite of many reminders. She had frequently been verbally abusive to the staff, something almost unheard of in the school. The teachers felt she had not made the necessary commitment to the alternative school and that she was taking time and energy that the other students should receive. The issue of Lisa's expulsion precluded other personal discussion in the small core groups which preceded the schoolwide community meeting, since it was the first expulsion issue in three years. I attended a core group meeting at which students took varying attitudes. Some felt Lisa had passed all bounds and that upholding the standards of the school required her expulsion. Others knew of her family difficulties and almost complete lack of close friends, and consequently worried about her return to the regular high school. One student said that the school was a very strong community and should give her the support and the prodding necessary to keep her attending class and being a member of the school.

The larger community meeting began with a statement by the director that the decision would be a community decision. She asked students to think about the issue from Lisa's point of view, from the staff's point of view, and from the point of view of the whole community. Then a spokesperson for the staff read a report recommending expulsion and giving the reasons for it. Lisa's initial response was quite instrumental and self-protective, a statement suggesting our description of Stage 2. She didn't like the regular high school and, she pointed out, for the past week she had attended classes regularly. When asked about the basis of her improved attitude, she said, "Out of fear."

The two students chairing the meeting asked for student discussion. Many hands went up. One of the first to speak was Sharon, who proposed that the school was strong enough as a community to form a support group for Lisa. Even if Lisa wasn't sufficiently self-disciplined to come to class regularly, others should help her and put some daily pressure on her to come to class. Other students then made comments supporting Sharon's position, one student saying he took pride in the community but would value it less if they didn't try to support Lisa. Other students were more critical of Lisa's behavior, expressing doubts about the community's ability to help her. One student commented, "No one else had an attendance problem like Lisa's. Why should the community tolerate it?" Another student said, "I didn't know this was supposed to be a therapeutic community," to which another responded, "It's not a therapeutic community. It's a community . . . That means we all care about each member of the school, with or without problems."

After still more discussion, Lisa was asked to comment. In tears, she asked to have another chance and stay in the school. It was as if a Stage 3 awareness was dawning in her as to what the school could be for her, that it could be a place where people cared. The discussion continued, other students remarking that being a caring community sounded good, but who would really take the responsibility? At this point several students individually volunteered to assume responsibility for Lisa. Her alternatives were outlined on the blackboard: (1) Stay in the school; (2) Stay in the school on probation, with an individual contract to be worked out with the staff; (3) Expulsion, with the chance to return the following year if she did well in the regular school. Lisa was then asked how she herself would vote, and answered, "Stay in the school on probation." Extensive discussion followed, with signs that some staff members were changing their minds. An hour and a half later a vote was called for. Lisa initially wanted to leave the room so she would not know who voted against her, but eventually agreed to stay. Of the seventy-six voting members present all but four voted for Lisa to stay. In the days after the meeting a contract between Lisa, her advisor, and a support group of students was worked out. Lisa met once a week with the support group; for the rest of the year she not only attended all classes, but her work improved and her abusive or disrespectful language disappeared.

CONCLUSION

Students who have participated in a just community speak well of their experience. One student who moved to Stage 5 talked about the effect participation in the Scarsdale democratic community meeting had on her:

> There is a big difference in me now. Before, I thought about what was good for me in the meeting. I didn't think consciously selfish. I just thought we should each vote for what we wanted and then you combine them and the best comes out somehow. Now I try to distinguish what is best for me from what is best for all the students or the community and decide on that basis.

The change she describes can be viewed as related to a theory of pluralistic interest group democracy governed by an "invisible hand" leading to a search for a consensus or Rousseau's "general will," a search never successfully engaged in by political states though it may have succeeded in some voluntary communities.

With regard to the experimental or alternative school as a voluntary community, the student continued:

> I think if you're being into the school, you're being into something that you give up certain rights or functions for the chance of belonging here. But there are different limits, there is no way the community should decide everything. Many things should be left to individual decision.

It is important to emphasize that I am not suggesting that secondary schools, public or independent, adopt the "free school" of the sixties, an ideology that failed. I am suggesting a quite different theory or ideology – that of democratic community – and I am suggesting that nothing less will make graduates active citizens of a democratic society. Of course, how the just community functions will vary with the nature and beliefs of the students and faculty in each individual school. However, if schools are to educate character in addition to promoting academic achievements, nothing less than such a community will do.

NOTE

1. This paper was presented at the Loyola-Mellon Colloquium Series on Moral Development, April 1984. A version of the paper appeared in M. W. Berkowitz & F. Oser (Eds.), *Moral education: Theory and application* (Hillsdale, NJ: Erlbaum), 1985.

REFERENCES

Blatt, M., & Kohlberg, L. (1975). The effects of classroom discussion upon children's level of moral judgment. *Journal of Moral Education*, 4, 129-161.
Colby, A., Kohlberg, L., Fenton, E., Speicher-Dubin, B., & Lieberman, M. (1977). Secondary school moral discussion programmes led by social studies teachers. *Journal of Moral Education*, 6, 90-117.
Dewey, J. (1966). *Democracy and education.* New York: MacMillan Free Press.
Downey, M., & Kelly, A. V. (1978). *Moral education: Theory and practice.* London: Harper and Row.
Durkheim, E. (1973). *Moral education.* New York: Free Press.
Gilligan, C. (1982). *In a different voice: Psychological theory and women's development.* Cambridge, MA: Harvard University.
Habermas, J. (1979). *Communication and the evolution of society.* Boston: Beacon Press.
Hartshorne, H., & May, M. A. (1928-1930). *Studies in the nature of character* (Vols. 1-3). New York: MacMillan.
Kohlberg, L. (1981). *Essays on moral development: Vol. 1. The philosophy of moral development.* San Francisco: Harper and Row.
Kohlberg, L. (1984). *Essays on moral development: Vol. 2. The psychology of moral development.* San Francisco: Harper and Row.
Lockwood, A. (1978). The effects of values clarification and moral development curricula on school age subjects: A critical review of recent research. *Review of Educational Research*, 48, 325-364.
Macmurray, J. (1961). *Persons in relation.* London: Faber and Faber.
Mosher, R. L. (Ed.) (1980). *Moral education: A first generation of research and development.* New York: Praeger.
Power, C. (1979). *The moral atmosphere of a just community high school: A four year longitudinal study.* Unpublished doctoral dissertation, Harvard University.
Rest, J. R. (1973). The hierarchical nature of moral judgment. *Journal of Personality*, 41, 86-109.
Royce, J. (1982). *The philosophy of Josiah Royce* (J. Roth, Ed.). Indianapolis: Hackett.

Growth and Regression in Cognitive-Moral Development of Young University Students

Georg Lind

In the late 1960s, a psychological study by Kohlberg and Kramer (1969) indicated that higher education may induce "moral regression" rather than moral growth in college students. It was reported that "between late high school and the second or third year of college, 20% of our middle class sample dropped or retrogressed in moral maturity scores" (Kohlberg & Kramer, 1969, p. 109). Psychologists, Kohlbergians as well as anti-Kohlbergians, have continued to discuss this finding, which is clearly at odds with the assumption of stage-wise invariant cognitive-moral development. Whereas there may be a considerable increase in the *use* of lower stage reasoning in moral interview situations, a decrease of *competence* of moral judgment from Stage 5 to Stage 2, as was reported, would be a real challenge to cognitive developmental theory as a whole.

Two of the central assumptions of cognitive developmental theory are (1) that there is an invariant sequence of moral development which does not allow for exceptions, and (2) that there is a fundamental parallel between the cognitive and the affective aspects of moral judgment (Kohlberg, 1969, 1984). Both assumptions, which are closely related to each another, are supported by empirical data, but there are also studies which have produced counter-evidence. In regard to the hypothesis of cognitive-affective parallelism, some studies indicate a systematic relationship between the two aspects, but other studies do not. Moreover, there are doubts as to whether these two aspects have so far been adequately conceptualized and measured. As I have argued elsewhere (Lind, 1982b; 1985b), in most studies the two aspects are either confounded and not distinguishable or are conceptualized as two ontologically separate entities. If adequately measured as aspects of moral judgment, a marked parallelism can be found (Lind, 1985d).

The hypothesis of invariant sequence is clearly supported by a number of excellently designed studies in spite of its high improbability, i.e., its *Gehalt* (cf. Kohlberg, 1979; Colby et al., 1983; Rest,

1979; for the Popperian concept of *Gehalt* and its application to theory evaluation, see Lind, 1985b). However, some findings – including Kohlberg's – cast doubt on the assumption that the stages of cognitive-moral development are "hard stages," that is, that there are no exceptions to the hypothesized sequence of development from Stage 1 to Stages 5 and 6. In consequence, various revisions or even substitutions for Kohlberg's original stage scheme have been proposed (cf. Broughton, 1970; Kohlberg, 1973; Gilligan & Kohlberg, 1973; Holstein, 1976; Gibbs, 1977; Murphy & Gilligan, 1980; Eckensberger, 1983).

The question of growth or regression in moral-cognitive development is not only of academic interest but is also important from the point of view of socialization theory. In the face of past moral failures of society's functional élite as documented in Ringer's *Decline of the German Mandarins* (1969) or Roszak's *Dissenting Academy* (1967), and in the face of such severe problems as economic crises, social injustice, and nuclear holocaust, widespread moral regression would indicate an alarming deficiency in our educational system, insofar as education is the most significant factor in the fostering of moral judgment competence (for a summary of research, see Lind, 1985c).

Unfortunately, neither the data-base nor its interpretation is unambiguous, and, hence, any derivation for educational policy must rely on rather tenuous assumptions. This ambiguity is due to the fact that, besides specific hypotheses, the cognitive-developmental approach implies, in part, a specific methodology in order to set up appropriate categories of data (cf. Kohlberg, 1969, p. 347; Broughton, 1978) – a methodology which is not yet fully developed. In moral judgment research, conventional psychometric criteria such as the criterion of "reliability" prevail, criteria whose implicit assumptions about human behavior, as we have tried to show elsewhere, are partly at variance with cognitive-developmental theory (cf. Lind, 1985a; Lind & Wakenhut, 1985).

Hence, when confronted with this problem of apparent moral regression related to educational gain, we must not concentrate solely on data and data comparison but must attend to the methodological problems engendered by our research question. In this essay I discuss critically several interpretations of the regression phenomenon and report on an empirical cross-validation study of German students, which we conducted using a new method of assessing moral development.

REGRESSION OR PSEUDO-REGRESSION?

Kramer and Kohlberg (1969) do not regard their cases of regression as contradicting cognitive-developmental theory, nor do they question the scoring method. They try instead to explain them theoretically in terms of intervening extra-moral processes. However, these explanations are not derived exclusively from cognitive-developmental theory, but are borrowed from Perry's (1970) work on ethical and cognitive development and from Erikson's (1966) theory of identity crisis and ego development. Kohlberg and Kramer speculate that moral development, in the sense of structural transformations, may terminate at the end of childhood, while ego-functions continue to become more important. According to this explanation, regression is not structural, but is only a temporary, functional phase "in the service of the ego." In fact, given this perspective, regression should be considered normal for the life-phase of identity crisis and "psychosocial moratorium," during which "new and non-conforming patterns of thought and behavior are tried out" (Kohlberg & Kramer, 1968, p. 116). This is an interesting speculation, but it should not be our first choice of an explanation, because such an eclectic and somewhat arbitrary amalgamation of different conceptual frames could diminish the explanatory power of cognitive-developmental theory as a whole. Two other lines of reasoning ought to be explored first. One suggests modifying the stage model in order to accommodate the postulate of invariant developmental order; the other suggests keeping, and perhaps extending, the Kohlbergian scheme as a common frame of reference within which either the methods of assessment or the empirical propositions of the theory would be modified. Let us examine these two alternatives.

One may conclude that the Kramer and Kohlberg findings undermine not only the hypothesis of general invariant developmental sequences and the assessment methods used, but, more dramatically, their entire conceptual framework. Consequently, those who advocate this proposition reject the original Kohlberg stage model, and posit a new conceptual framework in order to meet more adequately the demands imposed by the postulate of sequential order (cf. Gibbs, 1977; Haan, 1978; Eckensberger & Reinshagen, 1980; Murphy & Gilligan, 1980; Lempert, 1982). Kohlberg has also modified his system considerably, although he has only slightly reworded the stage descriptions themselves (Kohlberg, 1984). However, I do not believe that at this point there is any compelling reason – e.g., a better conceptual framework – for discarding Kohlberg's stage model, which has widened considerably our understanding of human cognitive-moral development. Moreover, a conceptual model cannot, as some authors seem to believe, be disproved by empirical data alone. Kohlberg's six stages are "ideal-types" that are the basis of theory construction and measurement, even if cases of regression occur and some stages are not matched by empirical cases. This point is especially obvious in connection with physical concepts. We would not consider that the concept of length was falsified because we observed that the size of an object shrinks or that a certain distance is not found in natural settings. On the contrary, the observation of both shrinkage and uneven distribution of distances depends on an a priori (non-empirical) concept of length. Analogously, cases of moral regression would contradict the hypothesis of invariant sequence but would not devalue the more general concept of stages. If we readjust our conceptual framework (i.e., our measurement system) every time we find such cases, we will end up in a Tower of Babel, full of mutually incommensurable stage concepts, and any scientific discourse will become impossible.

This leaves us with the second line of argumentation mentioned above, and with a new problem: the choice between two rather divergent interpretations of the Kohlberg and Kramer data. Should we interpret these data as indicating a true regression in moral development, or as a pseudo-regression which is the result of systematic measurement error which has actually inverted progression in cognitive-moral development? Here again the most responsible strategy, in our view, is to search first for methodological imperfections that can be remedied on the basis of an unchanged theory, instead of altering the theory or adding auxiliary hypotheses that could reduce the *Gehalt* (information value) of cognitive-developmental theory. Considering shortcomings of measurement methodology as a cause of regressions does not imply that only those methods are acceptable which produce the desired findings. The theory would become immune to any empirical critique and worthless if, as Kohlberg (1976) once suggested, one tried to save the theory by assigning "individuals to stages in such a way that the criterion of sequential movement is met" (p. 47). Our concern is with the concept of *theoretical validity*, which requires that we judge the research methodology on conceptual and theoretical grounds. Only if it is found that improvement of the theoretical validity of the methods eliminates regressions can the hypothesis of invariant sequence be considered "saved."

In reconsidering his research method in his publications since 1973, Kohlberg has identified various methodological causes for the occurrence of anomalies in the data. One such cause had to do with the original coding system which, in his opinion, has failed to distinguish clearly enough between "content" and "structure" (Kohlberg, 1973, p. 191; 1976, p. 43). Hence, he and his colleagues at Harvard completely revised the coding system (Colby & Kohlberg, in press). Although the findings are now more consistent with the hypothesis of invariant sequence, there are still a considerable number of persons who appear to regress (Kohlberg, 1979; Murphy & Gilligan, 1980). This fact would suffice to refute the hypothesis because, as Kohlberg (1973) has stated with admirable courage, "a single case of longitudinal inversion of sequence disproves the stage theory if it is not a manifest case of measurement errors" (p. 182).

Therefore, to account for the phenomenon of regression, Kohlberg and his collaborators have invoked the psychometric concept of random measurement error, whose effect is estimated on the basis of a test-replication within a short-term range (retest reliability). On these grounds, they were able to show in their longitudinal study (Colby et al., 1983) that the number of downward movements over a three-to-four-year interval is clearly lower than the number of changes within one month. This is an impressive result if one considers the critical comments on cognitive-developmental research made by psychometrically oriented psychologists. However, psychometric theory rests on assumptions which are themselves problematic (cf. Lumsden, 1976; Kempf, 1978) and, in our view, is based on an implicit view of human personality that is incompatible with cognitive-developmental theory. Moreover, there are still doubts as to whether or not the new scoring method has succeeded in distinguishing more clearly between content and structure (Eckensberger, 1983; Lind, 1985d).

The question remains: Does observed regression disprove the Kohlbergian hypothesis, or does it instead reflect an as yet unidentified measurement error? The centrality of this question, for cognitive-developmental theory as well as for practical problems in education, leads us once again to consider the problem of methodological adequacy. It may be that, in concentrating on problems of computing indices and analyzing data, we have overlooked other possible sources of measurement error.

Indeed, it has been suggested that the "regressions" may be due not so much to coding problems as to flaws in the assessment procedure. As early as 1970, Broughton pointed out problems pertaining to the design of moral interviews, and identified a "general lack of probing" (p. 6). Lacking relevant information, the psychologist can easily be misguided when classifying reasons according to moral stages. For example, instrumentalist answers are usually scored as Stage 2. But, as Döbert and Nunner-Winkler (1975, pp. 126-131) have demonstrated, instrumentalism is not unambiguously related to reasoning at Stage 2. Some subtypes of instrumental reasons can also be found in postconventionals, that is, in Stage 5 or Stage 6 subjects – if the interviews are so conducted as to provide sufficient information. For example, instrumentalist reasons may be given by postconventionals who argue "cynically," or by those who purposely understate their moral concerns in certain situations such as the interview situation. Colby et al. (1983), who have reanalyzed the original Kohlberg longitudinal data, also report evidence of "moral cynicism and relativism" (p. 72) which they consider irrelevant to the question of moral development.

However, whereas some authors regard this phenomenon solely as evidence of the subject's "metaethical position," we regard it also as a product of the method of assessment. Though they are hypothetical, the moral dilemmas presented usually engage the respondent, and it is assumed that they generally cause the subject to reason at the highest stage of moral judgment available to this person. Yet, the interview method may fail in some cases to elicit this engagement, with the result that the conversation remains superficial. In such instances the respondent may choose to avoid "high-sounding" reasons for defending his opinion on the dilemma. However, when reading these interviews, one wonders whether or not the respondent would stand by his instrumentalist reasons if he were asked to compare their inacceptability with his own or other people's Stage 2 reasons. Unless he or she would really prefer instrumental morality over principled reasoning, instrumentalist answers could be taken as a sign of non-moral factors (such as cynicism or understatement), or as a sign of a highly differentiated cognitive-moral structure. It may be misleading merely to count the number of times that a stage-typical concern was uttered. Often we might detect that the frequency of a statement does not correlate perfectly with its subjective significance. If the interview, or the computation of the individual's total score, is not designed to take this ambiguity into consideration, then non-moral utterances may be mistaken for moral judgment behavior, wrongly producing the impression of regression. Thus, to substantiate the explanation that regression is due to a measurement error, new kinds of information are needed. For this purpose, preference tests may produce important information beyond the data gained by interview methods.

EMPIRICAL CROSS-VALIDATION STUDY

Such new information is available from our comprehensive research into the process, condition, and effect of university socialization. (For further details, see Sandberger & Jetten, 1982).[1] The general guiding question of our research is: What supraprofessional attitudes, concepts *(Vorstellungen)*, and competences do university students develop – students who are considered what C. Wright Mills (1956) has called society's future "functional élite"? Do they acquire only professional or, as they are sometimes called, "cognitive" skills, or is it the case, as universities have claimed since Wilhelm von Humboldt, that they also develop the sociomoral competences appropriate to the "functional responsibility" of university graduates in society? Do students develop higher judgment competence, rationality, and social responsibility? How does university education foster the development of these qualities in students? To find answers to these questions our research has included a number of interdisciplinary perspectives and methodological approaches. It has been organized as a longitudinal, multinational study in which five European countries (Austria, the Netherlands, Poland, Yugoslavia, West Germany) have taken part. Here I shall report only on German students in the first phase of study, in which regression supposedly takes place.

As part of this comprehensive research, our study was designed to recapitulate the phenomenon of moral regression. We hypothesized that, if cognitive-moral development is really progressing invariantly, the following three statements should be empirically supported:

1. There should be a progressive change regarding the cognitive structure of moral judgment behavior. In their fifth semester, university students should demonstrate a higher competence to judge social dilemmas in accordance with moral principles than they do in their first semester of study.

2. However, cases of pseudo-regression may occur. By pseudo-regression we mean that, when subjects are asked to directly compare the acceptability of different stage-typical arguments, their preference for instrumentalist, preconventional reasoning may increase, but not to a degree that would exceed the significance of postconventional arguments.

3. In addition, these cases should prove to be pseudo-regressions and not real regressions, in that they should be confined, as

Kohlberg and Kramer (1969) have noted, to those previously judged as having developed a high degree of moral competence.

Only if these three predictions are fulfilled, can we regard the hypothesis of invariant developmental sequence as empirically valid. Normally, in the absence of pathogenic environments, we could then safely expect that the development of moral judgment competence does not invert. Otherwise we would indeed have to consider Kohlberg's stages of development as merely "soft stages" (Kohlberg, 1984; Vine, 1984). The test of these hypotheses is based on longitudinal data of 844 German university students coming from various fields of study: medicine, German studies, economics, natural sciences, engineering, and social welfare work. Here the first two waves of the longitudinal study, in the first and third years, are considered.

The data on moral development are obtained by my *Moral Judgment Test*, or, to use its German title, the *Moralisches Urteil Test* (MUT; Lind, 1984; cf. Lind & Wakenhut, 1985). This test is based on the new psychometric concept of "Experimental Questionnaires" which was developed in our search for new ways to make a structural assessment. It is an attempt to combine the transparency of questionnaires with the hermeneutic possibilities of multivariate experimental design (Lind, 1982). This new methodology may, on the surface, resemble classical attitude measurement. However, it should be noted that the rationale behind it is completely different. As an instrument for psychological research, Experimental Questionnaires are expected to meet the requirement of theoretical validity but not the criteria of classical test construction, since, as we have noted above, the hidden assumptions of the latter partially contradict cognitive-structural theory. In classical test construction, structure and behavioral consistency are attributed solely to the measurement instrument. In the interactionist concept of the Experimental Questionnaire, these aspects are conceived of as an attribute of the *interaction* of the instrument (situation) with the responding person.

The MUT has been constructed to assess both affective and cognitive aspects of moral judgment behavior. Unlike the Kohlberg interview, it asks the individual to directly indicate his or her preferences for stage-typical moral reasons. Unlike Kohlberg's method, but also unlike existing preference tests, the MUT enables us to measure simultaneously the affective content and the cognitive structure of moral judgment – to measure them as distinct aspects, but not as ontologically separate entities (Lind, 1985d). In this way it seems possible to circumvent some of the conceptual dilemmas of the

Kohlberg interview, and to gain an unconfounded measure – though not a "pure" one – of the cognitive component of moral judgment behavior, unlike classical tests of moral judgment, in which the cognitive component is confounded with properties of the measurement instrument or with the affective aspect.

The standard MUT employs a 2 x 2 x 6 experimental design. The test contains two dilemmas, a euthanasia dilemma by Kohlberg and a workers' dilemma which is taken from a German story. Each dilemma is followed by the question of whether the subject would tend to agree or disagree with the protagonist's decision. The respondent is then asked to indicate how acceptable he or she finds six arguments for and against this decision.[2]

With the experimentally designed MUT, the index for the *cognitive-structural aspect* can be computed by intra-individual multivariate analyses of variance. For each individual pattern of judgment behavior, the coefficient of determination is computed to indicate the degree to which moral or other sorts of criteria play a role in the individual's judgment behavior. These criteria are represented by the design factors on which the construction of the standard MUT has been based: *Stage* (the stage of each item of reasoning to be rated), *Pro-Con* (the reasoning's agreement or disagreement with the respondent's opinion on the dilemma presented), and *Dilemma* (the kind of dilemma at hand).

The indices for the cognitive aspects of moral judgment are constructed to range from 0 to 100. A scale value of "zero" on the *Stage* factor means that the respondent's judgment behavior is not determined by moral concerns; a value of "one hundred" indicates that his or her judgment is completely determined by moral considerations. Since this structural measure is conceptually different from Kohlberg's, we refrain from assigning stage numbers. Nevertheless, for the data obtained using the MUT we claim that the scores are *theoretically valid*. Among other things, studies with the MUT have corroborated the developmental hypotheses concerning moral judgment, in particular the hypotheses of sequentiality and of age-relatedness (Lind, 1984, 1985b).

The *affective aspect* of moral judgment is defined, as are classical attitudes, as the direction and the strength of the respondent's affective commitment to stage-typical moral concerns. For each of the six Kohlbergian stages of moral judgment, we have assessed the degree to which the subject accepts or rejects stage-typical reasons for and against a particular solution of the behavioral dilemmas presented.

The findings from our study of university students from their first to their fifth semesters shed some light on the question of progression or regression in moral-cognitive development. In general, there is no regression but a slight progression with regard to the cognitive structure of student's moral judgment behavior. Over the two-year period of university study, we could not expect great progress, yet there is a small but noticeable development toward a higher competence in judging social dilemmas by moral principles. The number of students whose judgment behavior has shown a high degree of determination by moral concerns (scale values 50 to 100) increases from 19.4 to 22.1 percent. This is a significant increase when one considers the large developmental scope of the Kohlberg stages.

However, in a number of cases we find what we have called a "pseudo-regression." When asked to directly compare the acceptability of different stage-typical arguments, some students increase their preference for preconventional reasons, while they reduce their acceptance of postconventional arguments. These apparent regressions could be predicted almost completely on the basis of the subject's initial moral judgment competence. For the most part, the regressions were found among those who had possessed a high degree of moral sensitivity in the first year of study. This becomes visible when we divide the total sample into three groups with initially low (score: 0-9; sample size: 36), medium (10-49; 496), and high (50-100; 312) determinations of judgment by the moral stage and analyze the changes in the pattern of acceptability of the six stages shown by our subjects. Figure 1 depicts the *change scores (C)* which were calculated from the number of increases *(I)* and decreases *(D)* of acceptability by this formula:

$$C = (I - D) / (I + D).$$

A positive value indicates a surplus of increase in acceptability, a negative number a surplus of decrease. The data show that it is only in the "high" group that regressions occur. The medium group and, even more clearly, the "low" group exhibit a pattern of developmental change expected by the theory. Whereas their preference for low stage reasoning decreases, their acceptance of postconventional concerns increases during this two-year period.

Moreover, we must note that the downward changes in regard to the acceptability of moral reasoning – in the "high" group – are only relative to the respondents' previous preferences. In *absolute* terms, nearly all students at the second assessment show higher acceptability of low stage reasoning, and hence a less morally determined judgment structure. Many more prefer postconventional over preconventional reasons and reveal a judgment structure which is more morally

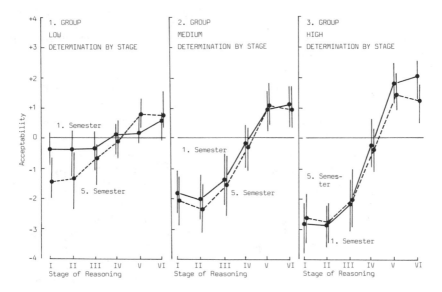

Figure 1. Pattern of *Relative* Change of Preferences of Moral Reasoning of Students with Initially Different Degrees of Moral determination by Moral Stages (*N* = 844, Change Scores).

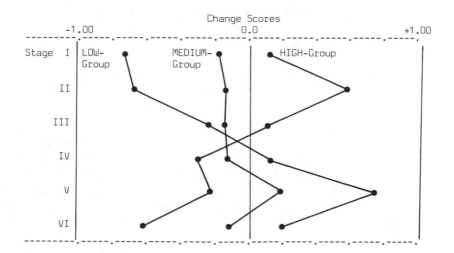

Figure 2. Pattern of *Absolute* Change of Preferences of Moral Reasoning of Students with Initially Different Degrees of Moral *Structuredness* (*N* = 844, Median and Quartiles).

structured than that of the other students who have made progress in the meantime. This finding is depicted in Figure 2, which presents the profiles of stage acceptability (median and upper and lower quartiles) for the students who initially exhibit a low, medium, and high determination of judgment by moral concerns at the time of their first and fifth semesters of study. Note that, since the changes are group specific, they cannot be discarded as an effect of statistical regression toward the mean.

To obtain information on the association – linear and non-linear – between the initial cognitive-moral structure and the change of pattern of stage acceptability during the period from the first to the fifth semesters, as well as on the statistical significance of this finding, we have submitted the data to a multivariate, polynomial analysis of variance (cf. Bock, 1975). (The calculation of statistical significance is reported here solely for conventional reasons, since it requires completely random sampling which, as in most other instances, is neither necessary nor feasible). In terms of multivariate, polynomial analysis, our major hypothesis states that (1) in general the slope of the line connecting the acceptability of each stage (see Figure 2) becomes systematically (i.e., linearly) steeper, and that (2) in the groups with initially low moral structuring of judgment, the change of steepness of the judgment profile – which indicates the degree of moral-cognitive development – differs in a predictable way from the change of the highly structured group. To make the results comparable to those of other studies, we have calculated coefficients of determination and, by taking the square roots, of correlation for all trends and effects.

Not surprisingly, the results are in line with the findings reported above. Only the linear and cubic effects of the semester x stage interaction effect on the acceptability of reasoning are significant and worth mentioning. The linear correlation between group-membership and change pattern is substantial ($r = 0.39$) and significant even if one sets the level at $p = 0.001$. An additional minor correlation can be found in the cubic polynomial ($r = 0.11$), which is also in line with the hypothesis and was to be expected because of the limited ranges of the response scales that cause ceiling effects at both ends of the scales.

CONCLUSION

In conclusion, I would like to discuss some possible implications of our findings. First, our findings clearly support the cognitive developmental hypothesis of invariant sequence. Like Kohlberg and Kramer's (1969) data and those of Rest (1979), our findings reveal that, in general, there is noticeable progress in cognitive-moral development at the beginning of one's higher education. In those cases in which the data seem to indicate regression, all our evidence suggests that this is not true regression. If there were genuine regression, we would expect it to occur with equal likelihood at all stages, and not to be confined to the initially highly competent subjects, a point already made by Kohlberg and Kramer (1969). Furthermore, in that case one would expect subjects to show regression in preferences for the stages of moral. judgment. However, neither of these possibilities was the case with our students. The strength of their preference for postconventional reasons remained greater than that of other groups, although they exhibited a relative devaluation of high stage reasoning and a slightly increased preference for Stage 2 reasons. Nevertheless, this fact may require further explanation. As Döbert and Nunner-Winkler (1975) have suggested, these students may be opposing moral oversophistication, or they may be using instrumentalist reasons to express cynicism. On the other hand, these students may have become more differentiated in their moral judgment, which appears as a lowering of their overall scores because of a lack of sensitivity of the method. The dilemmas presented and the reasoning required in most moral judgment studies constitute difficult tasks for adolescents but may not present such a challenge for highly educated young adults. Hence Kohlberg seems correct in attributing the regression phenomenon largely to methodological faults. Beyond a certain point, cognitive-moral development is easily misinterpreted when using insufficient methods of assessment. However, as our findings suggest, this seems a problem not so much of coding as of research design.

Second, our empirical research has again shown the usefulness of Kohlberg's stage scheme of moral judgment. The conceptual scheme of the six stages, as distinguished from their empirical verification, has been a valuable basis for recent research into moral judgment (cf. Broughton, 1978; Colby et al., 1983; Rest, 1979), as well as in the present study of the regression phenomenon. To clarify problems we had to find new ways – such as the use of experimental questionnaires – to design an instrument for the assessment of moral judgment competence. Yet there was no need to change the stage model. On the contrary, the conceptual framework provided by Kohlberg's stages was an important basis for our construction of the *Moralisches Urteil Test.*

Finally, our findings support the hypothesis that education and, in particular, higher education fosters the development of moral judgment competence (see also Rest, 1979; Colby et al., 1983; Lind, 1985c). The degree to which this is achieved may not seem sufficient in the face of society's present and future problems. The students themselves almost unanimously complained that, in their view, university courses deal too little with the political and ethical implications of their respective fields of study (Dippelhofer-Stiem, 1983, p. 108). But, as Kohlberg (1973) has said, the demands and opportunities that are provided by higher education may be indispensable conditions for the development of moral judgment competence, and, we would add, for the fostering of moral responsibility in society's future functional élite.[3]

NOTES

1. The research reported here is part of the Hochschulsozialisation research project, Sonderforschungsbereich 23, which is supported by the Deutsche Forschungsgemeinschaft and the University of Konstanz. The project is jointly conducted by Tino Bargel, Barbara Dippelhofer-Stiem, Gerhild Framhein, Georg Lind, Hansgert Peisert (project director), Johann-Ulrich Sandberger, and Hans Gerhard Walter.
2. The standard form of the test is reproduced in Lind and Wakenhut, 1985. Copies of the MUT as well as information on its analysis are available from the author.
3. I would like to thank John Broughton, Carol Harding, Gertrud Nunner-Winkler, and Thomas Wren, who have read and commented on earlier versions of this paper.

REFERENCES

Bock, R. (1975). *Multivariate statistical methods in behavioral research.* New York: McGraw-Hill.
Broughton, J. (1970). "College regression" in moral development. Unpublished manuscript, Columbia University Teachers College.
Broughton, J. (1978). Criticism of the developmental approach to morality. *SAS Catalog of Selected Documents in Psychology,* 8(4), 82, Ms. 176.

Colby, A., & Kohlberg, L. (In press). *The measurement of moral judgment.* 2 vols. New York: Cambridge University Press.

Colby, A., Kohlberg, L., Gibbs, J. C., & Lieberman, M. (1983). A longitudinal study of moral development. *Monographs of the Society for Research in Child Development,* 48(1-2, Serial No. 200), 1-96.

Dippelhofer-Stiem, B. (1983). *Hochschule als Umwelt.* Weinheim: Beltz.

Döbert, R., & Nunner-Winkler, G. (1975). *Adoleszenzkrise und Identitätsbildung.* Frankfurt: Suhrkamp.

Eckensberger, L. (1983). Research on moral development. *The German Journal of Psychology,* 7, 195-244.

Eckensberger, L., & Reinshagen, H. (1980). Kohlbergs Stufentheorie der Entwicklung des Moralischen Urteils: Ein Versuch der Reinterpretation im Bezugsrahmen handlungstheoretischer Konzepte. In L. Eckensberger & R. Silbereisen (Eds.), *Entwicklung sozialer Kognitionen.* Stuttgart: Klett.

Erikson, E. (1966). *Identität und Lebenszyklus.* Frankfurt: Suhrkamp.

Gibbs, J. (1977). Kohlberg's stages of moral judgment. A constructive critique. *Harvard Educational Review,* 47, 43-61.

Haan, N. (1978). The two moralities in action contexts: Relationships to thought, ego regulation and development. *Journal of Personality and Social Psychology,* 36, 286-305.

Holstein, C. (1976). Development of moral judgment: A longitudinal study of males and females. *Child Development,* 47, 51-61.

Kempf, W. (1978). Kritische Bemerkungen zu impliziten Voraussetzungen psychologischer Testtheorie und -praxis und ihrer Angemessenheit zur Erfüllung der Aufgaben curricularer Evaluation. Paper presented at the Symposium "Aspecten van Leerplanevaluatie," Velthoven, Oct. 3-4, 1978. University of Konstanz.

Kohlberg, L. (1973). Continuities in childhood and adult moral development revisited. In P. Baltes & W. Schaie (Eds.), *Life-span developmental psychology, research and theory.* New York: Academic Press.

Kohlberg, L. (1976). Moral stages and moralization. In T. Lickona (Ed.), *Moral development and behavior.* New York: Holt, Rinehart & Winston.

Kohlberg, L. (1979). *The meaning and measurement of moral development. Heinz Werner Memorial Lecture.* Worcester: Clark University Press.

Kohlberg, L. (1984). *Essays on moral development: Vol. 2. The psychology of moral development.* San Francisco: Harper & Row.

Kohlberg, L., & Kramer, R. (1969). Continuities and discontinuities in childhood and adult moral development. *Human Development,* 12, 93-120.

Lempert, W. (1982). Moralische Urteilsfähigkeit. *Zeitschrift für Sozialisationsforschung und Erziehungssoziologie,* 2, 113-126.

Lind, G. (1982). Experimental Questionnaires: A new approach to personality research. In A. Kossakowski & K. Obuchowski (Eds.), *Progress in the psychology of personality.* Amsterdam: North Holland.

Lind, G. (1984). Theorie und Validität des "Moralisches-Urteil-Tests." In G. Framhein & J. Langer (Eds.), *Student und Studium im internationalen Vergleich.* Klagenfurt: Kärntner Druck- und Verlagsgesellschaft.

Lind, G. (1985a). Attitude change or cognitive-moral development? How to conceive of socialization at the university. In G. Lind, H. A. Hartmann, & R. Wakenhut (Eds.), *Moral development and the social environment: Studies in the philosophy and psychology of moral judgment and education.* Chicago: Precedent.

Lind, G. (1985b). The theory of moral-cognitive judgment: A socio-psychological assessment. In G. Lind, H. A. Hartmann, & R. Wakenhut (Eds.), *Moral development and the social environment: Studies in the philosophy and psychology of moral judgment and education.* Chicago: Precedent.

Lind, G. (1985c). Moral competence and education in democratic society. In G. Zecha & P. Weingartner (Eds.), *Conscience: An interdisciplinary view.* Dordrecht: Reidel.

Lind, G. (1985d). Parallelität von Affekt und Kognition in der moralischen Entwicklung. In F. Oser, W. Althof, & D. Garz (Eds.), *Entstehung moralischer Identität, Soziogenese, moralisches Handeln und Schuld.* Munich: Peter Kindt.

Lind, G., & Wakenhut, R. (1985). Testing for moral judgment competence. In G. Lind, H. A. Hartmann, & R. Wakenhut (Eds.), *Moral development and the social environment: Studies in the philosophy and psychology of moral judgment and education.* Chicago: Precedent.

Mills, C. W. (1956). *White Collar.* New York: Oxford University Press.

Murphy, J. M., & Gilligan, C. (1980). Moral development in late adolescence and adulthood. A critique and reconstruction of Kohlberg's theory. *Human Development, 23,* 77-104.

Perry, W. (1970). *Forms of intellectual and ethical development in the college years.* New York: Holt.

Rest, J. (1979). *Development in judging moral issues.* Minneapolis: University of Minnesota Press.

Ringer, F. (1969). *The decline of the German mandarins: The German academic community, 1890-1933.* Cambridge, MA: Harvard University Press.

Roszak, T., ed. (1967). *The dissenting academy. Essays criticizing the teaching of the humanities in American universities.* Harmondsworth: Penguin.

Sandberger, J.-U., & Jetten, E. (1982). Between uncertainty and commitment: A comparison of first semester university students' occupational perspectives and values in five European Countries (FORM-Project). In M. Niessen & J. Peschar (Eds.), *Comparative research on education.* Oxford: Pergamon Press.

Vine, I. (1984). Moral maturity in socio-cultural perspective: Are Kohlberg's stages universal? In S. Modgil & C. Modgil (Eds.), *Lawrence Kohlberg: Consensus and controversy.* Brighton: Falmer Press.

The Moral Adequacy of Kohlberg's Moral Development Theory

Larry May

From the earliest disputes in ethical theory, we learn that there has always been at least as much controversy about what criteria and evidence would be employed to demonstrate which theory was better as about the substantive views supported by these theories. In the *Nicomachean Ethics*, Aristotle tried to show that the good of Plato's ethical theory was misconceived because it stressed what was ideal and hence beyond the ken of ordinary humans. Doctors do not study health by investigating what is eternally healthy, said Aristotle, but rather they investigate particular humans who are healthy. This is the way health and virtue are learned, and this is also the way a proper investigation into the nature of health and virtue should proceed. Thus, in the very first such theoretical dispute, there was intertwined a dispute about method of inquiry. The best moral theory, for Aristotle, not only provided the best solution to the moral problems of human beings, but was also the theory which most conformed with the evidence given by the actual decisions of most humans.

In this paper I will examine a claim to moral superiority or adequacy of a certain type of moral reasoning which has been put forth by the psychologist Lawrence Kohlberg. Since his argument, like Aristotle's, has intertwined considerations of method with substantive considerations, I will conduct my investigation on several different levels of analysis. This seems especially appropriate in view of Kohlberg's claim that his theory can be supported by psychological (empirical) evidence as well as by arguments from metaethics and normative ethics.

The term "moral adequacy" is employed by Kohlberg to indicate that a type of decision-making is able to solve or resolve the moral problems encountered by a given person. From the beginning Kohlberg assumes that a type or stage of moral reasoning will be more adequate if it can provide a means for resolving most, if not all, of the dilemmas encountered by individuals who are subjected to conflicting opinions about what is right or what is just. "Moral adequacy" is the preferred term employed by Kohlberg in his many arguments, although he occasionally admits that what he means is that a given type or stage of moral reasoning is "better" than, or "superior" to, other types or stages. Contemporary philosophers who call themselves empiricists, when faced with conflicting opinions in ethics, tend to become either relativists or social contractarians, subjecting these conflicting opinions to the deliberations of an ideal observer. Rawls (1971), with whom Kohlberg allies himself, introduced his procedure of reflective equilibrium because he found a plurality of principles which potentially conflict with one another, and because he wished to avoid relativism. Rawls assumed that there must be some natural way to assign relative weights to each principle, in order to show what would be naturally preferable to a rational person (1971, pp. 47-48). Rawls discussed which views or principles would be chosen under conditions of optimal rationality, and it seems clear that Kohlberg is interested in the same question in his discussion of moral adequacy.

I will begin this paper with a brief summary of some of the main tenets of Kohlberg's theory of moral development. I will then proceed to examine Kohlberg's psychological and methodological claims concerning the moral adequacy of his Stage 5 (and Stage 6)[1] of moral reasoning, showing that these claims do not support his conclusion. The paper ends with an investigation of the metaethical and normative claims advanced to support this same conclusion, showing that here also Kohlberg's claim to the moral adequacy of higher stage reasoning is not well supported.

KOHLBERG'S THEORY OF MORAL DEVELOPMENT

Since the 1950s, Lawrence Kohlberg has been collecting data on the moral judgments that people make when faced with dilemmas.[2] His original research project tested young adults who were asked to respond to various hypothetical cases, such as the Heinz dilemma. Over the last twenty-five years, Kohlberg has presented this dilemma, or variations on it, to thousands of people. Recently he has tried to present people with real-life dilemmas as well. Some of his studies have been cross-cultural (e.g., Turiel et al., 1978), and some have been longitudinal, tracing the responses to this dilemma given by the same people from childhood to adulthood (e.g., Colby et al., 1983).

The results of Kohlberg's studies have led him to draw the conclusion that there are distinct stages in the development of moral reasoning, and that these stages are universally present. The main evidence for the existence of the stages comes from the longitudinal data, and the main evidence for the claim of universality comes from the cross-cultural data. What he found was that the stages of moral development paralleled Piaget's stages of cognitive development. Kohlberg summarizes the results of these studies in the following way:

1. *Invariant Sequence:* "Under normal experiential conditions, moral reasoning state remains the same or moves up but does not move to lower stages . . . In only 2 percent of the interviews was there a change downward from time one to time two, and this change downward was small (less than one-half stage)."

2. *Hierarchy:* "As a higher stage comes into use, lower stages of thought are replaced as ways of resolving moral dilemmas."

3. *Structured Wholes:* "Individuals are consistent in their stage of moral reasoning regardless of the kind of moral dilemma presented to them, regardless of the moral issue on which a subject must take a stand." (1982, pp. 516-517)

The cross-cultural data have made these longitudinal studies of American male responses to moral dilemmas appear to represent a universal pattern of development. Kohlberg claims:

> It is this emphasis on the distinctive form (as opposed to the content) of the child's moral thought which allows us to call moral development universal. In all cultures, we find the same aspects or categories of moral judgment and valuing . . . (1971, p. 166)

Kohlberg has not been satisfied merely to describe types of experience, but has sought to move from these data to normative conclusions about the moral adequacy of the stages of moral reasoning. Kohlberg has argued that each higher stage represents a more adequate form of moral reasoning than does each lower stage. He has admitted that he has to provide more than just psychological data to move from descriptive to normative claims based on this evidence.

> Psychological findings and theoretical explanations of stage movement do not, of course, constitute direct proofs of greater moral adequacy of higher stages of moral reasoning, which must be justified in the language of moral philosophy and not just the language of psychology if we are to avoid the naturalistic fallacy. (Kohlberg, 1982, p. 523)

Philosophically, Kohlberg argues that there is an isomorphism between these psychological conditions of adequacy and the objective adequacy claimed for certain types of moral judgment by "the formalist tradition in ethics from Kant to Rawls" (Kohlberg, 1973, p. 633). Thus, Kohlberg claims that his psychological evidence of what is preferred by normal, rational adults is supported by, and lends support to, the "philosophical claim that a later stage is 'objectively' preferable or more adequate by certain moral criteria. This philosophic claim, however, would for us be thrown into question if the facts of moral stage advance were inconsistent with its psychological implications" (p. 633).

Of particular interest to the topic of this paper are Kohlberg's arguments against moral relativism and conventionalism. He has argued that the data support his view that the ordering or hierarchy of moral values is not relative, but that these values are primarily "reflections of developmental stages in moral thought."[3] In any event, there is less cross-cultural variation even in the substance of moral belief than is usually maintained, for "(a) almost all individuals in all cultures use the same thirty basic moral categories, concepts, or principles and (b) all individuals in all cultures go through the same order or sequence of gross stages of development, though varying in rate and terminal point of development." Whatever differences there are in moral valuing can be accounted for as "differences in stages of moral developmental status" (Kohlberg, 1981, p. 126).

In summary, Kohlberg believes that there are universal stages of moral development and that these stages constitute both a hierarchy of cognitive development and a corresponding hierarchy of objective moral adequacy. Examples of differences in moral belief or valuing can be understood merely as differences in stages of moral development of individuals. In particular, when faced with the opinions and experiences of cultural relativists or egoists, Kohlberg points to two "facts": these opinions have been rejected by most philosophers since Socrates, and these opinions are eventually rejected by the very people who hold them through the normal process of moral maturation. Consequently, it seems to be Kohlberg's view that all of the evidence, even that of the philosophers who reject Kohlberg's own theory, ultimately confirms the existence of universal moral principles which are reflected in his stages of moral development.

PSYCHOLOGICAL DATA AND MORAL
ADEQUACY

In this section I will analyze and criticize Kohlberg's claim that the psychological data support the contention that Stage 5 (and Stage 6) are more adequate than the lower stages. As I will reconstruct it, Kohlberg's argument has three premises:

1. Examination of all of the evidence reveals the fact that there are universal features of all moral reasoning.

2. Underlying this universal character is a deep structure which provides the basis for identifying distinct stages of moral development.

3. An examination of these stages reveals criteria of adequacy which support the conclusion that Stage 5 (and Stage 6) is (are) more adequate than the lower stages.

I will examine each of these premises and attempt to show that Kohlberg's claim that his higher stages are more adequate than the lower stages is not supported by this argument, which is based on the psychological data he has amassed.

Let me first turn to the point I began examining earlier, the claim made by Kohlberg that all the evidence supports the view that there are universal principles of morality. Part of the argument advanced in support of this view is that even those philosophers who have doubted that there is any universal structure to morality can be counted as testifying in support of Kohlberg's claim. Even the skeptics or relativists who stand opposed to the moral values of, say, justice and equity, reveal an acceptance of the existence of such universal features of morality by their very discourse.

Kohlberg cites many examples of supposed relativists who betray their own belief in universal features of morality. In response to the Heinz dilemma, for example, one psychology graduate student replied: "I think he should steal the drug, because if there is any such thing as a universal human value, it is the value of life, and that would justify stealing it." Kohlberg then asked her, "Is there any such thing as a universal value?" and she answered "No, all values are relative to our culture." Kohlberg's analysis of her reasoning is quite revealing:

> This response illustrates a typical confusion of the relativist. She starts out by claiming that one ought to act in terms of the universal value of human life, that it is logical and desirable for all men to respect all human life; but she fails to see that this does not conflict with the *fact* that all men do not always act in terms of this value, and so ends up by

denying the possibility of making a value judgment going beyond herself. (Kohlberg, 1981, p. 107)

According to Kohlberg, this woman confuses cultural relativism, the view that there are different beliefs held in different cultures, with ethical relativism, the view that we cannot adjudicate among these conflicting cultural beliefs.

While it may be true that this particular woman does not clearly distinguish between cultural and moral relativism, it is not clear that this is a good reason for Kohlberg to discount her testimony. Her denial that it is possible to make universally applicable moral judgments is indeed a claim to ethical relativism, and it is not necessarily mistaken, since it appears that she would hold this view quite independently of the truth of cultural relativism. As such it seems to be the kind of counter-evidence which Kohlberg should take seriously if he really believes that all of the relativists are simply mistaken in not accepting the universal character of morality.

There are two ways in which Kohlberg tries to show that all but an insignificant amount of the evidence supports his view. As I have just mentioned, he tries to show that some people are simply mistaken or in error about their intuitions, which rules out their evidence. This attempt is suspicious in my view, and seems to turn on metaethical assumptions which preceded his research (see Kohlberg, 1983, section 10). But there is also another way that Kohlberg has tried to dismiss some of the evidence which seems to disconfirm his theory. In the next few pages I will address Kohlberg's strategy of attempting to show that some intuitive evidence is not legitimate because it is not the product of reflective or cognitive judgment on the part of the people who claim to hold these intuitions. This strategy, as I shall show, turns on Kohlberg's assumption that moral judgments must be reflectively arrived at in order to be morally adequate.

In an important footnote to his essay "Justice as Reversibility: The Claim to Moral Adequacy of the Highest Stage of Moral Judgment" (1981), Kohlberg notes that the facts in a moral theory have a different status than do the facts in a strictly experiential scientific theory. He states: "We can attain consistency by revising the 'facts' (our intuitions about what is right in a concrete moral case) when they conflict with the principle of our moral theory . . . " (p. 195). Kohlberg's followers admit that they have been engaging in just this revision of the facts, and demanding it of others in order for their opinions to be counted. Indeed, Kohlberg's critics have been quick to point out that a lot of evidence which might be seen as disconfirming Kohlberg's theory can be reinterpreted to conform to the principles of the theory.

To understand better the change that occurs in the facts of moral experience due to confrontation with a principle of a theory, let me just mention the procedure of reflective equilibrium that Kohlberg, following Rawls, supports. This procedure requires that there be a constant interchange between intuitions and principles. For example, the type of intuitions considered would be the belief that there is a "primacy of the woman's right to life over the druggist's right to property" (Kohlberg, 1981, p. 200). These intuitive facts can be changed, and indeed must at least be subjected to the possibility of change, by reflecting on the principles of justice such as we know them to be. For Kohlberg, the main way in which intuitive adjustments are made is in light of higher stage analyses, in light of the insights which come from taking into account such higher stage principles as "reversibility" itself (what Kohlberg often refers to as "moral musical chairs"). When confronted with principles from a higher stage, individuals will come to make adjustments and changes in their intuitions, and these changed intuitions seem to have a greater factual legitimacy. In his most recent essay, Kohlberg claims that his researchers have been asking questions designed to probe and to focus specifically on "deontic question(s)" concerning the right, as well as the rights and duties, of the people interviewed (Kohlberg, 1983, pp. 92-93).

Thus, it appears that the facts which Kohlberg is interested in are the considered opinions of individual persons who have subjected their own ideas to something like a process of reflective equilibrium. Yet it has not been established that such opinions should be given a higher standing than those which are formed more directly and intuitively. More important, though, Kohlberg needs to establish that only the intuitions which have been subjected to reflective equilibrium are legitimate facts of moral experience. Until he does this, he has not borne out his claim that all evidence confirms his theory. Even if he reduces this claim to the weaker version that all data which are worth counting confirm his theory, he still needs more argumentation, especially to indicate how we are to know which evidence is legitimate and which not.

Kohlberg claims that his analysis of a great deal of evidence reveals a deep structure of moral reasoning. As I said at the outset, this structure is revealed through the fact that all peoples of all cultures develop through an invariant sequence of stages of moral reasoning. This stage sequence is a hierarchy, since lower stages of thought are replaced by higher ones. By analyzing these stages, Kohlberg claims to be able to demonstrate that there are universal categories or aspects of moral judgment. Such analysis is then drawn on to show that such thinkers as the female graduate student mentioned above are incorrectly understanding their own moral intuitions, and would come to see this if they were exposed to higher stage principles.

Kohlberg's claim that all evidence reveals universal features of moral reasoning rests rather precariously on another claim: that all moral judgments must display certain features, and this in turn is supported by the claim that he has uncovered the deep structure of the universal stages of moral development. But such an empirical claim would seem to depend on an analysis of all stages of moral reasoning, so that one could be certain to have discovered what underlies the stages, and hence to be able to support the claim to universality of a given aspect or category of moral reasoning. Yet Kohlberg is quite reluctant to admit that he has discovered all stages of moral reasoning.

Two recent admissions on his part clearly illustrate his reluctance to claim that he can demonstrate anything like closure on the stages of moral development. First, Kohlberg has written that it is at least possible that there is a seventh stage of development (sometimes called "agape"), which goes beyond the sixth stage of contractarian justice deliberations to Christian charity and altruism (perhaps even to supererogation, Kohlberg, 1981, ch. 9). Secondly, he has very recently claimed that his sixth stage may not be significantly distinguishable from Stage 5 within the normal population. With the exception of such figures as Socrates, Jesus, and Gandhi, there is substantial controversy over whether there are any pure Stage 6 individuals (Kohlberg, 1982, p. 523).

This brings me to my criticism of Kohlberg's second premise. Quite a bit of Kohlberg's theory turns on the interpretation of the facts of moral experience. Kohlberg has drawn from such facts the structure of his hierarchy of stages of moral judgment. But if the evidence from these experiences is not closed to the possibility of other stages, then there remains the possibility that the invariant deep structure of moral reasoning has not in fact been uncovered. It may turn out that the other stages display a quite different structure of reasoning than do the lower stages. What appears to be the deep structure given a six-stage categorization of the evidence of moral experience may change radically if there are seventh and even higher stages of moral reasoning yet to be discovered (or yet to be properly scaled by Kohlberg's researchers). Even if all the evidence at the moment points toward confirmation of Kohlberg's generalizations, this evidence remains insufficient to establish his universalist thesis.

The problem of the lack of closure on the highest stage then becomes most acute. Without such a closure, there is no good reason to think that the Kohlbergian normative criteria of universality, reversibility, etc., will not themselves be subject to change in light of even higher stage reasoning than Kohlberg has so far discovered. Hence, there is no reason to regard these criteria as any more fixed and settled than other principles or intuitions.

To make this claim more plausible, consider the possibility of a sixth or seventh stage of purely instrumental, but enlightened self-interested reasoning (see May, 1983). Kohlberg and others have indeed collected a fair amount of evidence of the existence of this type of reasoning, but they have ruled it out as not being a legitimate stage of "moral" reasoning. All five stages identified by Kohlberg already contain some of the features of this stage. Stage 2 is the closest to this stage, but it is clearly not enlightened. Stages 3 and 4 put a premium on obedience to conventional norms, but only so that the individual may gain the approval and support of those who are the guardians of these conventions. The postconventional stages seem to provide the most disharmony with the proposed stage, but even at Stage 5 such concerns as what one is obligated to do are explained in terms of "what one has contracted to fulfill in order to have one's own rights respected and protected" (Kohlberg, 1973, p. 637).

The way in which Stage 5 responses are characterized leaves open the possibility that the highest stage of moral reasoning employs prudential rather than universal principles. While it is true that these Stage 5 thinkers value the principle of reciprocity in their reasoning, it appears that they value this principle out of a concern for a higher principle, namely out of a concern that their own rights will be "respected and protected." Thus, reciprocity appears to be a principle which grows out of enlightened self-interest, rather than a principle which is adopted out of universal concern for all human beings. In fact, the Stage 5 responses which Kohlberg has documented could be understood as reflecting a movement toward, rather than away from, a highest stage of truly enlightened self-interest. A person would come to see, in this highest stage, that his or her own interests could best be protected in a system of maximal protection of rights for all. But the motivation to adopt such a system of rules would not be a concern for universal brotherhood (or sisterhood), but a concern for the self.

Some of the principles embodied in my proposed Stage 6 would resemble the principles of Kohlberg's proposed Stage 6, but in my conception the concern for self on the part of the person engaged in the moral thinking does not diminish in favor of a diffused concern for humanity in general. Most importantly, my proposed Stage 6 thinker would continue to engage in partisan rather than impartial reasoning – putting self and immediate family ahead of unspecified others. Since Kohlberg is so ready to follow the work of leading philosophers in ascertaining the highest stage of moral reasoning, perhaps he should be reminded that a number of past and current moral theorists regard partiality as an indispensable component in correct moral thinking. Philippa Foot[4] recently argued for just this conclusion, as did W. D. Ross (1930) much earlier in his quite influential work *The Right and the Good*. A concern for the self is not incompatible with other standardly recognized principles of morality.

In light of this discussion, let me briefly address the third premise in my reconstruction of Kohlberg's argument, that is, the premise that an examination of the stages reveals that the higher ones are more adequate than the lower stages. Stage 2 is characterized by Kohlberg as employing a concept of obligation "in which 'should' is a hypothetical imperative contingent on choice in terms of an end. In this sense, obligations are limited to oneself and one's ends." This is contrasted with Stage 5 where "obligations are what one has contracted to fulfill in order to have one's own rights respected and protected. These obligations are defined in terms of a rational concern for the welfare of others" (1981, pp. 215-216). Stage 5 is considered more differentiated and hence more adequate psychologically than Stage 2, Kohlberg claims, because in this higher stage a concern for others is distinguished from concern for the self. But it does not seem obvious that the Stage 2 thinker has failed to distinguish his or her own welfare from the welfare of others. Indeed, lack of concern for others is not the same as failure to distinguish others from oneself. Instead, it may be that the only salient difference between the individuals who hold to these conceptions of obligation is that the Stage 5 thinker recognizes that serving one's own interests requires that one show respect for others, as Kohlberg himself seems to indicate, so that "one's own rights are respected and protected," whereas the Stage 2 thinker does not. It seems quite reasonable to ask which one of these thinkers is at the top and which is at the bottom of the hierarchy?

In other words, why think that the more prudent or selfish the reasoning, the lower it lies on the scale of moral differentiation? Both the above thinkers put weight on their own interests. One is led to look only to his or her short-term self-interest, the other is led to look also to the interests of others, but both seem to be motivated by the same disposition: a regard for the self. Perhaps it is also less integrated to fail to take into account the others in one's life who may be affected by one's actions, but unless integration is itself a normative category (a possibility I take up in the next section), it is hard to see how the Stage 2 thinker's reasoning is less morally adequate than that of the Stage 5 thinker.

Before turning to the philosophical and normative claims made by Kohlberg in support of his theory, let me summarize the main points of criticism I have suggested. First, Kohlberg is not entitled to say that an examination of all evidence confirms his theory. At best, he is entitled to say that his theory is confirmed by most of the "legitimate" evidence, that is, by the evidence which does not contain mistakes or misconceptions, and discounting the judgments which have not been reflected upon. But even this weaker claim depends on the second premise, namely, that Kohlberg has successfully iden-tified five (or six) stages of moral development, each of which contains increasingly adequate development of various categories of moral judgment. Without this second premise, the first premise cannot be substantiated, because there is no basis for showing that the intuitions not subjected to reflective equilibrium are illegitimate. Yet the second premise itself rests on the problematic assumption that Kohlberg has identified all the stages of moral reasoning, and that he has culled from an analysis of these stages the universally present features of moral reasoning (and ruled out other features as not properly germane to moral reasoning). This assumption is at least potentially suspect, for there are other possible competing highest stages which would lend credence to the view that a concern for the self is *the* main feature of moral reasoning and the feature in virtue of which all forms of moral reasoning should be judged. This leads to the final criticism: Kohlberg has not provided sufficient psychological arguments to warrant the claim that the higher stages of moral development which he has identified are indeed better or more adequate than the lower stages, for the criteria needed to make this claim have not been shown, from an analysis of the evidence, to be clearly identifiable.

NORMATIVE ADEQUACY

Kohlberg claims, following Piaget, that higher stage reasoning is more adequate not only in the sense that it employs a more differentiated and integrated form of reasoning, but also, following Rawls, in the sense that it is truly morally superior to all other forms of reasoning. I will refer to this as normative adequacy. Specifically, Kohlberg claims that the higher stages display greater universality and reversibility (the normative features which correspond to the psychological features of differentiation and integration) than do the lower stages. As I will reconstruct it, Kohlberg's normative argument has the following premises:

1. People should choose principles of moral reasoning upon which all other persons would agree.

2. The only principle upon which all could agree, from one another's perspective, is the principle of "reversibility."

3. The highest stage of moral reasoning displays reversibility to the greatest extent and thus should be preferred as most adequate.

As in the previous section, I will examine each of these premises and attempt to show that Kohlberg's claim that his higher stages are more adequate than his lower stages is not supported by this normative argument.

Kohlberg's claim that the higher stages are normatively more adequate than the lower stages rests squarely on his claim that moral principles should be such that all people would agree upon them. Moral principles themselves are defined as "a general guide to choice rather than a rule of action" (Kohlberg, 1981, p. 174). Kohlberg believes that there has been relative agreement among philosophers over the years that formal principles of morality will include universalizability. Morality is formalistically defined to include universal principles. Against the claims of those who argue to the contrary, Kohlberg says, "To my knowledge, those who object to a formalist definition of morality have no positive alternative to offer except: (1) morality is in accord with my own system, or (2) morality is relative . . . Anyone who tries to criticize a formalist definition of morality must provide a stronger positive alternative" (1981, p. 173). Kohlberg explicitly argues that relativism in any of its forms is "in error" (p. 105), because it incorrectly identifies differences in moral principle as unalterable conflicts of moral value, rather than simply as different stage responses to the same dilemmas.

In most of his more recent writings, Kohlberg relies on this formalist tradition, from Kant to Rawls, to provide the normative basis of the otherwise empirical claim that higher moral stages display universalizability. It is not merely a matter of evidence or definition, but also of normative truth, that moral judgments should display universalizability. When all three of these factors (psychological, logical and normative) combine for the same conclusion, they constitute quite a powerful basis about which it is difficult to be skeptical.

But what is the positive argument advanced in support of this claim? The implicit argument seems to be that consensus and unanimity are the best test we have of the preferability and acceptability of a given normative principle. But like Rawls, Kohlberg is not interested in actual unanimous agreement, but only in the kind of agreement which could be reached among rational persons. And, as I suggested above, the reason for thinking that universalizability is most preferable stems ultimately from Kohlberg's view of the nature of morality. He claims:

1. that there are formal criteria which make judgments moral,

2. that these are fully met only by the most mature stage of moral judgment, so that,

3. our mature stages of judgment are more moral (in the formalist sense, more morally adequate) than less mature stages. Moral judgments, unlike judgments of prudence or esthetics, tend to be universal ... (1981, p. 170)

Rational people should come to recognize that the most adequate moral principle is the one which best meets the actual criteria of proper moral judgments, and universalizability is one of the most basic criteria of proper moral judgments.

Here it is most apparent that Kohlberg draws on his empirical work to provide support for his normative stance on the status of normatively proper moral judgment. In his essay "From Is to Ought," he claims that he is trying to develop a moral theory that is similar to certain economic theories "in which the theories of how people ought to make economic decisions and the way they do make economic decisions are very closely linked" (1981, p. 180). And the support for such a mixture of is and ought is found only in "the fruitfulness of the results" (1981, p. 180).

What this otherwise plausible approach to the study of morality lacks, however, is any fully defended criterion of "fruitfulness." One of the implicit tests for the failure of fruitfulness is that a given principle of morality cannot "handle or resolve certain problems that it acknowledges to be problems that it ought to handle, whereas another type of morality can do so." I will discuss this strategy of argument at length below, but for now it is necessary to point out that Kohlberg's early normative defense of the higher stages was based on the assumption that there was a sixth stage of moral reasoning corresponding to Rawls's view of justice as fairness. Even in his relatively recent (1978) essay, "Justice as Reversibility: The Claim to Moral Adequacy of the Highest Stage of Moral Judgment," Kohlberg depends to such an extent on the existence of this sixth stage that his normative argument does not succeed without it. The following quotation clearly illustrates this point and also shows that Kohlberg's recent uncertainty about the sixth stage casts serious doubt on this normative argument.

> First, all Stage 6 thinkers agree; all Stage 5's do not. If the purpose of moral judgment structures is to yield choices on which all reasonable people could agree, then they should use Stage 6 rather than Stage 5 structures. Second, and related, all Stage 6's can agree because their judgments are fully reversible: they have taken everyone's viewpoint in choosing insofar as it is possible to take everyone's viewpoint where viewpoints conflict. Again, if principles of moral judgment are to be chosen, they should be principles upon which all rational people could agree. (1981, p. 214)

In this statement Kohlberg shows the inadequacy of Stage 5, and yet it now turns out that Stage 5 is the highest demonstrable stage of moral reasoning. It is not clear that Kohlberg can now advance the same kind of argument in support of Stage 5 over Stage 4.

As the above quotation illustrates, Kohlberg holds that reversibility is the key to guaranteeing that moral principles are such that all rational people could agree with them, that is, that they be universalizable. Reversibility itself is defined as the following principle: "that we must be willing to live with our judgment or decision when we trade places with others in the situation being judged" (1981, p. 194). Initially, though, his argument appears to be circular. Kohlberg sometimes states it merely as part of the definition of morality: "Moral judgments involve role-taking, taking the viewpoint of others conceived as *subjects* and coordinating those viewpoints . . . " Secondly, Kohlberg claims that moral principles seek to resolve conflicts and hence to become more equilibrated, and the way that this is carried out is by morality becoming, again as a matter of definition, an enterprise which seeks agreement rather than conflict (1981, p. 197).

To assume that morality must involve role-taking and to assume that morality must also seek to resolve conflicts through assuming the roles of others, is to beg the question about which of the stages is normatively most adequate. For the very question at issue is whether stages that have greater role-taking and greater conflict resolution are indeed more adequate than stages that have less of these two features, or none at all. Indeed, if the lower stages are stages of moral reasoning, and if morality is defined as involving these two features, then these lower stages must also have role-taking and conflict resolution. But Kohlberg is not often clear on this issue, leading one to draw the conclusion on first viewing that the definition of morality proposed by Kohlberg begs the very question of whether higher stages are more normatively adequate than lower stages.

On closer examination it may be that, strictly speaking, Kohlberg does not beg the question at this juncture, for there does appear to be some role-taking and some "moral musical chairs" taking place in the lower stages: even in Stage 1 there is a deference to authority which clearly indicates that one understands one's role and can at least imagine what the role of the person in authority is. In order to better understand Kohlberg's normative thesis for the greater adequacy of the higher stages of moral reasoning, I turn now to a careful examination of the most developed version of this argument, that presented in *The Journal of Philosophy* in 1973.

In that essay, entitled "The Claim to Moral Adequacy of A Highest Stage of Moral Judgment," Kohlberg indicates that what is constant throughout all stages of moral reasoning is some kind of reciprocity, which by Stage 3 has become what he calls reversibility. In the Stage 1 thinker we find the reciprocity of "an eye for an eye"; but by Stage 3 we find the initial formulation of the Golden Rule: "putting yourself in the other guy's shoes regardless of exchange of interests or values" (1973, p. 642). But, Kohlberg holds, this Stage 3 thinking can also be shown not to be as fully mature and adequate as that at Stage 5 (or, even better, at Stage 6).

At Stage 3 the interpretation of the Golden Rule does not necessarily lead to fair decisions, Kohlberg tells us, and because of this lack of full reversibility, this interpretation of the Golden Rule is not as adequate as that which occurs at Stage 6 involving "ideal role-taking" (p. 643). The problem is that Stage 3 thinkers want to be able to resolve the Heinz dilemma, but their interpretation of the Golden Rule leads them to the impasse where "the husband reaches one solution if he puts himself in his wife's shoes, another in the druggist's" (p. 643). In contrast, by Stage 6 (and perhaps by Stage 5) the Golden Rule leads only to an imaginative attempt to put oneself in the other's shoes.

> In the Heinz dilemma, Heinz must imagine whether the druggist could put himself in the wife's position and still maintain his claim and whether the wife could put herself in the druggist's position and still maintain her claim. Intuitively, we feel that the wife could, the druggist could not. As a result it is fair for the husband to act on the basis of the wife's claim. (p. 643)

Stage 6 thinking is more adequate then Stage 3 because it is possible to resolve the dispute, a dispute that thinkers from both stages believe must be resolved, only by the use of Stage 6 thinking.

Kohlberg's view, like Rawls's, places a normative premium on maximal conflict resolution. I wish to indicate some problems with this assumption. First, this view ignores the possibility that there may indeed be moral dilemmas which cannot, or at least should not, be resolved in the way that Kohlberg and Rawls suggest. Moral dilemmas may often be true dilemmas. Consider the abortion dilemma. It may indeed be the case that there are truly irreconcilable claims that are made by the disputants: those taking the side of the woman's right to choose what to do with her life, and those taking the side of the fetus's right to life. If this is a true dilemma, then regardless of how much one may want to resolve the dispute in favor of one disputant or the other, to try to do so would be to attempt to resolve what cannot be resolved. The ensuing "solution" would not have any claim to adequacy over the failure to reach resolution which might occur in Stage 3 thinking about the problem. What this shows is that the "progress" toward resolving more and more dilemmas may be a sign of naive or unclear understanding rather than a sign of increased adequacy of moral judgment.

Perhaps more importantly, even if there could be a resolution of the abortion dilemma, it could be argued that this resolution should not be adopted. The Supreme Court of the United States reached a similar conclusion when considering *Roe v. Wade* in 1973. One could resolve the dispute in favor of the woman's right, but this would be dangerous since it would diminish the prescription against killing; or one could resolve the dispute in favor of the fetus, but this "resolution" would also be dangerous since it would diminish the prescription against the invasion of personal liberty. Instead of a resolution of the problem, what was called for was an acknowledgment that there should be no resolution. In general, the claim that all moral dilemmas can and should be resolved rests on an assumption about the nature of moral dilemmas which calls for a great deal of argumentation, much more, I propose, than Kohlberg has provided.

To support his view that moral judgments should be fully reversible in order to be fully adequate, Kohlberg draws an analogy between mathematical and moral reasoning:

> According to Piaget and others, the keystone of logic is reversibility. A logical train of thought is one which can move back and forth between premises and conclusions without distortion. Mathematical thinking is an example; A + B is the same as B + A. Or again, the operation A + B = C is reversible by the operation C − B = A. In one sense, the elements of reversible moral thought are the moral categories as these apply to the universe of moral actors. To say that rights and duties are correlative is to say that one can move from rights to duties and back without change or distortion. (1973, p. 641)

From this analogy Kohlberg tries to draw a conclusion about the need for full reversibility in moral reasoning. "If we have a reversible solution, we have one that could be reached as right starting from the perspective of anyone in the situation, given each person's intent to put himself in the shoes of the other" (p. 641). In what follows I wish to raise the following challenges to this claim:

1. Are moral reasoning and mathematical reasoning sufficiently analogous to warrant Kohlberg's appeal to mathematical reasoning in order to support claims about moral reasoning?

2. Does the analogy, if legitimate, suggest that moral decisions must be fully reversible to be fully adequate?

3. Does the analogy, if legitimate, suggest that it is the "intent" to take on other's roles that is important to the decision?

Norms in ethics are decidedly not much like norms or rules in fields such as mathematics. Kohlberg admits this. But perhaps the application of norms in both domains does follow the same structure. If so, must it be the case that from each person's perspective the same solution to a moral or mathematical problem can be reached? In one sense, it is true that mathematical solutions must be such that they are in principle true from all perspectives, for if mathematics depended for its truth on relative differences among people then mathematics would not have the status it is generally accorded. But in one important respect this is not true of mathematics, that is, it is not required that everyone actually be able to solve the problem from one's own perspective, especially if one lacks the requisite mathematical ability. Some of the natural perspectives of mathematical reasoners must be irrelevant to the legitimacy of the solution or else no complex mathematical solution could ever achieve legitimacy. Yet Kohlberg seems to suggest that this is not true for moral reasoning. If all perspectives must be considered in moral reasoning, then it is disanalogous to mathematical reasoning.

Secondly, does the analogy suggest that there must be one and the same solution reached from all perspectives, and hence does the analogy suggest that morally adequate judgments must be fully reversible? There is nothing that I can see in the analogy of mathematics that suggests that there might not be radically different perspectives which would solve problems in very different ways. Just as there are myriad logics, so also are there myriad types and number bases in mathematics, and there is no necessity that they should conform to one another. Logic and mathematics both demand only that there be consistency within a given system of ideas, not between one system and the next. Similarly, while the analogy does suggest that people reasoning from the same premises must reach the same moral conclusions, it does not suggest that each person, regardless of starting point or assumptions, should come to the same solution.

What is really at stake in this claim by Kohlberg is revealed in my third question. The issue is whether, in order to reason in a fully adequate manner, one must intend to consider all other perspectives. Here the analogy to mathematics provides some support for Kohlberg's view, but not enough. One need not actually adopt the other person's perspective, and one need not achieve actual unanimity of result with these others, but one must nonetheless take these perspectives into account (cf. Hare, 1981, ch. 7, entitled "Interpersonal Comparison"). If one does not at least consider all the alternative perspectives, one will have no basis from which to criticize one's own perspective, and hence one will be unsure that one's own perspective is the best or most adequate. But this consideration of different perspectives does not necessarily lead a person to adopt the perspectives of others, or even to have that intent. Hence, the analogy to mathematics does not help Kohlberg establish the supremacy of "reversibility."

This last point leads to a consideration of Kohlberg's third premise, namely, that the highest stage of moral reasoning displays reversibility to the greatest extent and thus should be preferred as most adequate. Kohlberg writes:

The notion that these claims correspond to a greater psychological equilibration of moral judgment becomes truly plausible in empirical study. A. Erdynast gave subjects instructions to assume the original position. This could not be done or was meaningless to highly intelligent subjects below Stage 5. Stage 5 subjects, however, would often change their choices after assuming the original position and would feel that the new solution was more adequate. (1973, p. 645)

In the Erdynast study we find people exposed to higher stage considerations or principles changing their opinions about the best solution to a given dilemma, then, importantly, claiming that the new solution is preferable because it is more adequate.

First of all, it is questionable whether the highest stage that Kohlberg has been able to identify does indeed display the greatest degree of reversibility. As I have indicated, with the bracketing of Stage 6 has come the problem that the highest stage of reasoning may not display a clearly greater degree of reversibility than that of the lower stages. In my analysis of the responses to the Heinz dilemma, the Stage 5 solution to the dilemma was characterized as follows: At "Stage 5, these problems are handled by the conceptions of prior rights and contractual agreements. Reversibility at Stage 5 means reciprocity of rights" (1973, p. 643). But Kohlberg still needs to show why he believes that reciprocity of rights displays more reversibility than does the Golden Rule interpretation at Stage 3. Kohlberg has provided a plausible argument for the claim that reasoning at Stage 6 is superior to reasoning at Stage 3, the argument that, although both forms of reasoning involve interpretations of the Golden Rule, that of Stage 6 is acceptable from the most perspectives and, hence, better in terms of reversibility. But he is on much less solid ground when the comparison is between Stages 5 and 3, for Stage 5 does not employ the same type of consideration as does Stage 3. Indeed, as characterized in this example, Stage 5 does not seem to display much greater reversibility than does Stage 3, since looking to prior rights and contracts is no more reversible than trying to put oneself in another's shoes. In fact Stage 5 may display even less reversibility than Stage 3, since Stage 3 clearly involves multiple role-taking, whereas, as indicated above, Stage 5 involves consideration of rights and interests of others *only* so that one's own rights and interests will be similarly respected.

Finally, some elaboration is needed about the preference displayed by the Erdynast subjects for Stage 6 reasoning. Preference alone, of course, does not conclusively establish greater normative adequacy. This is especially important as a criticism of Kohlberg's particular use of the preference argument since the preference is only for what one has been exposed to. We can only conjecture what the Erdynast subjects would have said of other possible higher stage considerations than the "original position" of Rawls's theory. Might they not also have displayed a preference for the stage of enlightened self-interest which I proposed in the previous section? As Mill pointed out, preference works as a legitimate normative criterion only when one has been exposed to all potentially higher experiences.

The answer to this question depends on empirical findings, but also on normative assumptions. It remains to be seen whether there would be a marked preference for my proposed stage of enlightened self-interest or for any other sort of higher stage, such as Habermas's communitarian stage. Nonetheless, by considering Kohlberg's other remarks we can anticipate how he might respond. When the evidence is lacking, he generally proceeds by demonstrating that one stage can be shown conceptually to be preferable to another. But his method is often suspect, for he continues to talk about preference as an ideal construct of those who are fully rational and who understand the nature of morality. Here again he comes close to begging the question. For Kohlberg, our preferences are to be considered legitimate only when we recognize that ideally moral judgments should be fully reversible and universalizable. But the very question under investigation was whether judgments that achieve maximum universalizability and reversibility are indeed to be objectively preferred. In order not to beg the question, Kohlberg cannot demand that only the preferences of those who agree with his definition of morality be counted. And yet even when he does restrict the evidence in this way, he is not able to show that there is unanimity of preference for his higher stage, as we see from the Erdynast study where "often," but not always, the subjects felt that the original position decisions were preferable. A proper empiricist respect for all of this evidence does not warrant Kohlberg's claim, and neither do the related normative arguments I have just rehearsed.

In conclusion, in this section I have tried to indicate a number of pitfalls, inadequacies, and shortcomings in Kohlberg's defense of the claimed normative superiority of the highest stages of moral reasoning. Specifically, I have argued that Kohlberg often comes close to begging the very question he is supposedly answering. His definition of morality assumes criteria of morality which display themselves fully only in the supposed highest moral stages. It is true that the lower stages also display some of the features, but it is not clear that Kohlberg has shown that he is employing an adequate definition of morality from the start. Kohlberg assumes, among many other things, that agreement about the resolution of moral dilemmas is a chief criterion of moral adequacy. However, it seems to me that this is surely not always true, and may not often be true, especially where there are genuine moral dilemmas. In such situations, a theory which allows for a plurality of quite different, perhaps equally adequate, moral resolutions seems better able to capture the experiential fact that these dilemmas simply do not have one resolution. Mathematical reasoning does not provide Kohlberg with an analogy sufficiently close to morality to help him out of this quandary.

Kohlberg argues that the higher stages are more normatively adequate because they display a greater extent of "reversibility" or what is commonly called reciprocity. Here the most serious internal criticisms can be brought to show the inadequacy of Kohlberg's normative arguments. I have tried to show that Stage 5 is not clearly superior to Stage 3 in terms of the criterion of reversibility. Reversibility itself is not clearly preferable to every other imaginable criterion of morality. This criticism is particularly telling when one realizes that most of Kohlberg's normative arguments, even as late as 1978, have been premised on the existence of a sixth stage which was virtually identical to Rawls's theory of justice. Such a stage was claimed to provide the perspective from which all other stages could be criticized for their inadequacies. However, Kohlberg's failure to confirm the existence of this stage has produced in persons such as myself a quite different critical perspective, one which challenges the adequacy of Kohlberg's own theory of moral development.[5]

NOTES

1. Throughout this paper I will refer to Stage 6 parenthetically since, contrary to what he previously claimed, Kohlberg has recently stated that he does not have solid empirical evidence for the existence of this stage as a distinct stage of moral reasoning within his subjects (cf. Kohlberg, 1982, p. 523).
2. For a good summary of Kohlberg's research as he himself understands its importance and philosophical significance, see Kohlberg (1982).
3. See Kohlberg's revised version of "From Is to Ought," which appeared as ch. 4 of Kohlberg (1981).
4. Philippa Foot argued this thesis in a paper delivered at Loyola University of Chicago, April, 1984.

5. I am grateful for help and encouragement I received from Marilyn Friedman, Marvin Berkowitz, Thomas Wren, and Carol Harding.

REFERENCES

Colby, A., Kohlberg, L., Gibbs, J. C., & Lieberman, M. (1983). A longitudinal study of moral development. *Monographs of the Society for Research in Child Development, 48*(1-2, Serial No. 200), 1-96.

Hare, R. M. (1981). *Moral thinking.* Oxford: Oxford University Press.

Kohlberg, L. (1971). From Is to Ought: How to commit the naturalistic fallacy and get away with it in the study of moral development. In T. Mischel (Ed.), *Cognitive development and epistemology.* New York: Academic Press.

Kohlberg, L. (1973). The claim to adequacy of a highest stage of moral judgment. *The Journal of Philosophy, 70,* 630-646.

Kohlberg, L. (1981). *Essays on moral development: Vol. 1. The philosophy of moral development.* San Francisco: Harper and Row.

Kohlberg, L. (1982). A reply to Owen Flanagan and some comments on the Puka-Goodpaster Exchange. *Ethics, 92,* 513-528.

Kohlberg, L. (1983). *Moral stages: A current formulation and a response to critics.* Basil: S. Karger.

May, L., "On conscience." *American Philosophical Quarterly,* 20, 57-67.

Rawls, J. (1971). *A theory of justice.* Cambridge: Harvard University Press.

Ross, W. (1930). *The right and the good.* Oxford: Oxford University Press.

Turiel, E., Edwards, C. P., & Kohlberg, L. (1978). A cross-cultural study of moral development in Turkey and the United States. *Journal of Cross-Cultural Psychology,* 9, 75-87.

Children's Conceptions of Morality, Societal Convention, and Religious Prescription

Larry P. Nucci

> Conventionality is not morality. Self-right-
> eousness is not religion. To attack the first
> is not to assail the last. (Charlotte Brontë,
> 1977 [1847], p. 3.)

When in the late 1970s John Paul II argued that the ordination of women was not an issue of justice or of human rights, but rather one of custom and tradition, he made a distinction not often acknowledged by psychologists who study the development of morality. Over the past decade, however, a body of research and theory has emerged which explicitly recognizes that people's conceptions of morality form a knowledge system distinct from their concepts of nonmoral social issues (Turiel, 1983). On that account, the focus of this chapter will be on social development. The differential development of concepts of morality and convention have been discussed in previous publications (e.g., Nucci, 1982; Turiel & Smetana, 1984; Turiel, 1983). In this chapter, the emphasis will be on related research on concepts of morality and religious prescription. The research asks two questions: (1) whether morality constitutes a conceptual and developmental domain distinct from concepts about religious behavioral standards akin to societal conventions; and (2) whether one's identification of the moral is ultimately independent of religious prescriptions.

The issues addressed in this chapter will thus bear on arguments raised by theologians and philosophers since Plato's time regarding the relationship between morality and religious values. From that philosophical and theological discussion have evolved two major positions. On one side of the debate have been orthodox theologians (e.g., Barth, 1957; Bonhoeffer, 1955) who have equated morality with obedience to the will of God. On the other side have been philosophers (e.g., Nielsen, 1973) and those theologians (e.g.,

Ramsey, 1966; Bultmann, 1966) who have viewed ethics as autonomous from theology.

I offer our findings with regard to children's concepts of morality and religious prescription as evidence to be considered in that debate. I do so conscious of what G. E. Moore (1903) has called the naturalist fallacy, and of Blasi's (1984) recent reminder that psychology cannot determine which philosophical approach gives "a more faithful picture of what morality should be" (p. 40). Thus, it is not my intention to suggest that what we observe children saying about God and morality is what we can then assume they ought to say. However, as Piaget (1965) has observed, such data can allow us to confirm or reject certain assumptions about the nature of human moral and religious values which undergird various philosophical positions. As Frankena (1973) reminds us, any philosopher's Ought carries with it a set of assumptions regarding human nature which are subject to empirical investigation. To the extent that the philosophical positions informing our research help to clarify our understanding of social development, psychology benefits. To the extent that our psychological research helps to resolve questions regarding the nature of human social and moral understanding, philosophy benefits.

DISTINGUISHING MORALITY FROM SOCIETAL CONVENTION

To begin a discussion of the issues at hand, it is necessary to clarify what is meant by the moral domain, and to differentiate morality from social or religious conventions. We distinguish between convention and morality as follows. Conventions (e.g., modes of dress, forms of address) are behavioral uniformities determined by the social system in which they are formed (Turiel, 1983). Over time, through accepted usage, these standards serve to maintain social organization. Longstanding social conventions can assume great importance in the lives of individuals, both as means of symbolic expression of group membership and as patterns of action that define the "good" person (Shweder, 1982). While conventions are important, they are arbitrary. This is because the actions they define are not intrinsically prescriptive: alternative courses of action could be designated to serve the same function. Accordingly, in the conventional domain, only violations of implicit or explicit regulations are considered transgressions (such regulations being alterable by consensus). For example, it is no longer a transgression for certain orders of Catholic nuns to wear trousers or knee-length dresses rather than habits. Concepts about social convention are structured by underlying conceptions of the social system (Turiel, 1983).

In contrast to convention, moral considerations stem from factors intrinsic to actions: consequences such as harm to others, violations of rights, effects on the general welfare. Thus, moral issues are neither arbitrary nor determined by social regulation. For an individual to determine, for instance, whether it is right or wrong to hit and hurt others does not depend on the presence of a rule, nor on the consensus of others. Instead, the individual may construct prescriptions about such acts out of features intrinsic to the acts, such as their consequences to the victim. Moral concepts are structured by underlying conceptualizations of justice and beneficence (Turiel, 1983).

Research on the Moral-Conventional Distinction

Support for the distinct domains model has been provided by results of over twenty recent studies. Nearly all of that research has focused on the individual's notions of morality and convention in secular contexts. The interested reader can find detailed summaries of most of those studies in reviews by Elliot Turiel (1983) and myself (Nucci, 1982). At this point, let me briefly list the major findings that have been obtained in those studies, before turning to a more thorough account of the results of studies examining the moral and conventional aspects of religious values.

Studies of the moral and conventional in secular contexts have demonstrated the following:
- Moral transgressions are viewed as wrong irrespective of the presence of governing rules, while conventional acts are viewed as wrong only if they are in violation of an existing rule or standard.
- Individuals view conventional standards as culturally relative and alterable, while moral prescriptions are viewed as universal and unchangeable.
- The forms of social interaction in the context of moral events differ qualitatively from interactions in the context of conventions. Specifically, it was found that children's and adults' responses to events in the moral domain focus on features intrinsic to the acts (e.g., harm, justice), while responses in the context of conventions focus on aspects of the social order (e.g.,

rules, regulations, normative expectations).
- Individuals view moral transgressions as more serious than violations of convention.
- Prosocial moral acts are viewed as better or more positive than adherence to conventions.

These studies have included subjects from 3 to 25 years of age. Yet, no age differences have been found in the criteria employed or in the tendencies of individuals to distinguish between the moral and the conventional. Similar findings have been reported for preschoolers and young adults alike. While the majority of these studies have been conducted in the United States, essentially the same results have been obtained with subjects in Korea (Song, Smetana, & Kim, 1985), the Netherlands (Turiel, in preparation), Nigeria (Hollos, Leis, & Turiel, 1985), and the Virgin Islands (Nucci, Turiel, & Encarnacion-Gawrych, 1983), demonstrating that the distinction between morality and convention is not limited to persons whose socialization experiences are within mainland United States culture.

The research described thus far is consistent with the contention that the moral and conventional constitute qualitatively differing forms of social events which are differentiated by individuals at all ages. Other research has shown that conceptions of morality and convention follow distinct developmental patterns and sequences. (With regard to moral development, see Damon, 1977, 1980; Enright, Franklin, & Manheim, 1980. With regard to the development of concepts about social convention, see Turiel, 1983.)

Related Research on Religious Values

There is then a substantial literature dealing with research on children's social concepts in secular contexts which indicates that morality constitutes a cognitive-developmental dimension irreducible to concepts about social convention. Let us now look at the evidence with respect to children's concepts of morality in the context of religious value systems.

Our studies are the first to examine this issue explicitly in terms of the distinction between morality and conventional values. Precursors to our work, however, are Middleton and Putney's (1962) study of the relationship between moral values and religious belief in American students, and Wright and Cox's (1967, 1971) subsequent research with English adolescents. Each of these studies made use of Middleton and Putney's distinction between "ascetic" morality, in which the consequences of actions such as smoking and drinking are

felt mainly by the actor, and "social" morality, in which the consequences of acts (e.g., stealing, lying) are experienced initially by
others. Middleton and Putney (1962) hypothesized that, since those
actions which they defined as social morality are intrinsic to the
function of living in communities, attitudes about such actions would
be common to believers and nonbelievers alike. In contrast, what
they defined as ascetic morality derives from religious traditions and
thus would be less strongly supported by nonbelievers than by
believers. Findings from each of the three studies supported that
general hypothesis.

In these studies subjects were asked to indicate whether they
considered a series of actions wrong, and if so, to what extent. In
each study it was found that believers and nonbelievers differed far
more in the extent to which they condemned violations of ascetic
morality than in the extent to which they condemned actions whose
consequences resulted in harm or injustice to others. Indeed
Middleton and Putney (1962) found no differences in the tendency
of believers and nonbelievers to condemn the latter class of actions.

Middleton and Putney's (1967) distinction between social and
ascetic morality shares some of the features of the distinction we
draw between moral and conventional forms of social values. Their
findings and those of Wright and Cox (1967, 1971) are consistent
with our hypothesis that morality (viz., what they have termed social
morality) is independent of religious prescription. That is, believers
and nonbelievers alike condemned transgressions of this type. On the
other hand, the data from these studies suggest that a considerable
aspect of religious values (viz., what they have termed ascetic
morality) is determined by the precepts of the religion as a conventional system. Thus, believers whose religions opposed actions
compromising ascetic morality were more condemnatory of such acts
than were nonbelievers.

This interpretation is further supported by Wright and Cox's
(1971) analyses of shifts in people's values as a function of shifts in
overall social attitudes. Their study illustrates that shifts in attitude
among English adolescents between the years 1967 and 1971 led to
greater liberalism with regard to "ascetic" values such as those at
issue in premarital sex, but continued condemnation of moral transgressions such as stealing, which have hurtful consequences for
others. These shifts in attitude, reported by Wright and Cox, were
found to follow the same pattern irrespective of subjects' religiosity.

While findings from the research just reviewed are consistent with
our hypotheses regarding religion and morality, they cannot be

viewed as dealing conclusively with the issues and questions raised in this chapter. The main limitation of those studies is that any conclusions to be drawn regarding the relationship between morality and religion must be inferred from comparisons of the judgments made by believers with those of nonbelievers rather than through a direct analysis of the reasoning of religious subjects.

In those studies, subjects were asked to generate severity judgments (degree of condemnation) of various actions. The pattern of agreements and disagreements between believers' and nonbelievers' severity judgments was used by the other authors, and later by myself (as in the preceding section) as evidence sustaining hypotheses of the universality of moral prescriptions (social morality) and the relativity of religious conventions (ascetic morality). The universality sustained by those studies, however, refers only to commonalities among group mores. Such data tell us nothing of whether the subjects themselves perceive certain actions as prescriptive and universally binding. Yet it is precisely the latter kind of datum that is necessary if our hypotheses regarding moral development and moral understanding in the context of religion are to be given credence. This is because criteria of prescriptivity and universality as developed in formalist ethics refer not to observed uniformities in norms across societies, religions, or individuals, but rather to a set of criteria employed by the individual to evaluate the moral status of actions. For us to say, then, that a prescription is treated as universal, it is not sufficient to show that most people – religious or not – condemn the act. Rather, we must demonstrate that the majority of individuals view the act as one which should be universally condemned.

As I reviewed earlier in this chapter, data of this kind have been gathered with reference to children's and adolescents' judgments about social, conventional, and moral issues in secular contexts. Without such data from religious subjects regarding religious values, we cannot rule out the possibility that religious morality as evidenced in the normative reasoning of religious subjects is something different from secular morality. That is, we cannot rule out the possibility that religious people not only view their moral prescriptions as requiring adherence, as unalterable, and as universally applicable, but also, unlike their secular counterparts, view their religious conventions as prescriptive and universally binding.

CHILDREN'S CONCEPTS OF MORALITY AND RELIGIOUS RULES

In order to address this possibility, we employed methods similar to those used in our research in secular contexts to examine concepts of religious, moral, and social values in children from four religious groups: traditional Roman Catholics, fundamentalist Christians, Conservative Jews, and Orthodox Jews. These denominations were chosen as exemplars of conservative religious belief systems within Western culture. Since these studies are ongoing, I am able to report now only on our investigations of the moral and conventional religious concepts of our Catholic and fundamentalist Christian samples. Our preliminary examination of the data we are obtaining from Jewish children and adolescents suggests, however, that similar patterns of thinking are exhibited by children from each denomination.

Morality and Religious Norms as Seen by Catholics

The first of these studies focused on traditional Roman Catholics. We chose practicing Catholics for this initial investigation of religious norms for three reasons: (1) Catholicism has a clearly specified set of acts that constitute wrongful (sinful) behavior; (2) Catholicism as a social system has a clearly designated authority and procedure for interpreting and determining what constitutes sinful behavior (i.e., the Pope, usually after consultation with other bishops, has the ultimate authority to interpret and hence determine matters of doctrine), and (3) Catholicism as one of the world's largest and oldest organized religions, has become an integral part of many sociocultural systems.

In the study we asked our Catholic subjects to make a number of judgments about actions considered sins by the Catholic church. Some of the actions such as stealing, killing, rape, slander, etc., entailed harm or injustice toward another and were classified by us as matters of morality. Other actions such as failure to attend religious services on Easter or Christmas, fasting prior to receiving communion, the use of contraceptives, masturbation, premarital sex between consenting adults, divorce, and ordaining women, entailed violations of worship patterns or social behavior prescribed by Catholicism as an institution. These actions were classified as nonmoral by us and akin to matters of social convention. To control for response bias, all items in the questionnaire were randomized.

Table 1

Percentages of High School and University Catholics Responding
"It Would Be Wrong" to Changeability and Relativity Questions Regarding Religious Rules

Type of Rule		Question — Would it be wrong or all right for the Pope and Cardinals to drop the rule about the acts listed below? It would be wrong...		Question — Suppose that another religion, religion B, has no rules or laws about the acts listed below. Would it be wrong or all right for a member of religion B to do the acts listed below? It would be wrong...	
		High School	University	High School	University
Moral:					
Hitting and Hurting	(M01)*	93	100	92	98
Rape	(M02)	98	100	98	100
Murder	(M03)	98	100	98	98
Kidnap and Ransom	(M04)	97	100	94	98
Stealing	(M05)	98	100	92	100
Damaging another's personal property (home)	(M06)	90	100	94	98
Selling dangerous defective car to unsuspecting buyer	(M07)	79	96	83	94
Slander	(M08)	90	98	82	98
Betray another's personal secrets	(M09)	90	96	92	94
Racial discrimination in hiring	(M10)	72	89	75	84
Ridiculing a cripple	(M11)	97	100	90	98
Allowing another to be punished for one's own misdeed	(M12)	97	100	96	98

		Question Would it be wrong or all right for the Pope and Cardinals to drop the rule about the acts listed below? It would be wrong…		Question Suppose that another religion, religion B, has no rules or laws about the acts listed below. Would it be wrong or all right for a member of religion B to do the acts listed below? It would be wrong…	
Type of Rule		High School	University	High School	University
Church Contentions:					
Not attend Mass (religious services) on Sunday	(C13)	46	42	39	12
Eating 15 minutes before communion	(C14)	38	34	19	12
Receiving communion without confession	(C15)	50	47	45	35
Year without communion	(C16)	57	38	36	14
Not attend Mass on Easter or Christmas	(C17)	62	54	48	31
Ordaining women	(C18)	39	16	29	8
Sexual Conventions:					
Premarital sex	(C19)	29	32	17	12
Masturbation	(C20)	43	18	52	14
Birth control (the "pill")	(C21)	22	16	27	8
Homosexuality	(C22)	64	52	47	39
Divorce	(C23)	18	31	22	27
Marital sex solely for pleasure	(C24)	21	12	25	6

Note: n = 25 males and 25 females for each of the four groups.

*Letters and numbers in parentheses are codes for identifying items on Tables 3 and 4.

The twenty-four moral and nonmoral (conventional) issues used in the study are listed in Table 1. It should be pointed out that nonmoral religious prescriptions are not, strictly speaking, conventions, since they are presumably derived from scripture and are not considered by the devout to be the products of social consensus. With Catholicism this issue is complicated by the existence of Church authorities (i.e., the Pope and the bishops) empowered to determine and interpret such issues for members of the Catholic faith. It was still our view that such issues would not be treated as matters of morality by our Catholic subjects.

Subjects were asked to make three kinds of judgments. First, they were asked to rate the seriousness of each transgression using a four point scale on which 1 = not wrong at all and 4 = very seriously wrong. This procedure paralleled that used in the Middleton and Putney (1962) and Wright and Cox (1967, 1971) studies. The remaining two judgments required subjects to employ criteria for identifying the moral (i.e., prescriptivity, universality) provided by formalist ethics. Subjects' judgments of the prescriptivity of various actions were evoked by asking (1) whether it would be wrong or all right for the Pope in conjunction with the bishops to remove the attendant moral and conventional rules, and (2) if it would be wrong or all right for a Catholic to engage in a given behavior once the rule was removed. Subjects' judgments of the universality of acts as constituting wrongful behavior were evoked by asking whether it would be wrong or all right for members of another religion to engage in the behaviors if the other religion had no rules or standards regarding the acts.

Subjects in this study were 100 sophomores attending religion classes at two Chicago Catholic high schools and equal numbers of undergraduates attending teacher preparation courses at the University of Illinois at Chicago. A preliminary set of questions determined that both groups of subjects were devout practicing church-goers (87.6% of the university Catholics received communion more than twice monthly; 92% at least once a month, which compares with 90% and 95.3% respectively for the high school sample). In addition, nearly all of the subjects in both groups adhered to the traditional Catholic beliefs that Mary was a virgin at the time of Christ's birth, that Christ is God and rose from the dead, and that Peter was the first head of the Church.

With regard to subjects' judgments of the seriousness of transgressions, we found that both the high school and college age Catholics rated the moral transgressions as more serious than violations of Catholic conventions (high school moral $\overline{M}$ = 3.55, conventional $\overline{M}$ = 2.28, t (99) = 21.09, p < .0001; college moral $\overline{M}$ = 3.65, conventional $\overline{M}$ = 1.85, t (99) = 27.79, p < .0001). This finding occurred despite the fact that according to Catholic dogma, engagement in a number of currently prohibited conventional behaviors entails the same severe penalty (i.e., damnation) as engagement in prohibited moral acts. These data are consistent with findings reported by Wright and Cox (1971) and indicate that the Catholic subjects based their judgments of the greater seriousness of moral transgressions on criteria other than the punishments assumed by Catholic dogma. It is our view that these Catholics judged the moral transgressions to be more serious because of the intrinsic effects such actions as hitting, stealing, slander, and rape have on the recipient of the act.

Findings for the high school and college age Catholics' responses to questions regarding the removal of Church rules are presented in Table 1. As can be seen in the table, the overwhelming majority of the subjects (on average 91.6% high school, 98% university subjects) viewed it as wrong for the Church authorities to remove rules governing moral transgressions such as hitting and stealing. In contrast, on average less than half of the high school (40.8%) and university (32.7%) Catholics viewed it as wrong for the Pope to remove the Church rules regarding conventional behaviors such as fasting prior to communion, the ordination of women, the use of contraceptives, or engaging in premarital sex. These differences were statistically significant (high school, F (1,22) = 137.21, p < .0001; university, F (1,22) = 213.66, p < .0001). The subjects' responses regarding whether or not it would be wrong to engage in the various actions once religious prohibitions were removed essentially paralleled the findings regarding the removal of the rules themselves. We conclude from these data that, to the extent that devout American Catholics grant the Pope and other religious leaders the authority to alter the standards for "good" or "right" Catholic behavior, this authority extends only to actions in the conventional domain. One possible explanation for this finding is that the majority of American Catholics, contrary to Church dogma, do not view the Pope as infallible in matters of faith. Our own data would tend to bear that out. Only 23% of our university sample and 28% of our high school subjects adhered to a belief in papal infallibility. These findings are in line with other surveys of American Catholic attitudes (NBC News, 1979). For the remaining quarter of our subjects, who professed a belief in papal infallibility, our findings may reflect an incredulity on their part that the Pope would make the error of removing Church rules governing moral actions. In either case, our findings are in line with the assumption that subjects generate notions of the prescriptivity of moral actions independent of the dictates of religious authorities.

With respect to relativity questions (i.e., questions about other religions), we found that Catholics tended to universalize only the moral issues. These data are also summarized in Table 1. On average 91% of the high school subjects and 97% of the university subjects viewed it as wrong for members of another religion to engage in acts entailing moral transgressions (e.g., stealing, slander) even if the other religion had no rules regarding the acts. In contrast to moral issues, less than half the Catholic subjects (on average 33.8% high school, 18.2% university) were willing to univer-salize Catholic conventions and treat as wrong engagement in such conventional actions by members of religions which do not regulate those behaviors. The tendency of the subjects to acknowledge the relativism of their Church's conventions is highlighted by findings that the percentages of subjects viewing the acts as wrong for members of another religion was significantly less than the percent-ages of subjects who viewed it as wrong for Catholics themselves to engage in the behaviors if the Pope removed the governing rules. In sum, the findings from this aspect of the study indicate that Catholics distinguish between Church conventions, which serve to organize the behaviors of persons who define themselves as Catholics, and those moral acts which have an intrinsic effect upon the rights or well-being of others, Catholic and non-Catholic alike.

The correlation among the three forms of judgments (seriousness ratings, rule alterability, act universality) subjects were asked to make was quite high. Spearman rank-order correlations for the subjects' treatments of individual items in response to aspects of the question-naire ranged from .90 to .99. These exceptionally high correlations are consistent with our assumption that the three forms of judgment derived from moral philosophy, which were employed as criteria for identifying the moral in this study, focused upon a common psycho-logical dimension.

The summative data from Catholics we reviewed thus far provide a pattern consistent with the proposition that morality is indepen-dent of religious prescription. Before concluding this section, however, I would like to focus on patterns in the data relevant to individual differences in persons' religious conservativism and vari-ability in the treatment of individual items that might present "gray" areas in the moral-conventional dichotomy. For the bulk of this discussion, I will be referring to data presented in Tables 2 and 3.

Each table was generated out of a relatively new application of Rasch scaling procedures (Master, Wright, & Ludlow, 1981), previously used mainly for calibrating items for tests measuring intellectual performance. In this case, the scaling procedure was used to generate an ordering of items according to subjects' perceptions of the alterability of governing rules (the tendency to say it would be all right for the Pope to remove the governing rule, in Table 2), and act universality (the tendency to view an act as wrong for persons of another religion which has no rule regarding the act, in Table 3). Tables 2 and 3 present plots of individuals along a continuum of religious conscrvativism (the tendency to treat rules as unchangeable, or acts as universally wrong). Individuals are plotted against item position on a scale of rule alterability (Table 2) or act universality (Table 3). The key to identifying individual items on the two tables is presented in Table 1.

One thing apparent in Tables 2 and 3 is that there is essentially no overlap among items from the two domains. A second thing evidenced in the two tables is that while there is variability among individuals in the tendency to classify items in terms of rule alterability or act universality, almost all of the variance is due to differences in the treatment of conventional items. Except for a few cases, each of the subjects including the "liberals" treated each of the table's moral items as prescriptive and universal. Inspection of the tables also illustrates the differences in subjects' treatment of conventional items as a function of the question that was asked. Table 2 presents a nearly normal distribution in the religious conservativism of subjects with regard to their tendency to view it as all right for the Catholic hierarchy to alter Catholic conventions. In contrast, Table 3 presents a skewed distribution (most markedly so for university subjects) in the tendency of subjects to universalize Catholic conventions. Subjects, including conservatives, were far more likely to treat conventional items as alterable and relative for outsiders (non-Catholics) than they were to treat the status of such items as variable for members of their own religion. The difference in the shape of the two distributions illustrates both the relativism of the conventional items (Table 3) and the importance many individuals attach to religious conventions in the governance of their own lives and in their pattern of worship (Table 2). Indeed, Table 2 may be viewed as a graphic illustration of one source of turmoil surrounding recent efforts to modify Catholic patterns of worship.

Table 2

Distribution of Catholic Subjects as a Function
of Conservatism and Rule Alterability[a]

	High School			University	
Raw Score	Item[c]	Subject Frequency[b]	Raw Score	Item	Subject Frequency
23		X			
22		X			
21	C19, C23, C24	X			
20	C21	XX	14		X
19		X		C24	
18	C14, C18	XXXX	13		X
17	C13, C20	XXXX		C20, C21	
16	C15	XXXXXXX	12	C18	XX
15	C16	XXXXXXXXXXX	11	C23	XXXX
14	C22	XXXXXXXX	10	C14, C19	XXX
13	C17, M10	XXX		C16	
12		XXXX	9	C13	XXXXXXX
11	M07		8	C17, C22	XXXXXXXXXXXXXX
10			7		XXXXX
9					
8	M08, M09, M06	X	6		XXXXXX
				C15	
			5		XXX
7	M01				
6		X	4		XXX
5				M10	
4	M02, M11, M12		3		
3	M04				
	M05, M03			M09	
2			2	M12	X
				M08, M07, M06	
				M05, M04, M03	
1			1	M02, M01, M11	

Note: n = 25 males and 25 females for each group.

[a] Subject conservatism is tendency to consider it wrong for the Pope to remove the governing rule. Higher score equals greater conservatism. Subject placement indicates tendency to consider alteration of rules governing items below that score as wrong. Rule alterability is tendency for subjects to view it as okay for Pope to remove the rule. Higher item score equals greater rule alterability.

[b] Each X equals one subject.

[c] Item description for each item code presented in Table 1; for each item C stands for convention, M for moral.

Table 3

Distribution of Catholic Subjects as a
Function of Conservativism and Act Universality[a]

	High School			University	
Raw Score	Item [c]	Subject Frequency [b]	Raw Score	Item	Subject Frequency
			19	C18	
			18	C24	XXX
			17	C13, C14, C19	XX
			16	C16, C20	X
22		X	15		XX
			14	C23	XX
21			13	C15, C17	
20	C14	X			XX
19	C19, C24	XX	12	C22	XXXXX
18	C18, C21	XXXX			
17	C13, C23	XXXXX	11		XXXXXXXXXXXXX
16	C15, C16	XXXXXX			
15	C20	XXXXXXX			
14	C17	XXX	10		XXXXXXXXXXXXXXXX
13	C22	XXXXX			
12		XXXXXX			X
11		XXXXXXX	9	M10	
10	M10				
9	M07, M08		8		X
8		X			
7	M11	X	7	M09	
6	M01, M05				
5	M04, M06		6	M07	X
			5		
4	M12		4	M01, M03, M06 M08, M11, M12	
3			3		
	M09		2		
2					
	M02, M03		1	M02, M05	
1		X			

Note: n = 25 males and 25 females for each group.

[a] Subject conservativism indicated by score. Subject placement indicates tendency to consider items from that score and below to be universal wrongs. Item universality is the tendency for subjects to treat an act as wrong for members of another religion even if that religion has no rule regarding the act. Lower scores indicate greater likelihood of being treated as universal.

[b] Each X equals one subject.

[c] Item description for each item code presented in Table 1; for each item C stands for convention, M for moral.

With regard to variance in the treatment of individual items within the conventional domain, there are four "gray issues" or items which stick out as being particularly important and likely to be treated as if they were moral. Three of these, receiving communion without confession, going a year without receiving communion, and not attending Mass on Easter or Christmas, represent violations of behavioral patterns that are basic to Catholic worship. As I mentioned earlier, conventions, though not intrinsically prescriptive, can take on deep significance in the lives of individuals committed to participation within a given cultural system. For devout Catholics to decenter sufficiently to treat these three behaviors as arbitrary and variable is in a sense to ask them to treat Catholicism itself, at least insofar as these conventional regularities are concerned, as alterable and relative. That devout Catholics can acknowledge this is evidenced in the subjects' responses to the act universality questions (see Table 3). It seems likely that in that context subjects were not asking themselves to "renounce" their own pattern of worship, but to acknowledge the Catholicism of those actions and the legitimacy of other religious patterns.

The fourth gray issue, homosexuality, is another matter entirely. While the act is not a matter of morality in that it does not meet our definition of morality as justice, it is likely that many subjects interpret the act of homosexuality as "unnatural" and not simply wrong because of social or religious standards. That the definition of sexual unnaturalness is largely consensual and cultural in origin is evidenced in the university students' treatment of the act as all right for persons of another religion if the religion does not prohibit homosexual behavior. Despite these data I hesitate to assume that homosexuality is treated by most people as a purely conventional issue. A more complete examination of individuals' notions of the propriety of homosexuality is now being studied by Elliot Turiel (personal communication). For our present purposes, it is not necessary to consider homosexuality as a moral issue.

Finally, one lesson to be drawn from Tables 2 and 3 is that our distinction between morality and convention does not mean that all individuals necessarily agree on every aspect of religious values. Indeed, some of the subjects plotted on the two tables would make Jerry Falwell appear liberal. The tables also suggest that factors such as age and education may affect individuals' conceptions of their religious values. Table 3, for instance, graphically illustrates that the university sample was considerably more "liberal" than were the high school students with regard to Catholic conventions. The two things most striking about these data in the final analysis, however, are (1) that individuals make a consistent set of distinctions between moral and nonmoral religious values, and (2) that there is little variance in individuals' identifications of actions in the moral domain. These findings are in keeping with our definition of the moral (Turiel, 1983). They are also consistent with the outcomes of each of the studies on moral and conventional reasoning conducted in secular contexts.

Our study of Catholics provided very strong support for our hypotheses regarding morality and religion. It must be said, however, that Catholicism, because of its organizational structure, seems ideally suited for the type of question we posed. Catholics, particularly since Vatican II, have become accustomed to the notion that Church regulations may be altered by the hierarchy and, hence, are relative to the historical period. As our research has shown, Catholics extend this relativity only to Church regulations that refer to matters of convention. Nonetheless, one might ask whether members of fundamentalist Christian religions, which eschew the notion of a temporal Church hierarchy and presumably derive their rules directly from scripture, would react in a similar fashion when asked about the alterability or universality of their religious conventions. Our subsequent study, therefore, focused on the thinking of fundamentalist Christian subjects.

Morality and Religious Norms as Seen by Fundamentalists

The fundamentalist Christians in our study were conservative Mennonites from a rural area of Indiana and a subgroup of Amish-Mennonites from the same area. The Mennonites constitute a religious denomination within the larger Anabaptist community which had its origins in the Swiss reformation. They are distinguished by their isolation from contemporary society and their rejection of modern technology. The children in our study all attended the same fundamentalist school overseen by congregational pastors and administered by an Amish principal. The beliefs and life-style of the conservative Mennonites and Amish in this population were the same, and were a bit less restrictive than the life-style adopted by their relatives in Pennsylvania. Among the beliefs and practices held by these children and their families were a number common to other Anabaptist groups such as the rejection of infant baptism and papal authority. In addition, these subjects adhered to a prohibition against radio or television in the home, and a prescribed plain mode of dress, the latter being more marked among the women than the men. Women, for example, were all required to wear a prescribed head covering following baptism, and were prohibited from wearing trousers. In most cases the girls in the study wore solid color calf-length homemade dresses patterned after those of their 17th century European ancestors. A total of 64 children participated in the study. Half the children were girls and half boys, equally distributed across four age-groups (10 to 11, 12 to 13, 14 to 15, and 16 to 17 years of age).

Each child was individually interviewed for approximately 90 minutes regarding his or her conceptions of four moral and six nonmoral religious prescriptions. Adolescents over the age of 14 were also interviewed regarding a seventh nonmoral prescription, the prohibition against premarital intercourse between consenting adults. A list of the issues used is presented in Table 4. For each issue the interview elicited subjects' responses to questions regarding the alterability of religious rules and the universality of the status of acts as transgressions. Since fundamentalists, unlike Catholics, do not acknowledge a Church hierarchy, prescriptivity and universality questions were supplemented by questions aimed at determining whether the status of acts as transgressions was contingent on God's word as recorded in scripture. Each subject was asked: "Suppose Jesus [God] had not given us a law about [the act], the Bible didn't say anything one way or another about [the act]. Would it be all right for a Christian to do [the act] in that case?"

The interview questions described thus far corresponded to the format of the questionnaire method employed in our study of Catholics, and provided data regarding fundamentalists' judgments of actions as moral or nonmoral on the basis of formal criteria (i.e., prescriptivity, universality). One limitation of the questionnaire method employed in our study with Catholics, however, was that we were unable to generate data regarding subjects' substantive definitions of either morality or convention. Our developmental model, in contrast, makes statements regarding the substantive definitions of morality and convention. It was these substantive definitions that formed the basis for our classification of items as conventional or moral prior to their presentation to the subjects both in the questionnaire given to the Catholics and in our subsequent interviews with fundamentalists. For instance, one of the substantive criteria used for defining an issue as one of morality was that the act must involve a matter of justice. A question which can be raised with respect to our study with Catholics, then, is whether the subjects' responses reflected substantive definitions of the moral and conventional status of the acts similar to those which we assumed.

In our interview studies with fundamentalist Christian children we addressed this limitation by asking subjects to provide justifications for each criterion judgment they made. It was expected that the justifications provided would correspond to the substantive criteria for defining actions as moral or conventional. Findings for subjects' criterion judgments are presented in Table 4. Their justifications are summarized in Tables 6-8. Definitions of the categories for coding justifications are provided in Table 5.

At this point in our analysis we have not applied inferential statistics to these data. On the basis of our descriptive statistics, however, we may draw some conclusions regarding our hypotheses. Let us begin by considering the data on Table 4 regarding subjects' judgments of whether it would be wrong or all right for religious authorities to remove the rules governing various actions. As can be seen in the table, subjects consistently stated that it would be wrong either for the authorities or for the collective membership of the congregation to remove rules prohibiting actions in the moral domain. This outcome is consistent with both our general hypotheses and our findings among Catholics. Subjects' responses to the same question with respect to what we considered religious conventions, however, appeared less consonant with our expectations, and, as a comparison with the data on Table 1 illustrates, fundamentalists' responses to alterability questions with respect to nonmoral items differ considerably from those provided by Catholics. For example, nearly as many 13- and 15-year-old Mennonite subjects said it would be wrong for either religious authorities or the congregation to alter the prohibition against work on Sunday as said it would be wrong to remove the rules against moral transgressions such as hitting and hurting others or damaging another's personal property.

This outcome appears to embody the fundamentalists' rejection of the notion of a temporal authority empowered to make such decisions. As we noted before, fundamentalists base their religious prescriptions on literal interpretations of Biblical statements assumed to reflect direct commands from God. Inspection of the justifications data on Table 6 indicates that such an orientation was operating as the basis for judging that it was wrong for church authorities or for the congregation to remove religious rules. The category "God's law" accounted for 60 percent of the justifications for such judgments with respect to moral issues and over 80 percent in the case of items we defined as nonmoral or conventional.

Table 4
Percentages of Amish/Mennonite Children Responding "It Would Be Wrong" to Rule Alterability, Act Universality, and God's Word Contingency Questions for Moral and Non-Moral (Conventional) Issues

	Question Type and Subject Age											
	Rule Alterability				Act Universality				God's Word Contingency			
Issue:	10-11	12-13	14-15	16-17	10-11	12-13	14-15	16-17	10-11	12-13	14-15	16-17
Non-Moral/Convention:												
Day of Worship	44	47	50	36	25	27	18	09	0	0	0	0
Work on Sunday	100	93	94	82	67	60	44	27	6	0	0	0
Head Covering	75	50	75	82	13	27	12	09	0	0	0	0
Baptism	71	79	88	82	25	57	18	27	0	0	0	0
Inter-faith Marriage	53	40	44	27	31	20	12	09	6	0	0	0
Women Preaching	53	36	44	91	19	07	18	30	6	0	12	11
Premarital Sex	-	-	75	90	-	-	25	45	-	-	11	14
M̄ Non-Moral*	66	58	66	67	30	33	20	18	3	0	2	2
Moral:												
Stealing	100	100	100	100	81	93	94	91	81	70	88	91
Hitting	94	100	94	91	88	86	100	100	81	70	88	82
Slander	88	100	100	100	81	100	88	100	75	78	88	89
Damaging Property	88	93	100	100	88	87	88	100	88	83	94	100
M̄ Moral	92	98	98	98	85	92	93	98	81	75	90	90

Note: *Rule Alterability:* "Would it be all right for the congregation to remove or alter the rule?"
  Act Universality: "Is it all right for members of another religion which has no rule about the act to engage in the act?"
  God's Word Contingency: "If God had made no rule about the act, would it be all right to engage in the act?"
*Calculated without premarital sex item.

Table 5
Definitions of Justification Categories

Social Consensus	If everyone agrees, then it should be altered, or it should remain the way it is because that's what everyone agrees should be done.
Religious Authority	The rule is one that is determined and maintained (and may be altered) by religious authority.
God's Law	The rule is determined by biblical statement or the word of God. The status of the act is determined by God's law.
System Dependent	The status of the act is determined by the rules and beliefs of the religious system.
Subject to Interpretation	The correctness of the act is a function of interpretation of scripture. The scriptural passage is open to alternative interpretations.
Personal Issue	The action is a matter of individual prerogative and private choice.
Historical Justification	The custom is long-standing and should be therefore maintained (for the sake of historical continuity). "We've always done it this way."
Prudential Concern	Issue of practical utility. Act leads to imprudent outcome (e.g., pregnancy, family discord).
Ignorance	The actor may be excused on the basis of ignorance of God's law.
Other's Welfare	Appeal to the interest of persons other than the actor ("Because somebody could have gotten hurt," "Nobody wants their money taken because they like to have lunch.")
Appeal to Fairness	References to maintaining balance of rights between persons ("I don't think it would be fair, where if someone earns money and the other guy would take it and keep it for himself when he didn't do anything. He didn't earn it.")
Obligation/Common Sense	References to feelings of obligation or personal conscience, or notion that the wrongness of the act is self-evident and binding.
Categorical Wrong	Unelaborated statement that the act is simply wrong.
Natural Order	This is the natural way of things. Part of God's plan.
Reciprocal Benefit	One wouldn't want the act to happen to self, so shouldn't act in such a way toward others.
Punishment Avoidance	Act is wrong because God or the authorities will punish the action.
Other	Non-classifiable justification.

Table 6

Justifications Provided by Amish/Mennonite Children for Rule Alterability Judgments (%)

	Judgment and Issue Type															
	It Would Be Wrong								It Would Be Right							
	Moral (Age)				Non-moral (Age)				Moral (Age)				Non-moral (Age)			
Justification	10	12	14	16	10	12	14	16	10	12	14	16	10	12	14	16
God's Law	71	70	60	41	93	86	83	89	-	-	-	-	0	3	0	0
Religious Authority	0	0	0	0	0	0	0	0	-	-	-	-	63	47	11	14
Social Consensus	0	0	0	0	0	0	0	0	-	-	-	-	22	34	78	64
System Dependence	0	0	0	0	0	0	0	0	-	-	-	-	0	0	3	0
Historical	0	0	0	0	0	0	9	5	-	-	-	-	0	0	0	0
Interpretation	0	0	0	0	0	0	0	0	-	-	-	-	6	3	3	14
Ignorance	0	0	0	0	0	0	0	0	-	-	-	-	0	0	0	0
Personal Issue	0	0	0	0	0	0	0	0	-	-	-	-	3	12	5	7
Prudential	0	0	0	0	0	4	6	4	-	-	-	-	0	0	0	0
Natural Order	0	0	0	0	5	2	1	1	-	-	-	-	0	0	0	0
Welfare	20	12	19	45	0	0	0	0	-	-	-	-	0	0	0	0
Fairness	2	10	6	9	0	0	0	0	-	-	-	-	0	0	0	0
Reciprocal	0	2	3	4	0	0	0	0	-	-	-	-	0	0	0	0
Obligation	0	0	6	0	0	0	0	0	-	-	-	-	0	0	0	0
Categorical	5	4	5	2	0	0	0	0	-	-	-	-	0	0	0	0
Punishment	2	0	0	0	0	0	0	0	-	-	-	-	0	0	0	0
Other	0	0	0	0	2	4	0	0	-	-	-	-	6	0	0	0

Note: Sample size at each age equals eight males and eight females.

Nonetheless, the justification data also indicate that a "revealed truth" orientation was not all that was operating in the alterability judgments of these Mennonite subjects. Approximately 40 percent of the justifications for saying that it would be wrong to alter or remove the rules governing moral actions focused on the intrinsic features of the acts as hurtful or unjust. With respect to those instances in which subjects said that it would be all right to remove the rules governing nonmoral (conventional) actions, the justifications conformed to our substantive definition of social convention in that they focused on the consensual and social organizational status of the norms.

If we turn from the alterability data to consideration of our findings with respect to the fundamentalists' responses to act universality questions, we find an increased differentiation between moral and conventional items. As can be seen in Table 4, actions we defined as depicting moral transgressions were judged to be wrong even for members of another religion which had no rules governing the acts. The percentages of subjects judging the acts as wrong ($\bar{M}$ = 92 percent) approximated the percentages for judgments that it would be wrong in response to rule alterability questions ($\bar{M}$ = 97 percent). In contrast, far fewer subjects responded that it would be wrong for members of another religion to engage in actions we defined as entailing violations of Mennonite religious conventions, if the other religion had no rules governing the acts ($\bar{M}$ = 25 percent). It would appear then that, as was the case with Catholics, the fundamentalists universalized moral issues, but viewed as relative their religious prescriptions regarding many nonmoral actions. Furthermore, as we had observed with the Catholics (see Table 1), the percentages of Mennonite subjects judging conventional actions as wrong in response to universality questions ($\bar{M}$ = 25 percent) was considerably less than the percentages for such judgments in response to rule alterability questions ($\bar{M}$ = 64 percent).

This latter outcome is somewhat puzzling in light of the God's Law justification the Mennonite children gave for judging that it would be wrong to alter the rules governing conventions within their own religion. It would appear from these data that the majority of our Mennonite subjects did not view God's laws regarding conventional actions as extending to members of other religions. Instead, they justified their judgments that it would be all right for members of other religions to engage in such acts (e.g., women *not* wearing head coverings) in terms concordant with our definition of social convention (see Table 7). That is, they saw such actions as system

Table 7

Justifications Provided by Amish/Mennonite Children for Act Universality Judgments (%)

	Judgment and Issue Type															
	It Would Be Wrong								It Would Be Right							
	Moral (Age)				Non-moral (Age)				Moral (Age)				Non-moral (Age)			
Justification	10	12	14	16	10	12	14	16	10	12	14	16	10	12	14	16
God's Law	25	51	23	18	89	92	86	72	-	-	-	-	0	0	0	0
Religious Authority	0	0	0	0	0	0	0	0	-	-	-	-	41	13	11	4
Social Consensus	0	0	0	0	0	0	0	0	-	-	-	-	5	0	8	6
System Dependence	0	0	0	0	0	0	0	0	-	-	-	-	37	53	58	62
Historical	0	0	0	0	0	0	5	3	-	-	-	-	0	0	0	0
Interpretation	0	0	0	0	0	0	0	0	-	-	-	-	5	8	9	15
Ignorance	0	0	0	0	0	0	0	0	-	-	-	-	0	8	8	7
Personal Issue	0	0	0	0	0	0	0	0	-	-	-	-	0	13	2	6
Prudential	0	0	0	0	4	4	5	10	-	-	-	-	0	0	0	0
Natural Order	0	0	0	0	7	4	0	7	-	-	-	-	0	0	0	0
Welfare	41	31	32	51	0	0	0	0	-	-	-	-	0	0	0	0
Fairness	4	5	13	11	0	0	0	0	-	-	-	-	0	0	0	0
Reciprocal	10	3	9	11	0	0	0	0	-	-	-	-	0	0	0	0
Obligation	0	5	9	0	0	0	0	0	-	-	-	-	0	0	0	0
Categorical	2	3	9	4	0	0	0	3	-	-	-	-	0	0	0	0
Punishment	8	0	0	0	0	0	0	0	-	-	-	-	0	0	0	0
Other	8	2	5	4	0	0	5	3	-	-	-	-	13	3	4	0

Note: Sample size at each age equals eight males and eight females.

Table 8

Justifications Provided by Amish/Mennonite Children for God's Law Contingency Judgments (%)

	Judgment and Issue Type															
	It Would Be Wrong								It Would Be Right							
	Moral (Age)				Non-moral (Age)				Moral (Age)				Non-moral (Age)			
Justification	10	12	14	16	10	12	14	16	10	12	14	16	10	12	14	16
God's Law	0	0	0	0	-	-	-	-	90	100	100	100	98	100	100	100
Religious Authority	0	0	0	0	-	-	-	-	0	0	0	0	0	0	0	0
Social Consensus	0	0	0	0	-	-	-	-	0	0	0	0	0	0	0	0
System Dependence	0	0	0	0	-	-	-	-	0	0	0	0	0	0	0	0
Historical	0	0	0	0	-	-	-	-	0	0	0	0	0	0	0	0
Interpretation	0	0	0	0	-	-	-	-	0	0	0	0	0	0	0	0
Ignorance	0	0	0	0	-	-	-	-	0	0	0	0	0	0	0	0
Personal Issue	0	0	0	0	-	-	-	-	0	0	0	0	0	0	0	0
Prudential	0	0	0	0	-	-	-	-	0	0	0	0	0	0	0	0
Natural Order	0	0	0	0	-	-	-	-	0	0	0	0	0	0	0	0
Welfare	50	39	53	70	-	-	-	-	0	0	0	0	0	0	0	0
Fairness	26	23	22	18	-	-	-	-	0	0	0	0	0	0	0	0
Reciprocal	3	23	9	6	-	-	-	-	0	0	0	0	0	0	0	0
Obligation	0	3	9	4	-	-	-	-	0	0	0	0	0	0	0	0
Categorical	8	6	2	0	-	-	-	-	0	0	0	0	0	0	0	0
Punishment	8	0	0	0	-	-	-	-	0	0	0	0	0	0	0	0
Other	3	3	5	2	-	-	-	-	10	0	0	0	2	0	0	0

Note: Sample size at each age equals eight males and eight females.

dependent, and subject to regularities established through consensus or by religious authority.

There were some indications in the data, however, that not all subjects viewing such actions as relative were also treating them as conventions. About 15 to 20 percent of the subjects 12 years of age or older excused the nonconformist actions of members of other religions on the grounds that these nonmoral laws of God were subject to interpretation or that members of other religions might simply be ignorant of God's law. Both justifications seem concordant with two other values held by these subjects: (1) one should not sit in judgment of others, and (2) one can make a distinction between those who are "saved" (chosen) and those who are not. Thus, the ignorant may be excused and the deviant tolerated, but they are nonetheless not part of the community (i.e., Mennonites) closest to God. What is interesting in this context is that in contrast to the relative tolerance shown regarding nonmoral issues, these fundamentalist subjects, like the Catholics, viewed it as wrong for members of other religions to engage in actions (e.g., slander) constituting transgressions in the moral domain. Instead of invoking God's law as the basis for such judgments, the majority of our Mennonite subjects were expecting even the nonbeliever to view such actions as wrong because of their intrinsic effects upon the rights and welfare of others.

Our last set of questions was intended to examine directly whether or not the fundamentalist children viewed morality as dependent on God's word. Subjects were asked: "Suppose Jesus [God] had not given us a law about [the act]. Would it be all right for a Christian to do [the act] in that case?" Subjects' responses are summarized in Table 4. As can be seen in the table, virtually none of the subjects at any age felt that it would be wrong to engage in any of the nonmoral behaviors if God (as indicated in scripture) had not provided any prescription or statement governing the act. These judgments are mirrored by the justifications data on Table 8 which indicated that essentially all of the reasons subjects provided for making such judgments are accounted for by the "God's law" category. For these fundamentalist children, then, the regulation of such actions by their religion is a function of the presence or absence of biblical injunctions regarding the acts.

In contrast, between 70 and 100 percent of the Mennonite subjects at each age stated that it would be wrong to engage in an action entailing a transgression in the moral domain even if there were no biblical prescription or statement by God concerning the act

(Table 4). The justifications data summarized on Table 8 reveal that subjects based those judgments on the intrinsic features of the acts as hurtful or unjust. This last set of findings suggests that even for the fundamentalist Christian, morality stems from criteria independent of God's word.

The following excerpts from our interviews with our Conservative Mennonite and Amish subjects illustrate the thinking of these children regarding the relationship between religious prescriptions and the regulation of moral and nonmoral (conventional) behavior. The first is from an interview with an 11-year-old Amish boy. The first portion of the interview deals with the Amish convention that women wear head coverings. The Biblical source of this convention is Paul's letter to the Corinthians (I:11). The boy's responses are given in the context of a story which tells of an Amish girl who attends a local public junior high school where none of the other girls wears a head covering. Children in such schools typically range in age from 11 to 14 years. In order not to be different, the Amish girl, Mary, decides not to wear her head covering to school.

The second excerpt presents this same subject's responses to questions regarding a moral issue, stealing. The two excerpts are as follows:

Subject DNWRM (11 years, 11 months)

Religious Convention: Women wearing head coverings. (WAS MARY RIGHT OR WRONG NOT TO WEAR A HEAD COVERING AT SCHOOL?) Wrong, because the Bible says you should, the women should have their hair long and have it covered with a covering and the men should have their hair short. (DO YOU THINK IT REALLY MATTERS WHETHER OR NOT A MENNONITE GIRL WEARS A HEAD COVERING?) It depends on if you are baptized or not. If you are baptized, you should. (HOW COME?) Because that's the way God wants it. (CAN THAT RULE ABOUT HEAD COVERING BE CHANGED?) Yes, I suppose it could. (WOULD IT BE ALL RIGHT FOR THE MINISTERS TO REMOVE THE RULE ABOUT WOMEN WEARING HEAD COVERINGS?) No. (WHY NOT?) Because God said that's how he wants it, and that's how he wants it. (IF THE MINISTERS DID REMOVE THE RULE ABOUT HEAD COVERINGS, THEN WOULD IT BE ALL RIGHT FOR GIRLS NOT TO WEAR THE HEAD COVERINGS?) If they were obeying the minister and not God, it would be, but if they were obeying God and not the ministers, then it wouldn't. (SUPPOSE IT WASN'T WRITTEN IN THE BIBLE THAT WOMEN ARE SUPPOSED TO WEAR HEAD COVERINGS, GOD HADN'T SAID ANYTHING ABOUT HEAD COVERINGS ONE WAY OR THE

OTHER, WOULD IT BE ALL RIGHT FOR WOMEN NOT TO WEAR HEAD COVERINGS THEN?) Yeah, it would be o.k. then, because if God didn't say so it wouldn't matter. (THE OTHER GIRLS AT MARY'S SCHOOL BELONG TO RELIGIONS THAT DON'T HAVE THE RULE ABOUT HEAD COVERINGS. IS IT O.K. THAT THOSE RELIGIONS DON'T HAVE THE RULE?) It's all right if that's the way their church is, believes. (WELL, THEN, IS IT O.K. FOR THOSE GIRLS NOT TO WEAR THE HEAD COVERINGS?) Yeah. (WHY IS IT O.K. FOR THEM BUT NOT FOR MARY?) Because she goes to a Mennonite Christian Church, she should obey the Mennonite laws. (COULD A WOMAN STILL BE A GOOD CHRISTIAN AND NOT WEAR A HEAD COVERING?) It depends on her, it depends on if she is really a good Christian and has accepted Christ. It depends on her, if she cannot find a head covering that suits her, but she thinks she should be able to wear it, then I'd say it would be all right to go without one, put your hair up. (WELL, THEN, WHY WEAR A HEAD COVERING?) Because if you are around people more often, like if one person doesn't have one and the other one does and they are both real good Christians and one goes, they are both walking and a guy comes up and says man, I can tell which one's a Christian out of them. This one over here has a covering and I can tell she is, but over here I don't know for sure because she doesn't wear one. I would have to do some questioning before I know for sure.

Moral Issue: Stealing. (IS IT O.K. TO STEAL?) No. (WHY NOT?) Because that is one of the Ten Commandments that God put in the law and gave to Moses and he expects us to obey these laws and if we don't obey these laws, we can know for sure that we will not go to heaven, we will absolutely go to hell. (WHAT'S WRONG WITH STEALING?) Having something that does not belong to us and taking it from someone else, it would just irritate you. Like, one time my sister stole my radio batteries. I didn't know where they were and then I found out that she had them in her tape recorder and I thought that these were the exact ones so I took them back. Actually, she had them in her drawer and she saw these were missing so she came back four hours later while I was in bed sleeping and she just grabbed them right out of there and put mine back in. By this time, she had worn mine down and they weren't working so I thought for sure that she had just wore hers out and so I went and stole mine back which were really hers. My conscience just bothered me until I returned them and took the other ones and I found out that these were the correct ones to be having anyway. (SHOULD THE RULE ABOUT STEALING BE FOLLOWED?) Yes, or else we will go to hell. And all of those will know, and those who are on earth already know that hell is a bad place. There's fire and brimstone and you could die down there! And everybody that goes there, they know that they are a sinful person. (SUPPOSE ALL THE MINISTERS DECIDED TO DROP THE RULE ABOUT STEALING SO THAT THERE WAS NO RULE ABOUT STEALING. WOULD THAT BE ALL RIGHT?) No. (WHY NOT?) Because God said that it wouldn't be expected of us and he expects us to obey him. (WOULD IT BE ALL RIGHT FOR A CHRISTIAN TO STEAL IF THE MINISTERS DROPPED THE RULE?) No, because you still wouldn't be able to go to heaven, you'd have to go to hell. (SUPPOSE THE PEOPLE OF ANOTHER RELIGION DON'T HAVE A RULE ABOUT STEALING. IS THAT ALL RIGHT?) No. (WHY NOT?) Because if they have their Bible, then they know about the law. (SUPPOSE THEY DON'T USE OUR BIBLE, THEY HAVE A DIFFERENT RELIGION AND IT DOESN'T HAVE A RULE ABOUT STEALING. IS THAT ALL RIGHT?) No, because God said that thou shalt not steal and that goes for everybody. (IF THEY DIDN'T KNOW ABOUT THAT RULE, WOULD IT BE O.K. FOR THEM TO STEAL?) No, because it would still make everybody unhappy. (IF GOD HADN'T SAID ANYTHING ABOUT STEALING ONE WAY OR THE OTHER, WOULD IT BE ALL RIGHT TO STEAL THEN?) No. (WHY NOT?) Because then if people would steal, then the world wouldn't be very happy. (COULD YOU SAY MORE ABOUT THAT?) Like when my sister stole my batteries, it really irritated me. If everybody's stuff kept getting stolen, everyone would be mad and say, "Hey, where's my stuff?" It would be terrible; nobody could keep anything that was theirs. I wouldn't like it.

What we can see in this 11-year-old subject's responses is that he acknowledges that the rule about head coverings is based on the word of authority (God), that it is relative to a particular interpretation or view of that authority's norms, and that it serves a social organizational function of distinguishing boys from girls, and Christians from others. In contrast with his views about head coverings, this Amish boy treated stealing as universally wrong, and wrong even if God did not have a rule about it. The wrongness of stealing, according to our subject, is that it leads to hurtful or unjust consequences. Thus, we see in him an early objective morality that differs from his understanding of nonmoral religious prescriptions.

A similar response pattern can be seen in the following excerpts from an interview with a 17-year-old Amish youth. In the first portion of the interview, he is responding to the same vignette regarding head coverings as was the 11-year-old previous subject. The second segment of the excerpt concerns a different moral issue, slander.

Subject PLBRM (17 years 10 months)

Religious Convention: Women wearing head coverings. (WAS MARY RIGHT OR WRONG NOT TO WEAR A HEAD COVERING AT SCHOOL?) She was wrong. (HOW COME?) Because a head covering, usually, symbolizes that she is a member of the church and she is to wear it all the time. (DO YOU THINK THAT IT REALLY MATTERS WHETHER OR NOT MENNONITE GIRLS WEAR HEAD COVERING?) I think that it matters. (AND WHY IS THAT?) I guess it is a symbol because of what God has done for them and they are then under submission. I guess, to be honest, as a boy, I don't know about that in detail, but I know one thing, that it is a sign of submission . . . (WHY DOES A HEAD COVERING MEAN THAT?) Well, in the Bible it says that the woman is supposed to keep her head covered and I think that if a girl is going by the standards of the Bible, then she should wear it. (WHAT DO YOU MEAN BY SUBMISSION IN THIS CASE?) For a married lady, it means that she is under submission to her husband and to God. For a girl, I guess it would be under her parents' submission, and to God also. (DOES THE RULE ABOUT GIRLS AND WOMEN WEARING THE HEAD COVERING HAVE TO BE FOLLOWED?) In the Mennonite church, it does. (WHY DOES IT HAVE TO BE FOLLOWED?) Because that is the right thing to do. (CAN THE MENNONITE RULE ABOUT WEARING HEAD COVERING BE CHANGED?) Yeah. (WHO COULD CHANGE IT?) Let's see, the minister could change it or the bishop of the church. (WOULD IT BE ALL RIGHT, THEN, FOR THE MINISTER OR THE BISHOP OF THE CHURCH TO REMOVE THE RULE ABOUT WOMEN WEARING HEAD COVERING?) I'd say no. (WHY NOT?) It wouldn't be right because the Bible teaches that they should be worn and if you drop it, I'd say that it would be more identifying with the world than doing the power of God. (WHEN YOU SAY IDENTIFYING WITH THE WORLD, WHAT DO YOU MEAN?) Well, like, you want to look like them, you don't want to be different and I guess that would mean . . . (WHY SHOULD A MENNONITE LOOK DIFFERENT?) I don't know, she would have to, she is really considered different, of course, she would dress different, of course. (WHY SHOULD THEY DRESS DIFFERENT?) So that people can see that they are not associated with the world. (IF THE MINISTERS AGREED TO DO THAT, REMOVE THE RULE ABOUT WOMEN WEARING HEAD COVERINGS, WOULD IT THEN BE O.K. FOR A WOMAN TO GO TO SCHOOL WITHOUT A HEAD COVERING?) No. (NO? WHY NOT?) Because of the same reason I said before; she would be identifying with the world rather than following the word of God. (THE OTHER GIRLS AT THE SCHOOL BELONG TO RELIGIONS THAT DON'T HAVE A RULE ABOUT HEAD COVERINGS. IS IT O.K. FOR THOSE RELIGIONS NOT TO HAVE THE RULE?) Yea. (IS IT

O.K., THEN, FOR THOSE GIRLS NOT TO WEAR A HEAD COVERING?) Yea, if their certain religion does not specify wearing it. (WHY IS IT O.K. FOR THEM, BUT NOT FOR MARY?) I often wondered myself, these people are Christians, too, and they are different, but I think that God said for each one because of the way they are and I think for the Mennonite it is just a choice that people have, there is not a rule that says that you have to stay Mennonite, but I don't think that it is any better than any other religion because they also believe in God. It is just that they have different standards and for the Mennonite to wear more plain clothes, I guess. Nowadays, it is not much different for the guys, it is hardly any difference. For the girl, it especially, I don't know, I often wonder too, if the girls ever think, you know, why can't I be like them? But I think that it is just their choice to show that they are, I guess, it is the different groups of people who believe differently in the Bible in a different way.

Moral Issue: Slander. (IS IT ALL RIGHT TO SLANDER?) No, it is not all right to slander. (IS THERE ANY RULE OR STATEMENT ABOUT THAT IN YOUR RELIGION?) Well, in the Bible it says that you are supposed to love everyone and I interpret that by meaning that you shouldn't speak against another person. (DOES THAT RULE HAVE TO BE FOLLOWED?) The rule can be changed, but, I personally don't think that it should. (SUPPOSE THAT THE MEMBERS OF THE MENNONITE CHURCH GOT TOGETHER AND DECIDED THAT THEY WOULDN'T HAVE THAT RULE ABOUT SLANDER ANY MORE. IS THAT ALL RIGHT?) No, I don't think that it would be. (IF THEY DID DROP THAT RULE, WOULD IT BE O.K. FOR THE MEMBERS OF THE CHURCH TO SLANDER OTHERS?) No. (WHY NOT?) Well, because that is violating one of God's principles in the Bible where it says you are supposed to love everyone and speak highly of them, of another person. (SUPPOSE THAT CHRIST HADN'T TOLD US THAT THAT IS WHAT WE ARE SUPPOSED TO DO. THEN WOULD IT BE ALL RIGHT TO SLANDER PEOPLE?) Well, I suppose that if he wouldn't have had that information, I suppose that you wouldn't know any better so you probably would. (WOULD IT BE RIGHT TO SLANDER, DO YOU THINK?) Well, it still wouldn't be right, but . . . (WHY WOULDN'T IT STILL BE RIGHT?) Well, it is putting another person down and if you really think about it, would you want someone else to do the same for you, like, talk about you, something that is not true, and I feel that's wrong. (SUPPOSE THAT PEOPLE OF ANOTHER RELIGION DID NOT HAVE A RULE ABOUT SLANDER. WOULD IT BE O.K. FOR THEM TO SLANDER?) I would say that it's wrong that they don't have a rule. (AND IF THEY DON'T HAVE A RULE, WOULD IT BE ALL RIGHT FOR THEM TO SLANDER?) No. (WHY NOT?) Well, like I said before, it's putting someone down, and I think that no one has the right to do that, and I think that applies to everyone. I mean, who would want that to be done to them. It's just wrong.

What is vividly portrayed in the preceding excerpts is that the children and adolescents we interviewed make conceptual distinctions between the moral and nonmoral issues dealt with by the precepts of their religion. The distinctions they made essentially paralleled the theoretical distinctions we have drawn between the moral and the social conventional. While it would be incorrect to reduce conceptions of nonmoral religious prescriptions to conventions, it would appear from our subjects' responses that concepts about such nonmoral religious precepts are coordinated with concepts about social convention, custom, and tradition. This is most evident in PLBRM's responses regarding the rules governing the head coverings worn by Mennonite women. In his responses, PLBRM evidences an understanding of the function of head coverings as a symbol of the hierarchical, sex-typed order of Mennonite society, and the subordinate relationship of that society to God. Both PLBRM's and DNWRM's responses are in fact structurally similar to same-age subjects' reasoning about secular social convention (Turiel, 1983).

In contrast with the normative system (rule based) reasoning exhibited by our subjects with regard to nonmoral (conventional) issues, their views of moral issues did not rest on the position taken by their religion nor on the presence of commands from God. Instead both DNWRM and PLBRM, as well as our other subjects, seem to have based their judgments about moral issues in terms of the intrinsic effects of the acts themselves. This outcome, as I suggested earlier, presents strong support for the view that morality is independent from religion and is not reducible to commands from God. In the final study to be reported in this chapter, we looked more specifically at the role of God's commands in determining the person's concepts of morality.

MORALITY AND GOD'S WORD

Beginning with Plato's account of Socrates' dialogue with Euthyphro, philosophical arguments suggesting that God's commands cannot in and of themselves determine what is moral have turned on what is known as the "open question." Put simply, the open question asks the following: "God commands X, but is X right?" To answer, one must invoke criteria for the good that are independent of God's word. In Nielsen's (1973) treatment of this issue, the case is made that in order for God's commands to be moral, it must at least be the case that God is good. From this premise, Nielsen argues that Judeo-Christian conceptions of God presuppose prior, independent conceptions of goodness which serve as criteria for differentiating God from Satan or from other preternatural forces.

Though it was not our purpose to analyze or test those philosophical positions, our research on religious children's conceptions of the relations between morality and God's word were informed by such discussions of the open question. In our final study in this series, we asked children whether God's commands could make right something which most children treated as morally wrong. Specifically, children were asked: "Suppose God had commanded [written in the Bible] that Christians *should* steal. Would it then be right for a Christian to steal?" We also asked the children whether they thought God would make such a command, and if so, why or why not? Subjects in the study were 64 fundamentalist Christians of the Dutch Reform (Calvinist) denomination. The children all attended a Calvinist parochial school in the Chicago area which sets aside periods during the day for Bible study, and which emphasizes adherence to Christian values as a core aspect of school life. It was our hypothesis that children's answers would reflect their efforts to coordinate conceptions of moral issues in terms of the intrinsic effects of such actions on others with their conceptions of God as omniscient, omnipotent, and perfect. In particular we hypothesized that children would: (1) reject the notion that God's command to steal would make stealing morally right and (2) reject the notion that God would command Christians to steal as a normative behavior.

Our analyses of subject responses revealed that indeed the majority of children at each age rejected the notion that God's command to steal would make it right for a person to steal. At ages 10 to 11 and 12 to 13 years, 69% of subjects responded in this way, while 81% of subjects at ages 14 to 15 and 16 to 17 years gave such responses. These results were concordant with findings from our previous studies indicating that, while the presence or absence of God's commands determined subjects' judgments of the right or wrong of nonmoral religious behaviors, judgments about the right or wrong of moral actions appeared to be independent of God's word. The following excerpt from an interview with a 15-year-old girl is typical of responses provided by children who rejected the notion that God's command to steal would make stealing right.

Female (15 years, 7 months)

(SUPPOSE THAT GOD HAD WRITTEN IN THE BIBLE THAT CHRISTIANS SHOULD STEAL. WOULD IT THEN BE RIGHT FOR CHRISTIANS TO STEAL?) Probably, I think people would maybe do it. Because, if it was written in the Bible and that's what God said that we should do, then people would probably do it. I mean more often. 'Cause that's what God said, and it's easier to do than to go against God. (SO, IF GOD SAID IT, PEOPLE WOULD DO IT. BUT WOULD THEY BE RIGHT TO DO IT?) No. It still wouldn't be right. (WHY NOT?) 'Cause you're taking from somebody else, and it still wouldn't be right. After all, who would want that to happen to them? (DO YOU THINK GOD WOULD COMMAND US TO STEAL?) No. (WHY NOT?) Because, it's not the right thing to do, and he's perfect, and if he's stealing, he can't be perfect.

In the responses of this 15-year-old subject we see that, although she believes that people might engage in stealing in response to God's command, such an action would continue to be morally wrong because of its effects upon the victim. Furthermore, she coordinates her moral position with her notion of God's perfection by rejecting the notion that God would make such a command, since to do so would negate his status as a perfect being. In the following excerpts we see evidence that such thinking for some of these Christian children constitutes the very criteria for worshiping God.

Male (15 years, 4 months)

(DO YOU THINK GOD WOULD SAY THAT WE SHOULD STEAL?) No. (WHY NOT?) Because he's good in every way, and he wouldn't encourage people to do wrong. (BUT IF GOD SAID TO STEAL, WOULD IT MAKE IT RIGHT?) Well, I'd still have doubts about it. If you knew it was from God, then you might think it was right. But, I really – I probably wouldn't – ah – worship God – if he said – if he encouraged us to do bad things. (HOW DO WE KNOW THAT WHAT IS WRITTEN IN THE BIBLE IS THE WORD OF GOD AND NOT THE WORD OF THE DEVIL?) Well, because we realize that many parts of the Bible are just good common sense, and that they are things that we would normally think. Like the Ten Commandments, that's right to you even before you understand the Ten Commandments. So, if a person told you to do what was right, you'd realize that this was a person who was good. (I SEE, AND DOES GOD HAVE TO BE GOOD?) Well, yes, because worshiping an evil being would not be a very intelligent thing to do.

Male (16 years, 6 months)

(SUPPOSE THAT GOD HAD WRITTEN IN THE BIBLE THAT CHRISTIANS SHOULD STEAL. WOULD IT THEN BE RIGHT FOR CHRISTIANS TO STEAL?) No, then he wouldn't be a just God. And there are, I'm sure there are people who would go against him, then, if he were an unjust God, even though he had absolute power.

We see in the thinking of these children a rejection of the Nietzschean dictum that might makes right, as well as of Euthyphro's position that morality is determined by God's commands. Instead, what appears to be evidenced in these interviews is an attempt by children to coordinate their notion of the just Judeo-Christian God with what they *know to be morally right.*

While such was clearly the case among the majority of the subjects, a significant minority (approximately 30% at the younger ages) stated that God's command to steal *would* make stealing morally right. Such responses were of two types. The first type provided by three of our younger subjects reflected a failure to coordinate conceptions of morality and God's perfection with conceptions of God as omnipotent. The following set of excerpts from one young girl serves as an illustrative example.

Female (10 years, 8 months)

(HOW DO WE KNOW THAT WHAT THE BIBLE TELLS US TO DO IS REALLY THE RIGHT THING?) You have to believe. (SUPPOSE GOD HAD MADE A COMMANDMENT THAT WE SHOULD STEAL. WOULD IT THEN BE MORALLY RIGHT TO STEAL?) Yes. (SO, WHO WOULD BE THE BETTER PEOPLE THEN, THE ONES WHO STOLE OR THE ONES WHO DIDN'T STEAL?) The ones who stole. (WHY WOULD THEY BE THE BETTER PEOPLE?) Because they were obeying God's law. (WHY SHOULD PEOPLE OBEY GOD'S LAW?) Because God is the only God. He made us, and he made the world, and he rules the world, and we are supposed to do what he says.

In this first portion of the interview, our young subject focused on God's power and authority as the criterion for her judgment of the right or wrong of stealing. In the very next section of the interview, however, her focus shifted to God's goodness and an evaluation of moral actions in terms of their consequences.

(DO YOU THINK THAT GOD WOULD TELL US TO STEAL?) No. (WHY NOT?) Because God is – he's supposed to be good. (IS

STEALING GOOD?) No. (WHY NOT?) Cause – it's bad. It's not right. You're taking another person's stuff and they would probably get upset. I know I don't want my stuff stolen.

In this transcript we see two seemingly contradictory positions coexisting in the thinking of our 10-year-old subject. On the one hand she evaluated the wrongness of stealing on the basis of its effects on the victim and coordinated that evaluation with her expectation that God would not condone stealing since God is good. On the other hand she evaluated the right or wrong of stealing in terms of God's commands. She did not conjoin her notion of God's goodness with his omnipotence, but simply focused on the latter criterion to the exclusion of the former when evaluating the morality of actions commanded by God. This mode of thinking was continued in the remaining portion of her interview.

(DO YOU THINK IT WOULD BE RIGHT IF THE CHILDREN AT SCHOOL HIT AND HURT EACH OTHER?) No. (WHY NOT?) Because hitting hurts! (SUPPOSE THAT GOD HAD SAID THAT CHILDREN SHOULD HIT ONE ANOTHER. DO YOU THINK IT WOULD BE RIGHT THEN FOR CHILDREN TO DO THAT?) Yes. (HOW COME?) Because God said. (BUT WOULDN'T IT STILL HURT TO HIT?) Yes. (THEN WOULD IT BE RIGHT OR WRONG TO HIT?) It would be right. (HOW COME?) Like I told you, because God said.

The thinking of this 10-year-old girl was not seen in any of our subjects over 14 years of age. However, since only three subjects provided responses of the form just described, we cannot conclude whether such reasoning is a function of developmental level or if it simply reflects an alternative mode of conceptualizing the relationship between morality and God's word.

The second type of reasoning provided by children who felt that God's command to steal would make stealing morally right resulted from efforts to coordinate notions of morality and God's perfection with conceptions of God's omniscience. In these subjects the assumption is maintained that God is good, and that his command to steal would reflect good intentions and an ultimately good outcome. Since God is all-knowing, only he can anticipate and comprehend an outcome which may simply be beyond the grasp of temporal consciousness. In the reasoning of these subjects, one sustains faith in the goodness of God without requiring that his ends be comprehensible to the faithful. Such thinking is provided in the following excerpt from an interview with a 17-year-old girl.

Female (17 years, 6 months)

(HOW DO WE KNOW THAT WHAT IS IN THE BIBLE IS REALLY THE RIGHT THING TO DO?) I believe that the Bible is the word of God and that God knows everything and God made us, so what he said must be true. (IT MAY BE TRUE, BUT HOW DO WE KNOW THAT WHAT GOD IS SAYING IS REALLY MORALLY RIGHT, IF HE SAYS ACT A CERTAIN WAY THAT THAT'S THE MORALLY RIGHT WAY TO ACT?) He created us, so he knows what's best for us, so whatever he says must be the best thing to do. (SUPPOSE THAT GOD HAD WRITTEN IN THE BIBLE THAT CHRISTIANS SHOULD STEAL. WOULD IT THEN BE RIGHT FOR CHRISTIANS TO STEAL?) If God said so, I guess it would be, yes. (HOW COME, WHAT WOULD MAKE IT RIGHT?) Because God is the author of everything and he's holy, and whatever he would say has to be right. (SUPPOSE GOD HAD SAID THAT CHRISTIANS SHOULD MURDER. WOULD IT THEN BE RIGHT FOR CHRISTIANS TO MURDER?) It would be the same as with stealing. If he said it, it would be all right because he's God and he knows everything. He knows the end of everything and if he said that it was all right [subject sighs and laughs nervously], I guess it would be. (YOU SEEM A LITTLE BIT CONFLICTED.) Well, I mean, I know it would be hard for me to be able to handle it, because there's things in his word that I already don't understand. But, you just have to take it by faith and believe that he is God, and he knows what he is saying.

This subject's thinking nicely illustrates how a deep conviction and faith in God's goodness coordinated with a belief in God's omniscience can lead a person to accept conclusions about the moral rectitude of actions commanded by God which run counter to the person's own intuitions about the actions. The reasoning of such subjects, however, is not structured by an unreflective acceptance of God's authority. On the contrary, the subjects' notions of God's moral authority stemmed from their assumptions about the inherent goodness of the Christian God. Should that assumption be challenged, then God's authority in moral matters would be called into question. This reasoning is illustrated in the remainder of the interview.

Female (17 years, 6 months), continued:

(HOW DO WE KNOW THAT WHEN WE ARE "HEARING THE WORD OF GOD" THAT WE ARE HEARING GOD'S WORD AND NOT THE DEVIL?) Well, the Bible is the only test you could give it, and the Holy Spirit inside you. (WHAT DO YOU MEAN, THE HOLY

SPIRIT INSIDE YOU? HOW DOES THAT HELP?) I believe the Holy Spirit leads me and convicts me. If I don't believe something is – goes along with, or is part of God's character, than I'll check it out in the Bible and pray about it, and ask for guidance. (DO YOU THINK MURDER IS PART OF GOD'S CHARACTER?) No, but if it said in his word that it was all right to kill, then God must be a different kind of God. (SO, IF HE WERE A DIFFERENT KIND OF GOD, WOULD IT BE RIGHT TO DO IT – TO KILL?) Well, I don't know. That changes the whole thing. So I don't know.

In summary, for all but three of the children in this study, there was clear evidence that fundamentalist Christian children evaluate moral issues on the basis of criteria independent of the word of God. Consistent with our developmental hypothesis, and consonant with findings from our other studies, the children's notions of morality focused on the intrinsic justice and welfare outcomes of actions. On the basis of such "objective" criteria, the children established a moral position which constituted the conceptual framework from which they apprehended the moral aspect of the just Judeo-Christian God. In each of our 64 transcripts, we saw evidence that fundamentalist Christian children attempted to coordinate their notions of God as perfect with their conceptions of the morally good. Thus, for these children, concepts of God did not structure moral knowledge so much as they were coordinated with and informed by the children's independent moral understandings.

CONCLUSIONS

In this research we have seen evidence that children's conceptions of morality are not reducible to their knowledge of or adherence to religious rules. Instead, our research indicates that children's moral, societal, and religious concepts comprise distinct facets of their notions of right and wrong. The findings of this research parallel those of our previous studies of children's conceptions of secular values and lend further support to the developmental hypothesis that children's conceptions of morality constitute a domain distinct from notions of societal convention and other nonmoral behavioral norms (Turiel, 1983). Though our research findings are also consonant with philosophical views that morality is autonomous from theology, neither our findings nor our conclusions may be seen as shedding any light on the nature of God, or on whether God plays a role in establishing the moral nature of humankind. Such questions are beyond the reach of scientific inquiry.

This research is a first step toward a comprehensive account of the development of children's moral concepts and their notions of religious rules. In this report I have discussed the thinking of Christian children. In our current work we are extending this research to interviews with Jewish children. Our preliminary analyses suggest that those data will be consistent with the findings reported here. With that research we will have a more comprehensive view of the development of children reared in the Western religious tradition. It will remain, however, for other studies to show whether our findings will be sustained for children of non-Western religions.

REFERENCES

Barth, K. (1957). *The doctrine of God: Church dogmatics: Vol. 1, part 2.* Edinburgh: T. & T. Clark.

Blasi, A. (1984). *How should psychologists define morality? On the negative side-effects of philosophy's influence on psychology.* Paper presented at the Second Ringberg Conference on Moral Development, July, 1984, Ringberg, Bavaria, Germany.

Bonhoeffer, D. (1955). *Ethics.* New York: Macmillan.

Brontë, C. (1977). *Jane Eyre.* New York: New York University Press. (Original work published in 1847)

Bultmann, R. (1966). Reply to D. Heinz-Horst Schrey. In C. W. Kegley (Ed.), *The theology of Rudolf Bultmann.* New York: Harper & Row.

Damon, W. (1977). *The social world of the child.* San Francisco: Jossey-Bass.

Davidson, P., Turiel, E., & Black, H. A. (1983). The effect of stimulus familiarity on the use of criteria and justifications in children's social reasoning. *British Journal of Developmental Psychology, 1,* 49-65.

Enright, R., Franklin, L., & Manheim, L. (1980). On children's distributive justice reasoning: A standardized objective scale. *Developmental Psychology, 16,* 193-202.

Frankena, W. K. (1973). *Ethics* (rev. ed.). Englewood Cliffs, NJ: Prentice-Hall.

Hare, R. M. (1952). *The language of morals.* New York: Oxford University Press.

Hollos, M., Leis, P., & Turiel, E. (1985). *Social Reasoning in Nigerian children and adolescents.* Unpublished manuscript, University of California, Berkeley.

Kant, I. (1959). *Foundations of the metaphysics of morals.* (L. Beck, Trans.). New York: The Liberal Arts Press.

Kohlberg, L. (1981). *Essays on moral development: Vol. 1. The philosophy of moral development.* San Francisco: Harper & Row.

Masters, W., Wright, B., & Ludlow, L. (1981). *Credit: A Rasch program for ordered categories.* Unpublished computer program manual. Department of Education, The University of Chicago.

Middleton, R., & Putney, S. (1962). Religion, normative standards, and behavior. *Sociometry, 25,* 141-152.

Moore, G. E. (1903). *Principia ethica.* Cambridge: Cambridge University Press.

NBC News. (1979). *Poll No. 122.* New York: Author.

Nielsen, K. (1973). *Ethics without God.* Buffalo, NY: Prometheus Books.

Nucci, L. (1982). Conceptual development in the moral and conventional domains: Implications for values education. *Review of Educational Research, 49,* 93-122.

Nucci, L., Turiel, E., & Encarnacion-Gawrych, G. (1983). Children's social interactions and social concepts: Analyses of morality and convention in the Virgin Islands. *Journal of Cross-Cultural Psychology, 14,* 469-487.

Piaget, J. (1948). *The moral judgment of the child.* (M. Gabain, Trans.). Glencoe, IL: Free Press. (Original work published 1932)

Piaget, J. (1971). *Insights and illusions of philosophy.* (W. Mays, Trans.). New York: Meridian Press.

Ramsey, I. T. (1966). Moral judgments and God's commands. In I.T. Ramsey (Ed.), *Christian ethics and contemporary philosophy.* London: SCM Publishing Co.

Rawls, J. (1971). *A theory of justice.* Cambridge, MA: Harvard University Press.

Shweder, R. (1982). Beyond self-constructed knowledge: The study of culture and morality. *Merrill-Palmer Quarterly,* 28, 41-69.

Song, M.-J., Smetana, J. G., Kim, S.-J. (1985). *Korean children's conceptions of moral and conventional transgressions.* Unpublished manuscript, University of Rochester.

Turiel, E. (1983). *The development of social knowledge: Morality and convention.* Cambridge: Cambridge University Press.

Turiel, E., & Smetana, J. G. (1984). Social knowledge and action: The coordination of domains. In W. Kurtines and J. Gewirtz (Eds.), *Morality, moral behavior, and moral development.* Somerset, NJ: John Wiley & Sons.

Wright, D., & Cox, E. (1967). A study of the relationship between moral judgment and religious belief in a sample of English adolescents. *Journal of Social Psychology,* 72, 135-144.

Wright, D., & Cox, E. (1971). Changes in moral belief among sixth-form boys and girls over a seven-year period in relation to religious belief, age and sex differences. *British Journal of Social and Clinical Psychology,* 10, 332-341.

Religious Dilemmas: The Development of Religious Judgment

Fritz Oser

In general, the scientific community interested in religion has concerned itself with two general sorts of objects of analysis. On the one hand, the focus has been on religious content, texts, revelations or customs, and explanations in light of psychoanalytical theory. On the other hand, there have been attempts to analyze why people believe, and whether religion is either a residue of infancy to be overcome in adulthood or, following Erikson, something to be connected with the development of a person's identity.

Until now few investigations have been undertaken to examine the role religious belief plays in attempts to solve life problems, problems of death, and problems of change and contingency. The cognitive religious structure which a person may have built up through his or her own life history and which can give meaning to existence has rarely been an object of research. However, the research carried out over the last seven years by myself and my colleagues has addressed the question of how this cognitive religious structure can be described across phases of development, and how it can be explained in terms of genetic epistemology and educational transformations. In particular, I have been concerned with how different contents affect the structure and, still more specifically, the process by which dilemmas elicit different aspects of the complex interweaving of a religious cognitive structure.

ELEMENTS OF A RELIGIOUS JUDGMENT

Taking a structural approach, I have posited a set of operations which deal with what I have called contingency situations, namely, the relation of the human person to the ultimate, as that relation obtains within a concrete situation calling for a solution unavailable through objective means. A good example is the reaction of individuals at the interface of life and death who use elements such as trust, meaning, timelessness, etc. to make sense of their situation. In the course of dealing with the situation, factual aspects are clearly prominent, such as a physician's prognosis, as are psychological aspects, such as sublimation of fear through defenses. However, religious aspects such as a deliberate facing of questions of freedom versus dependency or of hope versus despair are also prominent when situations involving life and death are encountered.

Using interviews in which we confronted subjects with contingency situations, my colleagues and I have inductively derived seven elements of the religious structure. Each of these elements is presented as a continuum and is considered to have its own developmental course, to be discussed in a later section of this essay.

The first element is the bipolar dimension of "the holy versus the profane." These two poles are familiar themes in the study of religion, which generally regards the dimension constituted by them as present in all cultures. Research in the history of religion has typically dealt with the function of these categories over time. Thus Eliade (1954, pp. 21ff.) states that in each context in history, human beings believed that there is an absolute reality, the holy or the sacred which "transcends" the world and reveals itself through special places, words, texts, and gestures. This insight can be traced back to Durkheim (1915), who wrote of the sacred and the profane as follows:

> In all the history of human thought there exists no other example of two categories of things so profoundly differentiated or so radically opposed to one another. The traditional opposition of good and bad is nothing beside this; for the good and the bad are only two opposed species of the same class, namely morals, just as sickness and health are two different aspects of the same order of facts, life, while the sacred and the profane have always and everywhere been conceived by the human mind as two distinct classes, as two worlds between which there is nothing in common. The forces which play in one are not simply those which are met within the other, but a little stronger; they are of a different sort. In different religions, this opposition has been conceived in different ways. Here, to separate these two sorts of things, it has seemed sufficient to localize them in different parts of the physical universe; there the first have been put into an ideal and transcendental world while the material world is left in full possession of the others. But howsoever much the forms of the contrast may vary, the fact of the contrast is universal. (pp. 53-54)

In our own research we have not attempted to analyze the function of this element but rather have looked at the process used in finding an equilibrium in contingency situations with respect to these two poles. In short, we asked how the mind connects the holy with the profane. We have concluded that in higher stages the holy is always mediated by the profane. Subjects at the higher stages of development integrate the two opposites in such a way as to gain insight and to clarify their relation with the ultimate. However, this is not true at earlier stages, such as Stage 3, where the typical response is, "Either it's holy or profane, but it can't be both," presumably because a child from 5 to 7 years is unable to distinguish these two dimensions.

The remaining six elements have not been as clearly formulated in the history of religion as this first one has. However in each case it is proposed that each element, which can be stated as a dichotomy, is first experienced developmentally as undifferentiated; later as a pair of opposites, one being the negation of the other; and only during the highest stages of development is the dichotomy resolved and the opposing forces seen as necessary parts of a unified structure. The remaining six elements are briefly described below.

The second element is that of "Freedom versus Dependency." At a higher stage subjects reconstruct reality as an amalgamation of freedom and dependency. In the middle stages subjects can see only one or the other aspects of this element and think of them as opposites. However, in the lower stages subjects lack the cognitive capacity either to connect or separate the two aspects, and instead see only one or the other, depending principally on the mediation of adults, e.g., parents and teachers.

The other elements derived from our interviews can be characterized with equal brevity.[1] Expressed as bipolar dimensions, they are: "Hope versus Absurdity," "the Everlasting versus the Temporary," "Trust versus Anxiety (or Mistrust)," "Explanation versus Mystery," and "Transcendence versus Immanence." Each of these is problematic in its own way, both for the subject and for the theorist. For instance, Erikson, though a developmental theorist, regarded Trust versus Distrust only as an element present at the beginning of life, failing to see it as a continuous, lifelong dimension of meaning-construction.

In the present essay I shall use the term "religious judgment" to refer to the reasoning by which subjects reconstruct reality from the point of view of these seven elements. The capability of doing so is a transcendental capacity, in the Kantian sense of a condition of the possibility and reliability of mutual understanding, of self-understanding, and of general thinking about why things happen. These seven elements, which as I have said were devised inductively from interview protocols outlining subjects' decision-making and justifying processes, are what Kohlberg calls "issues." The issues relevant to moral judgments include life, property, law, punishment, conscience, obedience, contract, affiliation, among others. The issues for a religious judgment are, I propose, best thought of as the seven elements just mentioned. A religious judgment includes these elements in a more or less complex, accentuated, and equilibrated way, depending on the subject's developmental status. Hence a special task of our research has been to ascertain how persons of different ages relate these elements to one another, forming a more or less richly structured whole and thereby constructing *stages* of religious development.

STAGES OF RELIGIOUS DEVELOPMENT

Our research suggests that religious development is a sequence of five stages, which for purposes of this essay can be described briefly and somewhat anecdotally in terms of responses we have gathered in interviews involving ten different dilemmas. I must emphasize at the outset that the five stages of religious development are depicted by using the most important aspects of each one. The reader is asked to sort out the more formal aspects of each stage and to give less importance to the content. For example, my use of a title like "Deism" for Stage 3 is not intended to imply that Stage 3 is exactly like an Aristotlelian (or even Enlightenment) form of deistic thinking about an absentee God that can be known by reason alone, but rather that parts of the conceptual structure of adolescents and other young persons at that stage are *similar* to such thinking.

The five stages can be concretely described in terms of the realization, which presumably occurs to all children at some point during their childhood, that there are other children in the world who are bereft of one or both parents, typically because of divorce or death. In the first dilemma, the interviewer asks the question of how God could have been so unfair as to let this happen. The following descriptions and examples of the reasoning processes used in answering this question nicely illustrate the stages of religious development which we have discovered in the responses to this and other dilemmas.

Stage 0:

The child is not able to differentiate between events caused by human error and those caused by something nonhuman. In response to the above cited question, the child could respond as follows:

They did it like that.

It's just that way. They're poor.

Someone did it.

God did it.

This lack of differentiation between human and transcendental causality occurs prior to the point at which we begin to exhibit "higher reversibility."

Stage 1:

The term "higher reversibility" refers to the clear differentiation between the human and the nonhuman. The method of differentiation between these two on the part of the subject is the hypothesis of a covert or manifest intention, whose discovery is the liberating element. Some examples of thinking at this level are:

The parents are at fault; they didn't want to be together anymore. Now the children are suffering for it.

Maybe God wanted it this way.

It's a punishment, and God did it. He always does things like this with some people.

The new freedom at this stage is that there are reasons for things happening, and "I" can discover them. The reasons are to be found either in human inadequacy or in the ultimate will (God), for instance:

Maybe the father didn't like the mother or the children anymore.

Maybe the father didn't believe in God anymore.

Maybe God forgot them?

Maybe God doesn't like these people too well, but I don't really believe that; that doesn't have to be so.

We call this stage the "Deus ex machina stage."

Stage 2:

The Stage 1 explanations are felt to be no longer adequate. Higher reversibility now means that the reason itself must be found embedded within a means-end scheme. This is, for example, a preventive model or a give-so-that-you-get concept, as can be seen in the following answers from a 12-year-old girl:

Maybe God wants the children to get a different father; then this person would love them more than their own father did.

God thinks that it's better this way. It is his will. Otherwise the father may have killed his own children some day.

Maybe God wants this to be a lesson for them, and they will understand it later.

In contrast to the children at Stage 1, this girl says that she has thought about these questions in the past. It is clear in these responses that the subject perceives there is another reason beyond the obvious one, which is not easy to identify. Hence a new, cognitively more adequate approach is needed to explain this situation. Higher reversibility means here that situations are approached and interpreted from this point of view, i.e., there is a hidden cause.

Using the classical Latin expression for give-so-that-you-get, we call this the "Do ut des stage."

Stage 3:

The person at this stage is no longer contented with the concept of a hidden cause. Critical thought emerges in this period, as can be seen in the following responses from a 16-year-old:

That people die, that parents separate from one another and leave "divorce waifs" behind, all of this falls within the area of a human being's responsibility. God cannot be made responsible for this.

It is ridiculous to say that everything which does not work out in this world must be viewed as if there were a hidden reason for it. Human beings must take their fates into their own hands.

God has nothing to do with the pain of separation. One should pray to God without asking anything for these people or their children. In this case, we human beings have to do something.

In other words, the person at this level interprets situations from the viewpoint that responsibility for causality is within the realm of the human being. On one hand subjects have a solid mode of inferring causalities, on the other hand they can eventually accept or reject a realm of the ultimate.

We call this stage "Deism."

Stage 4:

At this level, one is no longer contented with the structural a priori nature of Stage 3. At this point, there again is another higher reversibility to be found which stands in the middle between immanence and transcendence. The human being is not his or her own origin or creator. Therefore, the gap between human responsibility and the realm of the ultimate is experienced as a bond which interferes with freedom, as the following response shows:

There is always a possibility of preventing "divorce waifs." This is exactly where the unseen, god-like call in us lies: to engage ourselves in activities which would benefit mankind, for example, to provide family therapy or financial support.

At this level, part of human existence is understood in terms of human potential, and a second part is understood in terms of the ultimate, taken as the condition for the possibility of human freedom, interactional understanding, and action possibility. "God's vessel" and "God's instrument" are two expressions typical of this type of thought, whose outcome is the conception of a plan in which the world is continually developing toward goodness. Moreover, the Stage 3 belief that one can direct one's life endures throughout this stage as well.

We call this stage "the correlational stage" or "stage of the divine plan."

Stage 5:

At Stage 5, the binding together of the human and the ultimate of Stage 4 is objectified. The place where this binding occurs is human love and communication, a point whose traditional theological expression is the idea that God became man *among* us. The highest possible reversibility is the interpretation of human reality in the light of the existence or absence of communicative love. In one subject's words:

> When we are concerned about such children and counsel such parents, we are giving them the opportunity to grow. Only through such actions does the ultimate emerge in this world.

The reversibility of this highest level is based on the stable and continuous presence of an anthropologically religious attitude.

We call this stage "the perspective of religious autonomy through absolute intersubjectivity."

The general features of the stage description presented so far can be summarized as follows.

(1) Structural wholeness. The subject uses his or her perspective as a regulating system that helps one to cope cognitively with challenging and religion-related situations in one's life.

(2) Transitions. Transitions from one stage to the next will occur when the structure of the given stage is inadequate for the resolution of a real life-critical situation, so that it needs to be replaced by a new, more complex and more adequate structure.

(3) Hierarchy. The stages form a hierarchy in the sense that the sequence of stages is irreversible. Furthermore, there is no skipping of stages. However, relatively few people actually reach Stage 5, this being the richest and most complex stage as well as one which liberates the subject from authoritarian representations of the ultimate.

(4) Self-regulation. The subject forms and makes use of the structure by means of a self-regulating process. This process is an interpretative one, whereby reality is reconstructed under the viewpoint of the man-ultimate relationship.

Empirical studies describing or validating the stage concept have been carried out, including a cross-sectional study in Switzerland with age groups from 6 to 75 years, a cross-cultural study with subjects in different religions (Buddhists from Tibet, Hinduists from Rajasthan, Imanists from Rwanda, Muslims and orthodox Jews from

Israel), a study with atheists, a study referring to the religious family climate, and, finally, a series of intervention studies stimulating higher stages of religious judgment development. (Further information on these and related studies is available from the author.) This body of empirical research shows a clear age trend of the developmental concept and a high stability of the construct within subjects. But what about the content? How do the dilemmas influence the fundamental structure of the religious judgment? Can we say that this structure is universal? Can we say that persons with no religious commitment have a structure of religious judgment? In order to answer these questions, we must look at the dilemmas and their content stimulus.

CONTENT AND STRUCTURE: THE DILEMMAS

In order to determine the subjects' religious cognitive structure we studied their responses to a series of dilemmas. These are stories that put the subjects into a simulated situation in which the relationship to an ultimate reality is under stress. The questions posed to the subject dealing with the given situation address the seven elements described above. I would like to present here two of our dilemmas in order to delineate their fundamental structure. The first is the Paul dilemma:

> Paul, a young medical doctor, has just successfully taken his exams. He is very happy. He has a girl friend, whom he promised to marry. His parents have rewarded his success by paying for a trip to England. Paul sets out. No sooner has the plane lifted off than the captain announces that one engine is damaged and that the other engine does not function reliably. The plane loses altitude. All safety measures are immediately taken: oxygen masks, life vests, etc. First the passengers cry out; then it is deathly still. The plane dives rapidly. Paul's whole life races through his head. Now he thinks: It's all over.
>
> In this situation he thinks of God and starts praying. He pledges that he will dedicate the whole of his life for the poor in the Third World if he is saved, that he will give up his girl friend if she doesn't go with him, and will renounce a high income and prestige in our society.
>
> The plane is smashed in the emergency landing in a field. Paul is saved miraculously. On his return home, a lucrative position is offered to him in a private clinic. He was selected from ninety candidates on the basis of his abilities. Paul recalls his promise to God. Now he does not know what to do.

The second is the Judge dilemma:

> A well-known judge in a small town was very lucky. He possessed a huge house, his wife and three children were healthy and all loved each other, and he had an excellent reputation. He was a devout man, prayed every day, and spent a lot of money for the sake of the poor.
>
> One day, he made a mistake in his professional career: he accepted bribes from a client. As a result, he lost his job and his reputation. Later on, his daughter became severely ill and died of her illness. Finally, his wife left him too. So his whole life was destroyed.
>
> He sold his house and went to another town. There, he was, by chance, invited by a church committee to read a text in front of the community. But he was very reluctant. After all, should he get into religion again and pray and participate in such a community? He felt that God was not with him in those difficult times. What should he do in this situation?

If we inspect these two dilemmas closely, we see first that the structure of both is universal. What does this mean? First of all, it means that there is no appeal to special beliefs, to revelation or an esoteric content. The dilemmas deal with a certain relationship, that of man to an ultimate, in a commonly understandable context and social setting. Secondly, it means the elements can be generalized and transported across cultural boundaries, so that the dilemmas fit every culture. For example, in Rwanda we adapted the Paul dilemma so that instead of promising to go to the Third World, Martin pledges to give up a scholarship and to stay home. Similarly, the accident may be a snakebite, etc., rather than an airplane crash. Thirdly, it means that the dilemmas are not gender specific, but are told just as easily with women as with men in their center. My colleague Schildknecht, for example, has used a version of the first dilemma featuring a nurse, well loved by many children in the hospital at home, who promises to work for the Third World. (Schildknecht found that dialogues at each age are much more intense and controversial when using this version of the dilemma.) Fourthly, the name used to signify the ultimate can be changed to correspond to a culture's belief system. Thus we use the word "God" when presenting the dilemmas in our culture, since this term is familiar enough to be understood by everybody. In sum, our claim of universality is the claim that the dilemmas are able to elicit a cognitive structure because they are understandable at first sight and no special knowledge is necessary in order to respond to them.

Our empirical work has shown that the more universal a dilemma is, the more likely it is that the age-stage trend will show a high functional correlation. Conversely, as would be expected, the more culture-specific a dilemma is, the more we obtain cohort effects, such that the monotonic relationship in the age-stage trend gets destroyed. For example, we have compared the age trend of the Paul dilemma to that of another dilemma, the "Marriage Dilemma," in which a Protestant Swiss clergyman intends to marry a Catholic woman from a South American country. If he does so, the woman can never return to her native country since she will lose her citizenship and will be excommunicated from Catholicism. The woman feels guilty in the face of God, but the clergyman insists on the marriage. What should she do? . . .

Figure 1 shows that the dilemmas of Paul and the Judge have a nice monotonic upward movement. But the Marriage dilemma connects the highest stage with an age mean of 17.5, which means that younger people score higher on this dilemma than older people do. In other words, younger subjects much more easily relate general, religiously interpreted love to the situation than do older subjects, for whom the rule-guided adherence to a church is more important. Thus we see that the Marriage dilemma is culture-specific, lacking the generality of the Paul dilemma as well as that of the Judge, which consist of situations that could possibly happen to anyone.

I would like now to turn to another problem, concerning the stage structure of the dilemma itself. Even in the case of a universal dilemma such as that of Paul or the Judge, one might object that the dilemma itself has a Stage 2 character, which influences the subject to make certain sorts of responses. In other words, should we demand that the dilemmas be neutral with respect to the stage structure of their protagonists? Such a demand would be based on the objection just posed, namely, that Paul's reacting with a promise to God is a Stage 2 reaction on his part, as is the Judge's asking himself whether he should pray. But this objection is ill-conceived, as I shall now try to show.

The objection fails to recognize that the dilemma only describes a way of acting, not a way of reasoning. Paul is afraid; he makes a promise to God; he does not know what to do. The story contains no justifications. Consequently, we can make no inference from the protagonist's action to the nature of his judgments. The action itself has no stage structure. Logical or psychological arguments would be needed to explain why this action occurs, and why any one person would or would not act in a certain way. Considering the dilemma

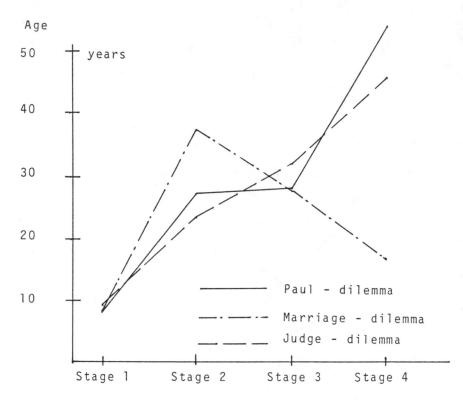

Figure 1. The relationship of stage and age in three religious dilemmas.

itself to have a Stage 2 structure is altogether wrong: only the recon-
structing arguments and their justifications can give insight into the level
of reasoning.

Instead of arguing that the story itself contains a Stage 2 structure, it would be more to the point to examine the questions which
are put to the subject after the dilemma has been presented. These
questions are meant to stimulate the subject's thinking in a specific
way, namely, in terms of the elements mentioned above. Let us
examine these questions:

1a. Should Paul keep his promise to God? Why or why not?
1b. Must one really keep a promise to God? Why or why not?
1c. Do you believe that one has duties to God at all? Why or why not?

2. What do you say to this statement: "It is God's will that Paul go to the Third World" (i.e., that he keep his promise)?

In the foregoing story two sets of demands oppose each other: first, Paul's girl friend and the job offered to him; second, God and his promise to God.
3a. Which of these two demands do you feel to be more significant, or how do you experience the relation between the two demands?
3b. What is more significant in this world: man or God?

Let us suppose Paul tells his (religious) parents of his experiences and of the difficult situation in which he finds himself. They implore him to obey God and keep his promise.
4. Should Paul follow the advice of his parents? Why or why not?

Paul feels duty bound to a religious community (church, sect, etc.) and is strongly committed to it. The spiritual attitude and the precepts of this community require that the call and the will of God must be accepted by man, that Paul should keep his promise unconditionally.
5a. What does this demand mean for Paul? Must he, as a believing person, be led in his decision by the dictums of this community? Why or why not?
5b. Must one be led in one's fundamental decisions by the principles or demands of a religious community? Why or why not?
5c. Which duties does one have vis-à-vis a religious community at all? Why?
5d. May a person oppose the demands of a religious community by his personal freedom? Why or why not?

Let us assume that Paul does not keep his promise, after many sleepless nights and a time of uncertainty and despair as to how he should act, and that he accepts the promising position in the private clinic.
6. Do you believe that this choice will have any consequences for Paul's future life? Why or why not?

Shortly afterward Paul has a head-on collision with another automobile. The accident was disastrous and it was his fault.
7a. Did this accident have any connection with the fact that Paul did not keep his promise to God? Why or why not?
7b. Do you believe that God is punishing Paul for not keeping his promise? Why or why not?
7c. If this is so, will God intervene directly in this world? If not, does God manifest himself in this world? In which way?

Suppose Paul starts out his career as a doctor and decides to donate one tenth of his income every month to charitable organizations.
8. Do you believe that Paul, in his own way, has kept his promise after all? Why or why not?

These questions have in common the feature that they separate the subject from the dilemma and ask: "What would *you* do in this situation?" The questions do not ask for knowledge but for positions. They do not refer to the subject's "second-hand religious life," which as William James (1902, p. 8) states, "has been made for him by others, communicated to him by tradition," but rather to "the original experiences which were the pattern-setters to all this mass of suggested feeling and imitated conduct." Thus the answers to the questions reveal a cognitive structure which is completely different from the structure of the dilemma. If we ask "Is it God's will that Paul go to the Third World? Why or why not?" the subject must reconstruct his or her *general* position and apply it to Paul's situation. While the subject reveals a stage structure, the text retains action-oriented structural stability. Confronting someone with a dilemma thus invites that person to deal with this dilemma in terms of his or her particular cognitive religious structure.

But this raises a new issue. If Paul promises something to God, is this not a moral dilemma rather than a religious one? In other words, if there is such a thing as religious structure how does it differ from a moral one? Careful consideration of the matter in the light of the religious elements mentioned above suggests that to promise something to an ultimate, and to keep or not to keep that promise, is more than a moral issue: the ultimate is not visible, touchable, arbitrary, etc., but instead is powerful, has created man, is utterly reliable, and so on. Thus, even if there could be an interpretation of the dilemma based on strictly moral elements, the relationship at its center is more fully determined by the seven religious elements. In effect, the promise merely serves as an excuse for discussing the relationship. The questions which stimulate the discussion have been designed to incorporate the seven elements, and hence go beyond the justice issue. As we observed in our study, if the questions are changed, the whole interview changes. For example, when we left out the reference to God, the subjects responded more often in a moral or socially oriented way.

THE ULTIMATE AS THE REFERENCE POINT

I shall conclude by addressing one last question: Does everyone have a religious stage structure? In other words, is it reasonable to assume that the cognitive religious structure is universal? How do the dilemmas of Paul and the Judge relate to this question?

One of the major criticisms of our stage concept lies in the assumption that our stages are stages of dealing only with what in another era was called theodicy, that is, that branch of philosophical ontology which is concerned with justifying the ways of God to man. But if we define religious judgment as the way a person conceives the man-ultimate relationship in a concrete situation, then the most important reference point is the ultimate. To the degree that the seven elements refer to this ultimate, they serve as distinguishing marks of the category of "religion." On the one hand the search for equilibrium between the elements is not specifically religious; however the reference to an ultimate (rather than to a concrete subject or object) gives a religious tone to the judgment which embodies that search. On the other hand, the structural point of these assertions does not lie in the reference to this or that ultimate, but in the way of "acting upon" this or that ultimate in the corresponding contingency situation. Stage 4, for instance, implies that the self-responsibility of man in the corresponding situation is brought into question by an a priori acceptance of a given (in this sense, given by an ultimate) condition of the possibility to act.

Now we see the theorist's dilemma. Taking into account a specific interpretation of the ultimate, for instance that it is a personal God, is indeed significant for the thinking of a person and also for the determination of his or her religious judgment with regard to the content. But the same basic structure of the religious judgment can obviously be constructed with a different (but equally specific) chosen content (see Fetz & Oser, 1985). The ultimate can be a personalized God, an unpersonalized divinized being (for example, a mystical principle of divine reality or Pantheism), a power of destiny (Tyche, various forms of causality), Nature (stream of life, self-organizing matter), Society (as an integrative whole, universal plan), and so on. With this assumption, we can go in two directions with our research: one is that of analyzing the differences proper to each stage when different ultimates are used as reference points; the other direction is that of investigating the similarities of the structural features. The second way is very difficult to follow; however, if those thinkers are correct who claim that the very act of conceiving a world presupposes an ultimate as a reference point, the second way should be as possible as the first. Furthermore, this claim provides the philosophical basis for our methodological assumption that everyone makes religious judgments even if he or she does not know exactly what the ultimate is. Even the assertion that one does not believe in any ultimate at all, whatever might be its validity, constitutes a religious judgment, albeit a negative one. It becomes clear that religious judgment in this sense has nothing to do with a judgment about religion, but with the reconstruction of meaning given the concept of an ultimate.

It is important that everyone concerned realizes that the dilemmas employed in our investigations always refer to an ultimate. Otherwise subjects try to solve the problems posed in the dilemmas without referring to an ultimate. Although it is true that we can and indeed often do try to solve problems in this way, it leaves us with a residue of unresolved questions. In our society we learn to live with such ambiguities, to hide the theodicy problem, to compensate for and to defend ourselves against final questions. Nevertheless, even discussing religious explanations in a negative manner indicates that we understand what religious reasoning is, an understanding which, I propose, is accounted for psychologically by the schema of religious structures. It is through these religious structures that we can achieve cognitive religious equilibrium, which then becomes part of our identity.

NOTE

1. Further description of these elements, as well as additional data from our empirical studies, are available upon request from the author.

REFERENCES

Durkheim, E. (1915). *The elementary forms of the religious life.* New York: Free Press.

Eliade, M. (1954). *Die Religion und das Heilige. Elemente der Religionsgeschichte.* Salzburg: O. Müller.

Fetz, R., & Oser, F. (1984). *Development of world view and religious judgment: Their influence on morality.* Paper presented at the Second Ringberg Conference on Moral Development, July, 1984, Ringberg, Bavaria, Germany.

James, W. (1902). *The varieties of religious experience: A study in human nature.* New York: Longmans, Green and Company.

Index